BORN IN A WAR BETWEEN DARK AND LIGHT

VIVIAN GENDERNALIK

Contents

TIME IS RUNNING OUT TO WAKE FROM DEMON LIES   **7**
    End-Time Vision Of Global Wickedness   9
    The Day That Followed Full Of Supernatural Signs   14
YOU'RE BORN INTO THIS WAR   **19**
DEMONIC PRINCIPALITES ARE ENTIRELY REAL   **29**
    Potent Information Demonic Principalities Are Real   29
    Science Has Already Proven God And Devil Real   31
SOME OF MY DEMON ENCOUNTERS   **39**
    Paranormal Times in Apartment 5-110   45
    Wed Devotee of the Occult & Demon Times Started   49
    Living In A Demonic Stronghold   57
YOUR MISSION OPERATION MAKE IT TO HEAVEN   **71**
    Not All Commanders Mean What They Order Except Jesus 72
    The Gift of Salvation   78
    Don't Skip Instructions   81
FINAL GRACE TIMER NEARING LAST TICK   **85**
    Dream 1, 1972   88
    Dream 2 1979   90
    Dream 3, 1982   93
    Dream 4, 1991   94
    Dream 5, 1984   95
    Dream 6, 1987   97
    Dream 7 1992   100
    Dream 8, 2011   101
DEMON DOCTRINES COMING TO A CHURCH NEAR YOU 107
    7-2 Demon Doctrine: After Cross No Guilt   114
    7-3 Demon Doctrine: Once Saved, Always Saved   126
    7-4 Demon Doctrine: Living By Pharisees' Righteousness 131
    7-5 Demon Doctrine: How God's Law Is Put On Hearts   146
    7-6 Demon Doctrine: Deceive You Are His Sheep   160
    7-7 Demon Doctrine: Fool You With Paulism   164
        Paulism Trademark   167
        Revelatory Nugget of the Paulism Disclaimer   173
    7-8 Demon Doctrines: How You Enter Heaven   175
        Fundamental Foundation   175

Wrongfulness of Imputed Righteousness	186
UNEXPECTED MARY SHRINE DEMON PHOTO	**195**
Hail Jesus	227
Hail, Holy King	228
WHEN PEOPLE TURN INTO DEMON PAWNS	**231**
September 12th, 1982	233
April 2012	258
January 2014	264
BE AFRAID, BE VERY AFRAID	**281**
March 9, 2013 - Ruler Of Principality Upset	283
On The Dark Side's Hit List	291
God Is Always Victorious	313
Grieved By Various Trials Testing Faith	320
Supernatural Dates	325
YOUR FREE BONUS GIFT	**329**
SINNER'S PRAYER	**331**
AUTHOR CONTACT INFORMATION	**332**

BORN IN A WAR BETWEEN DARK AND LIGHT
He Is Coming Book 1
Copyright © March 9, 2014 Vivian Gendernalik

Published by Holy Force
www.holyforce.org

I have done my best to make certain this book was done as professional as possible. However, a small publisher as myself does not have the resource to use the costly services of editors or proofreaders or typesetters, and works on a very limited budget. Thus, if you do find any errors in grammar or spelling or misplaced text or any other kind of error your help is appreciated in pointing out what is wrong so I am able to do the required corrections. However, any such editorial problem which may be discovered does not in any way affect the quality of the material.

This book is copyrighted material. All rights reserved. It is against the law to make copies of this material without obtaining specific written permission in advance from the author. Infrequent copying of a page, or brief quotation for personal use or group study is allowed and supported, and permission will be given on request when submitted to the author with description in the manner in which it will be used. But for commercial profit or advantage this book may not be reprinted or copied. As well as, no part of this publication may be reproduced, stored in any retrieval system including search engines such as powered by Google Inc, Yahoo or MSN, electronically reproduced, or transmitted in any form or by any means such as by portable scanners, or e-books or PDF formats, electronic, mechanical, photocopying, recording or otherwise such as YouTube audio or visual readings, or website downloads or article snippets or features, without prior written permission from the author. Scripture quotations marked ESV are from The ESV® Bible (The Holy Bible, English Standard Version®), copyright © 2001 by Crossway, a publishing ministry of Good News Publishers. Used by permission. All rights reserved. Scripture quotations marked GNT are taken from the Good News Translation - Second Edition, Copyright 1992 by American Bible Society. Used by Permission. Scripture quotations marked GW are taken from GOD'S WORD®, © 1995 God's Word to the Nations. Used by permission of Baker Publishing Group. Scripture quotations marked HCSB are taken from the Holman Christian Standard Bible®, Copyright © 1999, 2000, 2002, 2003 by Holman Bible Publishers. Used by permission. Holman Christian Standard Bible®, Holman CSB®, and HCSB® are federally registered trademarks of Holman Bible Publishers. Scripture quotations marked KJV are taken from the Kings James Bible Version. Scripture quotations marked NCV taken from the New Century Version®. Copyright © 2005 by Thomas Nelson, Inc. Used by permission. All rights reserved. Scripture quotations marked NIRV taken from the HOLY BIBLE, NEW INTERNATIONAL READER'S VERSION®. Copyright © 1995, 1996, 1998 by Biblica. www.biblica.com All rights reserved. Scripture quotations marked NIV are from the Bible Version Quotations designated (NIV) are from THE HOLY BIBLE: NEW INTERNATIONAL VERSION®. NIV®. Copyright © 1973, 1978, 1984 by Biblica. All rights reserved worldwide. Scripture quoted by permission. Scripture quotations marked NKJV are taken from the New King James Version®. Copyright © 1979, 1980, 1982 by Thomas Nelson, Inc., publishers. Used by permission. All rights reserved. Scripture quotations marked (NLT) are taken from the Holy Bible, New Living Translation, copyright © 1996, 2004, 2007 by Tyndale House Foundation. Used by permission of Tyndale House Publishers, Inc., Carol Stream, Illinois 60188. All rights reserved. Scripture quotations marked RHE are from the Douay-Rheims Bible Version.

Cover design by Vivian Gendernalik
Image of man at finish line © ShutterStock.com
All photographs and material were given by the author unless otherwise acknowledged.
ISBN-10: 0991303288
ISBN-13: 978-0-9913032-8-1
E-book ISBN: 978-0-9913032-0-5

Acknowledgment

First of all, I want to give special thanks here to God, the Father, Jesus, and the Holy Spirit, for their absolute support, guidance and help not only for this book, but throughout my entire life where I so many times tread like a fool where angels fear to go.

Next I want to give special thanks to my mother, Olga Pulido, and to my aunt, Hope Pulido. Without their crucial help which allowed me to remain in my house after my husband's death during a wrongful foreclosure, the writing of this book would not have happened. Nor would have my fighting song War been done I include as a bonus download with this book with the aim to charge up and motivate listeners to stand firm in this battle against the darkness.

I also want to thank my late sister-in-law, Linda Sue Nesmith-Pulido, for coming from heaven to give me a God-sent message that would fuel me to do this book.

Chapter 1

TIME IS RUNNING OUT TO WAKE FROM DEMON LIES

> By the same word the present heavens and earth are reserved for fire, being kept for the day of judgment and destruction of ungodly men.
> —*2 Peter 3:7, NIV*

**WHAT I AM ABOUT TO TELL YOU
IS ALL TRUE, EVERY LITTLE DETAIL.
I urge you to hear me out—while there is still time.**

In 1972 I had an open vision that changed me forever when God transported me to his day of wrath, and showed me how deserving his wrath will be on that day he will end the world from the state of evil prevalent at that time amongst the majority of the global population, a population who accepted demonic lies to sink to such depravity.

Yet he presented it to me in a way of mercy that involved my standing in the gap for those vast numbers of people I saw, in which he will allow them one more chance to repent and turn from evil, and save those who do from the day of his wrath when he certainly will follow through destroying all sinners as is written in Scriptures.

> Behold, the day of the Lord comes, cruel, with wrath and fierce anger, to make the land a desolation and to destroy its sinners from it.
> —*Isaiah 13:9, ESV*

This open vision took place when I was 13 years of age,

followed with a day of supernatural signs as if a confirmation the vision was really of God, a vision which opened my eyes to the depths of depravity which can lie hidden within people and merit destruction, and about the righteous judgments of God against such wickedness, and transformed my entire perspective of what really matters.

> Remember that some people lead sinful lives, and everyone knows they will be judged. But there are others whose sin will not be revealed until later.
> —*1 Timothy 5:24, NLT*

At the time the vision took place, I was Catholic and attending a Catholic elementary school, and in the final year, which was eighth grade. By my eighth grade year, when the incident took place, I had gotten a rather infamous reputation and was known by teachers who I did not even know.

My usual greeting from a new instructor was, So you're the one that ran away, and they would take up the same disapproving attitude of the residing faculty, an attitude which would not have lasted for long had the prior monsignor's still been around, who had been my wise-hearted friend in a sea of overly-stern nuns who viewed guilt first instead of innocence.

I won't forget this one time especially when he had gently but with full authority of his position, lifted his hand up to stop the nun ready to take me to the backroom for a spank when it came my time in the long line of children showing their report cards to the nuns and my card had shown a few D's for my conduct.

Patting me affectionately on the head, with a fatherly smile to me, he had told the surprised nun, "This is very good for Vivian," an intervention that had made me feel loved.

So I was not a quiet average little girl and if there was any blame to whose fault it was for instigating the plan to run away, it was easily shifted to me without my getting to prove otherwise.

Here in this photo on the next page I am in my school uniform, making 'bunny ears' behind the head one of my favorite nuns, picture taken at that very elementary school, 4 months before my vision from God.

Chapter 1: Time Is Running Out To Wake Up From Demon Lies

Thus, you can see the teenage girl who I was when I had that encounter with God over his reasons for ending the world, having  a reputation trailing me for being rowdy and a renegade.

Yet, early on, I was, without consciously knowing it, setting up Biblical ground for the Lord to interact with me. I remember at age 6 that the last thing I would say before I went to sleep was, "Good night, Jesus," and kiss the air. After this was a habit for a while, I got the unexpected delightful surprise, one I shall never forget, one time when I kissed, I felt whom I had no doubt was Jesus kiss my lips in return as a loving parent would. There was absolutely no doubt at all of his identity; I did not have to wonder. Needless to say, it was amazing. So it seems my consistent expressions of love to Jesus, caused me to be at a place for God to use me for his purposes.

End-Time Vision Of Global Wickedness

Through this 1972 open vision I am discussing here and the supernaturally-filled day that followed, my whole rebellious, wild and moody lifestyle was to be affected and changed. Although I had experienced spiritual encounters before, one related above when Jesus met my goodnight kiss one time, and another not mentioned here that took place nightly for 2+ months, this was the event that changed me, partly because I saw God is a God of righteous judgments and I witnessed sinners undergoing a frightening condemnation. As a child I did not know these things as we did not read Revelation as children in Catholic school; our teaching was limited to the catechism for the most part geared to children.

I still retain my original 1st draft of that account I wrote a year after it, now the pencil handwriting very faint 40-plus years later on the yellowed crinkled note paper I wrote it on. The incident took place nearing day break while I slept in the room shared with my 2 older sisters. I was 13 years old at the time and we lived in Miami, Florida. The life-changing events for me took place that day afterwards at the Catholic school I attended, life-changing because they confirmed to me that what I had gone through was real.

As I slept in the lower bunk bed beneath my oldest sister who had the top bunk bed, my other sister across the room in her own single bed, I found myself in an open vision that seemed as real as if I was doing these things in my physical body to which this day I am uncertain if I was or not because it was as real an experience as I am sitting here typing. I discovered I was on my knees in total dark, as if transported directly from my bedroom to this unknown, pitch-black place.

Then my awareness widened and I found myself in my school room, still kneeling, but next to the teacher's desk. All the desks were empty and I knew, even though I couldn't see from the lack of light, by some kind of supernatural awareness that so was the entire building empty and dark.

It felt as if the experience was taking place right then in real live time as the time I was supposed to be asleep in my bed, dark outside as it was dark like it should be in my bedroom, if in fact I was out of my body and my body was still there sleeping, same exact time. However, like John in Revelation, I couldn't tell if I was there in the body, or if this was my spirit there only, or the most lucid dream ever that strangely coincided exactly with real time in all 3-dimensional detail which I had never experienced before. Because it was so life-like, I felt I was actually physically there. I could feel the hard floor in contact with my legs in my pajama pants, and as far as I could tell I was really there.

Not even the smallest light was on anywhere in the classroom, the brick, 2-story school building and room where I knelt dark exactly as it was really happening at that time of night. It seemed to be 3 to 4 a.m. just by the total quiet and darkness. Only the lightning bolts accompanied by shattering thunder occasionally lit the otherwise dark and desolate classroom that was my normal classroom during the days.

For a few seconds I was alone until I heard a voice, medium of tone and full of power. Without having to be told I knew the voice

Chapter 1: Time Is Running Out To Wake Up From Demon Lies

belonged to no other than God. I had never heard God talk before, but I didn't have to be told it was God, I just knew.

God told me he was going to end the world, and when he said that, I thought he meant right that night. However, he did not specify that as he went on elaborating on the evil that was going on within the world.

As he spoke my young mind could not perceive the horror of the things he said. But towards the end of his talk to me, I could not find a reason to debate his decision, as his decision was totally justified by the level of evil he revealed.

Instead of the conversation coming to a close as I anticipated, God split the room starting from the center of its floor until I found myself kneeling at the outer most atmosphere of the world.

The sky below grew darker as he showed me the people on the earth living out their daily lives: talking, working, laughing and so on. No more than five seconds past when he switched the scene to the end of the world and how the people's souls would look then.

They were ugly, repulsive, horrifying for me to look at from my high perch. They no longer looked like people, because their ugliness within them had so transformed them, they had turned into repulsive creatures.

It didn't matter how likable or attractive that person had seemed on the outside, inside every one of them turned out to be deformed from their sins to the point they had become contorted into creatures that were far from human and were ugly and vile, not one standing upright but deformed and changed so extreme they lost all human traces. Really they looked like a sea of demons if you hadn't seen the transformation they were people and what you were beholding was their true insides from their massive sinning.

I could see them as they were: a vast, pitiable multitude with arms outstretched, both shrieking and screaming out to me, asking for forgiveness. I received the impression without words that these were people who had thought the devil's lies were entirely fine, people who were shocked to find the Bible was literally correct, which seemed from my view millions and millions. They had bought the demonic mistruths and had become ugly creatures in sin over their lives, and now they suddenly discovered they were in righteous judgment and condemned rightfully before a Holy God.

This was in 1972, before computers, cell phones, big screen televisions, DVDs and even vcr players being affordable for the average person, medias which give methods of transmitting visual messages that are not family-rated on the individual person level, and personalized, that allowed people to privately indulge in all kinds of perversions and sins on a scale that exist now, but not back then, scale wise. Though throughout human history, people have not been puritanical and have greatly sinned, they have not done so on the tremendous scale of mass involvement that computers and cell phones and easily-created affordable mediums like DVD, mp3, etc allow today.

In 1972 if you wanted pornography, you had to travel by car to one of those stores in the bad parts of the city, or get embarrassed getting one of the 3 magazines available in select bookstores.

If you wanted to bully someone, you could only do so by traveling in person. There were no cell phones with cameras available to humiliate or tempt people with. So from my frame of reference, I couldn't understand then how so many people could have such vile interiors, could be all so corrupt.

In the early 70s, those kinds of sins happening stayed secret for the most part, but today, you are just about considered a nerd if you don't interact in these kind of activities, which is now considered many a person's right and healthy expression thanks to the enemy's very layered and well-crafted plans to make sin seem right and not sinning seem wrong.

But there far below me, giving me a great view that seemed somehow to scan the world, were multitudes and multitudes of people who by sin were deformed creatures inside, no denying this from my supernatural view. The mass sea of corrupted people I was looking at were shown in their spiritual condition at what would be officially the end of the world, as in Biblical end, the end described in Revelation of which I had no teaching then at 13. I understood from the sight I beheld that people were sinners, however, sin would prevail so much as the day of the Lord got closer that they were going to get even worse, become ugly beasts when that end time would finally arrive.

Chapter 1: Time Is Running Out To Wake Up From Demon Lies

There had been such a difference the way the people looked on the outside and the true states of their souls when the end of the world would be. When I had seen them with their physical bodies gone, and just as their soul man, they were like ugly creatures, depraved and evil. Everyone looked different from each other, but they were all repulsive---their true nature was offensive and vile.

Then they began a unified chant asking for one more chance, just one more, over and over, until I realized that all the souls that I could see, which were many upon many, that saving them from destruction was being left all up to me.

I couldn't bear the sight any more and turned away quickly from them to God. The morbid view closed itself back into the school room leaving me where I had been originally situated, next to the teacher's desk.

Then I turned to God and began to plead with him out of the very depth of my soul to give these people one more chance. From the state of their corruption, I personally felt that the situation was hopeless and my feelings of desperation continued to grow, however, I kept on pleading for them.

What moved me most was their terrible shrieks and screams for forgiveness. I couldn't help but be moved no matter how vile they were.

They were a sight to pity, and I feel now my own pity was God's pity for them, his mercy working through me despite their clear inner vile nature, and their deserving condemnation. It brings to mind the Scripture where Jonah was angry God had not destroyed the wicked in Nineveh who clearly were deserving of destruction, and God replied, "But Nineveh has more than a hundred and twenty thousand people who cannot tell their right hand from their left, and many cattle as well. Should I not be concerned about that great city?" (Jonah 4:11 NIV)

Like those clueless people in Nineveh, God was revealing a concern for all these depraved people I was viewing, millions and millions of people who had lived in clueless sin that led to his righteous wrath and destruction. By their ugly transformation into some other kind of creatures when God showed them to me how they really appeared, it was clear not just one sin changed them like that, but living in sin so long it had transformed them into deformed evil creatures within. Yet, like Nineveh, they did not know one hand from the other, and had lived clueless about their lives of sin, total pawns of the devil.

At any moment God had the power to destroy them; just one word they would get their justly-due punishment. By his staying his mighty hand and showing me by the situation it was my job to help them, it was apparent this was God's mercy, his setting up this way for them to be delivered despite they deserved immediate destruction. But it was also clear, those who would not respond to this final mercy chance, would get God's eternal wrath.

The storm outside was really lashing about. It was at its top fury when one dazzling flash of lightening filled the room. At that moment I found myself in a half kneeling, half begging position in my lit up bedroom, for real, for physical real, in the brilliant flash of a blinding lightning bolt exactly as had filled the classroom, followed by a clap of roaring thunder.

I was awake for another ten minutes expecting more lightning and thunder, but that was the end. Instead soothing pitter patter of gentle rainfall followed, as if a sign of God's mercy, lulling me to sleep. There had been no difference between the last second in the classroom and my time finding myself in the same position in my bed: at that age I did not know about visions or getting spiritually translated, so I thought it was real, felt it was real, but could only name it 'dream incident' because open visions and closed visions were not terms taught in Catholic elementary school.

The Day That Followed Full Of Supernatural Signs

When I awoke in the morning, I immediately fell to my knees thanking God the world was still there. Even though the scene from the end of the world he had shown me I knew had been the future at some unknown time, I still wasn't entirely 100 percent sure he could withhold his hand for that length of time, due to the level of evil he had first shown me which justified his holy wrath at that very moment.

When my mother called me and my two brothers, who were still of the age to attend the grade school, to go to the car for the

Chapter 1: Time Is Running Out To Wake Up From Demon Lies

normal ride to school a mile away, I told her I wanted to walk, not telling her, though, the reason why, because I was happy to see God had not ended the world, so grateful for his mercy, and the precious world was still there. Although she looked at me queerly, she consented.

I strolled happily to school, stopping often to look at flowers, inhale the fresh morning air, and laugh at the iridescent rays of the sun that played on the street I walked. It was a gorgeous day that could validate any miracle.

When I reached my school there was still a half hour before classes. So I strode into the church. Using my lunch money, I lit a few candles, spending the time in thankful prayer.

It was, however, when I was inside my class that I noticed something unusual about myself. I was looking at the classroom door half swaying between shutting and opening. Its indecisive manner led me to wish it would open fully. At that thought, it did as if an invisible person pulled it back. Amazed, I wished it to close. Instantly it did just like that same person complied with my desire.

By now my emotions were rising as my teacher was deciding who was going to read. In my mind I directed her to pick me, and she did!

For the rest of the day everything obeyed my thoughts, or that is how it seemed to my mind ignorant of Old Testament stories how God worked directly through prophets like Elijah so at their word to strike someone with fire, fire would come down from heaven, with the prophet not the power, but it being God responding to the prophet for a confirmation to those God was really behind the prophet's word.

But to uneducated me who had only seen something like this done by the magician Uri Geller popular back then in the USA, it appeared as if by my thought the door opened and closed several times, not knowing God sometimes would do whatever sign a prophet said to others in order to prove that prophet was a servant of his, and confirm a message a prophet had received was indeed from God.

So to me it seemed that the teachers would follow my thoughts to pick me, pick someone else. I played with what I thought were my newly found powers, not having known anything about the supernatural signs God can sometimes give to confirm he has spoken through a person.

I believe because I was an unguided, untrained young girl that God for a short while did this for me, though I was not speaking any of these things in his name but just thinking for these things to happen, in order that I could be sure the encounter I had had with him and what he had said, was a valid supernatural word I could and should take seriously.

Without any person to instruct me on what I was experiencing that whole day, my young mind could only think I had a sudden development of psychic powers. However for the first time I was fully conscious of the contrary behavior of all the people around me to God's will. Their behavior was definitely often in clash with a Holy God and never before had I perceived this.

I am sure if I had had someone trained in the prophetic, they would have cleared up my wrong thinking, and instructed me in what was really going on. And perhaps if I had had such guidance it might have gone further, but I believe God cut off that overt outright response from him to my every proclamation by that day's end to keep me from the error of my mind I now had psychic powers.

That morning I told two of my friends at school only, out of fear of being ridiculed, but I mostly wanted to tell one of the priests. At my lunch time, having spent my lunch money earlier to pray on the candles and unable to buy food, I used that time to go to the rectory to tell a priest about this monumental vision, and how after experiencing it that it seemed I could now move things with my thoughts.

I remember sitting across the priest telling him these things, about the door opening and closing as I wished, about the teacher following my thoughts to pick me, pick so and so. He told me that it was a dream and nothing more, and he had no comments to say on my experiences with moving things and people with my thoughts. And that was an effective end to any guidance.

Not until decades later when I became familiar with the Bible did I understand what I experienced that day, which was an open vision from God, the following supernatural events isolated to just

Chapter 1: Time Is Running Out To Wake Up From Demon Lies

that day to correlate it as a true experience. At the end of the school day, nothing more responded to my thoughts, as if God called it a day validating something special had happened to me more than just a waking dream, perhaps because God knew I would find no guidance concerning any open vision from my spiritual leaders at that Catholic school as I might have found at another denomination believing in gifts of the Spirit visiting people today.

At the end of that day I was a changed teenager. It gave me the desire to live a religious life and I actively explored becoming a nun.

I spent time at the convent at my school, asking questions about becoming a nun; I corresponded with several convents across the United States to get an understanding about what becoming a nun required. For several months I exchanged letters with various nuns while I seriously considered this as my calling, while spending time at my local convent learning and make rosaries while considering this lifestyle.

This also improved my relations with the nuns at my school who went from a disapproving attitude, to an totally approving attitude by the end of that school year when they knew I was contemplating life as a nun, although none knew about my experience that day, the priest's negative response completely suppressed my desire to share what I held as a very special experience. The only thing that kept me from joining was I knew I was not set up to wake at 4 am, live in cold weather having lived in Florida all my life, and be ready to live a gypsy life going to whatever convent in the world I was ordered to go to, for as little or as long as told, and gladly, as obedience to one's religious superiors was the foundation of that life.

Since that time I have had other supernatural experiences which have led me to firmly believe we are in the last days. As I had seen in the vision it definitely appears God's judgment is on the horizon, and because of that the demonic principalities are increasing their warfare against us to snare as many as possible to embrace the depravity and evil God had let me see within the people as acceptable, and view righteousness as an offense.

It is for these reasons I have felt driven by God to write this book as fast as I possibly can while there is yet time for those who will listen to break free of the enemy strongholds gripping many in delusions that the warfare with the demonic principalities against all human souls is some kind of myth.

Through some of these supernatural experiences of mine, which include facing hostile demonic principalities, having a prophetic dream heralding the approaching end of the Lord's grace to the disobedient, and capturing on photo what appears evidence of a demonic principality deceiving billions, I will reveal just the opposite, which is the war to deceive people into various sins that disqualify them from heaven is tremendously and terrifyingly real precisely as our Lord Jesus said in Scriptures, and provide the scriptural ways how to overcome those enemy wiles, and despite all their wicked schemes, be counted ready when the Lord comes.

> This is why you also must be ready, because the Son of Man is coming at an hour you do not expect.
> —*Matthew 24:44, HCSB*

***

Chapter 2

YOU'RE BORN INTO THIS WAR

> When Adam sinned, sin entered the entire human race. Adam's sin brought death, so death spread to everyone, for everyone sinned.
> —*Romans 5:12, NLT*

Some nations in wars draw the line in harming children, seniors, and women and they adhere to Geneva Convention rules, and in those wars you can hope on certain kinds of civil behavior. The enemy engaged in a war against you, however, is truly your worst enemy right from your conception of life from God.

In his book, *Dead To Live Again*, Ronald Posey describes how the spirit of babies sent by God are attacked on their way to earth because the enemy wants to destroy any life created by God.

From the moment of your creation the enemy is out to attack you, and sometimes if there is a plan God has made for you to work in his kingdom known from the beginning, you can come under even more intense attacks, even when you are a tiny helpless baby.

In my case, Satan used a nurse to try to interfere with my birth, perhaps because it was clear God had a plan to use me for his kingdom work.

My mother related the story to me as this: the evening prior to my due date, on her own mother's advice, my mother had checked into the hospital not because she had shown signs of labor, but because it was nearing my scheduled birth.

That was clearly wise advice my grandmother gave to my mother, as close to 6 a.m. the next morning my mother felt me pushing to come out, without experiencing any labor pains or cramps.

At that point my mother told the nurse, a middle-aged woman, who was also in the room tending to another woman also having a baby that she felt me coming out.

The nurse shouted back at my mother, "Don't do that!"

Then she told my mother a stream of profanities, and then went on shouting, "You cannot do that! I am busy with the other girl, you have to wait! Close your mouth, don't open your mouth, close your mouth!"

Over and again she kept shouting like this to my mother, as if that alone would prevent my passage.

"The baby is already coming out!" my mother screamed back, as I was actually emerging to the world.

"No, you have to wait for the doctor!" the nurse shouted back.

"This is stupid as I can't do anything about it!" my mother yelled back as I came out despite the nurse's anger, and was born at precisely 6 a.m. on August 15, 1958.

The seasoned nurse later was never apologetic and stayed aggravated by my bad timing, displaying fruits revealing the source working in her at the time of my birth as the enemy, as there is no rational reason why a nurse whose job it is to assist mothers giving birth, trained with the medical knowledge, would be enraged to the point to lose all professionalism and hurl a stream of profanities to a young woman having a baby in a hospital setting where I was born, cursing that woman for giving birth at that time, and then remaining angry about it afterwards.

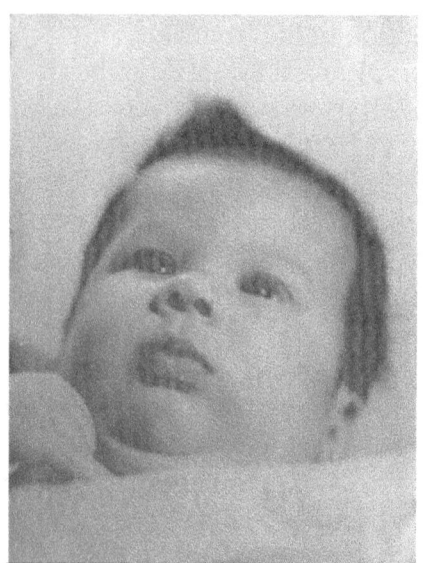

Me as that baby the nurse was so irritated to see born.

Such behavior points to demonic origins, showing a textbook example of demon spirits actively attacking a baby on its way to be born, to destroy if

Chapter 2: You're Born Into This War

possible, if not at least harm in some way a baby which they may even have seen would lead to a future threat to their ranks.

Left, my mother at the year the nurse screamed at her profanities as she gave birth to me, and me bottom center baby, between my 2 sisters, cousin above in his cowboy costume, and my father to the right.

Demons routinely use people to do their work often without that person knowing they are being a mouthpiece for the demonic as I detail in chapter 9, providing more examples from my life of this phenomenon which can grip a person and turn them into what I call a demon pawn.

Anything that is against God that a person utters is of demon origin, and the person does not have to be of bad character, that person just can let his or her guard down to follow a demonic thought as in the case of Apostle Peter.

> Peter took him aside and began to rebuke him. "Never, Lord!" he said. "This shall never happen to you!" Jesus turned to Peter and said, "Get away from me, Satan! You are a dangerous trap to me. You are seeing things merely from a human point of view, not from God's."
> —Matthew 16:22-23, NLT

Thus your arriving into this war as a newborn infant gained you no sympathy points with this enemy to perceive you as a helpless victim of the powers that be, and extend to you any mercy.

This enemy is all about defacing, blaspheming and deriding anything God has given life to for His purpose on earth, aiming to harm even tiny babies in the womb.

Bishop Earthquake Kelley relates in his book *BOUND to LOSE DESTINED to WIN*, how his own father, a voodoo priest living in the USA, demanded his mother have an abortion as he was not a wanted baby in an already large family. I separately saw Bishop Kelly relate in a televised interview how for close to two hours the doctor was unsuccessful in aborting him which he learned later on when he had an NDE and met Jesus in heaven, was due to the Lord himself holding his hand over his fetus to prevent the doctor from aborting him, and destroying the plan God had meant for his life.

> We know that we are children of God, and that the whole world is under the control of the evil one.
> —*1 John 5:19, NIV*

Bishop Kelly's own story is another example how people under control of the devil are unwittingly performing the devil's work to destroy any children to be born sent by God to aid the world in the battle of good and evil.

Was the doctor performing abortions himself evil? Not necessarily, but for certain the doctor had let himself follow a path that led him to do work respected of the world as important for pro choice, which was in total enmity with the plans of God which are to bring into the world children, all set with plans he has marked for them.

> Unfaithful people! Don't you know that to be the world's friend means to be God's enemy? If you want to be the world's friend, you make yourself God's enemy.
> —*James 4:4, GNT*

If the enemy treats even unborn babies as threatening targets to eliminate or detrimentally harm, you can have a better

Chapter 2: You're Born Into This War

understanding of the kind of war your parents conceived you into, an understanding that hopefully will get you to not harbor wrong ideas of your safety in their presence, to expect any sort of compassion and decency from them.

Instead of blaming God for the travails of the world, the blame rightly sits on Satan and his kingdom.

> "For I have no pleasure in the death of one who dies," says the Lord God. "Therefore turn and live!"
> —*Ezekiel 18:32, NKJV*

The key item to keep foremost in your mind concerning this war is that our Lord Jesus Christ has accomplished for us on the cross all that is needed for us to obtain liberty if we are captives and obtain deliverance from every trouble stemming from the enemy.

> The Spirit of the Sovereign LORD is upon me, because the LORD has appointed me to bring good news to the poor. He has sent me to comfort the brokenhearted and to announce that captives will be released and prisoners will be freed.
> —*Isaiah 61:1-2, NKV*

For this singular purpose, which is to completely abolish all schemes of our enemy, is why the Son of God came down from his glorious throne.

> He who sins is of the devil, for the devil has sinned from the beginning. For this purpose the Son of God was manifested, that He might destroy the works of the devil.
> —*1 John 3:8, NKV*

Thus it really is an affront to Jesus to try to brush under the rug any focus on the works of the devil and teachings Jesus left for us to follow to overcome them through what he painfully suffered to set us free from. He didn't come down to fill people with good feelings and peace; he came down to turn people against one another, to set the world on fire, to break people out of the bondage of the enemy.

> Do not think that I have come to bring peace to the earth. I have not come to bring peace, but a sword. For I have come to set a man against his father, and a daughter against her mother, and a daughter-in-law against her mother-in-law. And a person's enemies will be those of his own household.
> —*Matthew 10:34-36, ESV*

Therefore, to reject teachings about the threat of hell as the Lord relates in the Scriptures is to be an anti-Christ.

> Whoever is not with me is against me, and whoever does not gather with me scatters.
> —*Luke 11:23, NIV*

If you understand your participation in this battle started at your conception, you can have a better picture of the ruthlessness of your adversary towards you, that it goes all the way back to when you were a defenseless fetus, on to a defenseless infant, all those times the enemy ready and seeking to destroy you.

From the moment you were created, you were swept up into a highly-dangerous hostile battle, with a literally diabolical enemy out to destroy all humans. Knowing this, allows you to operate with the veil of ignorance ripped from your eyes, and see the true full threat of such an enemy that has zero qualms in destroying humans at all stages of their lives.

From your very conception, this unseen enemy has kept watch on you, plotting against you ever since to take your life.

> For I was born a sinner -- yes, from the moment my mother conceived me.
> —*Psalm 51:5, NLT*

Chapter 2: You're Born Into This War

Since you are born into this war, you are in either one of two positions: captive or fighting soldier, one or the other.

As the end days near, the war to destroy you has increased even more, as it is increasing against people everywhere. The battle you were born into from the moment you were conceived in sin is against Satan's kingdom, his rulers in power and all their soldiers.

> For we are not fighting against people made of flesh and blood, but against the evil rulers and authorities of the unseen world, against those mighty powers of darkness who rule this world, and against wicked spirits in the heavenly realms.
> —*Ephesians 6:12, NLT*

The war is very real, and the enemy, although largely not seen by humanity, is very real.

> Be careful! Watch out for attacks from the Devil, your great enemy. He prowls around like a roaring lion, looking for some victim to devour.
> —*1 Peter 5:8, NLT*

New Testament Scriptures alone provide enough proof for you to believe they are real and no other witness should be necessary to convince you to take who they are and what threat they are to you, enormously serious. However, they are so crafty that too many people still disbelieve, people who profess to be Christians, yet dismiss the words of Jesus, himself, concerning the demon principalities under Satan's rule, and the threat they work to lead you to, which is hell.

That is why I will speak freely of personal encounters I have had with demonic principalities in this book, to work against the strongholds they have erected to make you disbelieve and be unaware of the grave danger you are in and to realize that not just the good things in the Scriptures are true, but the terrifying things Jesus and the Apostles warned about also are true, things put to save you from them.

One of the ways the enemy tries to get you to dismiss the warnings is to scoff against any message to believers dealing with fear. The enemy wants you to scoff at fear, treat it as bad, and entirely forget there is fear that saves you, a fear that is good, a fear full of messages you want to pay attention to with all you are worth and follow what they are telling you in order to live.

An example of good fear that saves is the fear you feel at the edge of a dangerous height. Without that fear you might disregard the danger and make a fatal mistake. That fear keeps you alert and on guard, and gets you to resist coming too close to an unwise position where an accident can happen if you lose your balance. The fear you feel there is one to protect you from harm.

It is the same with the fear the Lord Jesus teaches to have about God. That fear is the fear that saves you by keeping you from making fatal mistakes next to an omnipotent power.

> Don't be afraid of those who want to kill you. They can only kill your body; they cannot touch your soul. Fear only God, who can destroy both soul and body in hell.
> —*Matthew 10:28, NLT*

It is also the same with the fear of hell sentence. That fear is a fear that moves you to resist doing offenses that can take you to its depths, and is a healthy fear to save you from such a fate.

> Instead, all that is left is to wait in fear for the coming Judgment and the fierce fire which will destroy those who oppose God!
> —*Hebrews 10:27, GNT*

Some reactions of fear happen automatically when you observe the threat such as coming to the edge of a steep cliff. Other fears happen only through indirect education about the threat if it is one that is unseen, such as acquiring an educated fear about entering an environment contaminated with a deadly bacteria or full of dangerous levels of radiation in order to have the

Chapter 2: You're Born Into This War

healthy response to take the measures necessary to keep yourself safe against such unseen threats.

Therefore, do not let the enemy lie to you that any message of fear regarding your salvation is not of God, and not Biblical and cause you to harden your heart and not receive the life-saving instructions in the Scriptures that teach that we are wrestling against a people that truly exist in the unseen world, a people that is fanatically hostile and full of hate to us.

There is no safe region in this planet you can escape to and be free of this war, no place as this enemy is in power over the entire world.

> The LORD said to Satan, "Where have you come from?" Satan answered the LORD, "From roaming through the earth and going back and forth in it."
> —*Job 1:7, NIV*

All your days left in this earth as a person of flesh and blood, you will continually face persistent attacks of the enemy in one form or another to ruin your life, with intent to destroy you, and that's the kind of war you were born into.

> Since the children have flesh and blood, he too shared in their humanity so that by his death he might destroy him who holds the power of death--that is, the devil— and free those who all their lives were held in slavery by their fear of death.
> —*Hebrews 2:14-15, NIV*

***

Chapter 3

DEMONIC PRINCIPALITES ARE ENTIRELY REAL

You will open their eyes and turn them from darkness to light and from Satan's control to God's. Then they will receive forgiveness for their sins and a share among God's people who are made holy by believing in me.'
—*Acts 26:18, GW*

To have any kind of fighting chance in this war, you need a primer 101 on demon reality. You need to be caught up to speed demons are real, and the demonic principalities are real.

Potent Information Demonic Principalities Are Real

As an eye-witness myself of their reality, I will relate to you myself some of my encounters as part of this proof. However, before I do, I want to touch briefly on some potent information on these realities from others, including what could be scientific evidence already established that not only demonic principalities as real, but prove God is real.

I will start with Roger Morneau, who related in his book, *A Trip Into The Supernatural*, about when he was involved in an underground demonic cult with direct interactions with Satan, that the best strategy the devil came up with to conquer people was to stay hidden, unlike in the early ages when demon activity was out in the open.

Now Roger Morneau, who has since passed away, later became a Seventh-Day Adventist based on a remark a priest of Satan reported the devil had said, which was that because the Adventists observed the Sabbath according to the Old Testament, meaning on Saturday, that God gave them special help so no evil spirit could ever deceive them in any way---which by the way refutes a later book called *Beware of Angels* by Mr. Morneau where he told the story of a devoted Seventh-Day Adventist deceived by demons to commit murder. So much for Satan's claim to that satanic priest, right? See? He is the Father of Lies.

> --He was a murderer from the beginning, and has nothing to do with the truth, because there is no truth in him. When he lies, he speaks out of his own character, for he is a liar and the father of lies.
>
> —*John 8:44, ESV*

But when Morneau had been told this Sabbath angle which purportedly afforded special protection from God which kept Adventists from demonic deceit, he was a young man who had no knowledge of the New Testament Scriptures which reveal the true deceit behind that reverse psychology the Father of Lies planted which are Colossians 2:13-18, Romans 14:5-6, Galatians 4:10, Ephesians 2:15, Mark 2:27 and Galatians 5:4.

What would be the purpose of such a deceit? One such purpose would be to get people to falsely believe that just by belonging to a denomination they cannot be deceived by the enemy, and thus let down their guard in that way, and believe anything they get is from God without testing it to Scriptures.

Ordinances, which are those rules dealing with food, days and such rituals, Christians are free from, and if you look further into that denomination you see more ordinance-type rules pertaining to foods, in that a vegetarian diet is what gives health from a loving God. However, Romans 14:3-6 shows we are not to despise a fellow Christian brother who abstains from a certain food, or who esteems one day above the other, as God has accepted him and we are not to pass judgment.

Thus, knowing how Satan is the master of deceit, I just want to state by my quoting Mr. Morneau, I do not endorse the views he expressed concerning that denomination. Yet I do recommend, in that light, that you read his experience with the demonic which largely took place before he converted to that denomination, in order to further gain information on the reality of the demonic principalities in work in today's world.

As far as the strategy Morneau shared of the devil to keep the demonic principalities hidden, you have to admit, this is a very clever move to conceal their existence, as for many people if they don't see something with their own eyes, or at least get reports back from sources they trust, they will not and cannot buy that fact, if and I stress IF, it has to do with the supernatural, because routinely and without question, people accept the world of microbiology where a whole dimension of things exist affecting them, they never will lay eyes on.

Science Has Already Proven God And Devil Real

You don't get ridiculed near as much accepting data from a scientific source as from a religious source, never mind the track record in science that has more than once scrapped entire systems of scientific beliefs when new data has wiped away the former criteria.

The irony of this, though, getting to the scientific evidence, is there actually exists an accepted scientific phenomenon which gives strong proof of the supernatural forces of good and evil, as in God and the devil. Yet, despite this existing evidence which people have overlooked or not connected to supplying this evidence, here many people believe science can never prove the supernatural world is real, or that God really exists and that the evil principalities exist, and thus feel these subjects will always remain issues of faith.

But I say science may have already established good proof in the Schrödinger Cat phenomenon, a thought experiment by Austrian physicist Erwin Schrödinger which revealed strong evidence that matter as in sub-atomic particles, can be influenced by one's thoughts or expectations.

Go beyond the surface, dare to consider the implications this phenomenon presents: just flip around this quantum mechanics behavior non-spiritual classification to go beyond the obvious superficial, the obvious surface, to the implications beneath that, which is not that the observer's thoughts or expectations are the final influence, but the observer's thoughts act as the catalyst to the real driving force behind what moves the atomic particles.

In other words that the cause of the influence is spirit interaction with the observer, that spirit has substance and influence itself, is not imaginary and actually is the foundation of control to existence itself.

While Erwin Schrödinger interpreted the thoughts or expectations of the observer to be the influence, I say he did not look beyond the physical interpretations to consider the apparent influence as result of a reaction from an unseen force meeting that observer's thought or expectation, resulting to that source as the actual influence.

While it would seem it was the observer enacting the influence, in fact, the implication is a greater power, an unseen power, could be fulfilling that expectation, and causing the influence on the subatomic particles, in fact to all matter, one power source for life, one power source for destruction.

Thus expectation for evil, results in an evil source delivering that behavior, and an expectation for good, results in a good source, the true source of influence, delivering that expected good---in other words, in the example for expectation of a good desire, what the principle of true faith is about, as in the kind Jesus said would move mountains, God as that source that fulfills true faith.

In the Scriptures on Jesus raising Lazarus from the dead, through Jesus words to God before he commanded Lazarus to come out of the tomb, Jesus revealed that believing would result in seeing the glory of God, and in that implying the glory of God's power to do all things asked in real faith.

He went further to reveal that the command he was about to give to Lazarus would be heard by God, the Father, whose ears always listened to whatever Jesus said, thus making clear that because God listened to ALL Jesus said, that whatever Jesus told Lazarus to do, God would thus fulfill immediately.

Here then we have Jesus the observer full of expectation, speaking that expectation, and the true source, the Father, revealing his glory, which is his power, causing the physical matter in decay to regenerate and a dead man come to life.

Then Jesus said, "Did I not tell you that if you believed, you would see the glory of God?" So they took away the stone. Then Jesus looked up and said, "Father, I thank you that you have heard me. I knew that you always hear me, but I said this for the benefit of the people standing here, that they may believe that you sent me." When he had said this, Jesus called in a loud voice, "Lazarus, come out!" The dead man came out, his hands and feet wrapped with strips of linen, and a cloth around his face. Jesus said to them, "Take off the grave clothes and let him go."
—*John 11:40-44, NIV*

"You don't have enough faith," Jesus told them. "I tell you the truth, if you had faith even as small as a mustard seed, you could say to this mountain, 'Move from here to there,' and it would move. Nothing would be impossible."
—*Matthew 17:20, NIV*

This faith principle Jesus gave, further Bible Scriptures reveal the believer is not the source of power that moves the mountain, but his or her strong enough faith, and God the one fulfilling that faith.

But when he asks, he must believe and not doubt, because he who doubts is like a wave of the sea, blown and tossed by the wind. That man should not think he will receive anything from the Lord; he is a double-minded man, unstable in all he does.
—*James 1:6-8, NIV*

And whatever we ask we receive from Him, because we keep His commandments and do those things that are pleasing in His sight.
—*1 John 3:22, NKJV*

What is faith, but the type of expectation seen to result in an influence of matter as in the Schrödinger Cat phenomenon, delivering to the observer of faith, that expectation, just as that quantum principle.

> To have faith is to be sure of the things we hope for, to be certain of the things we cannot see.
> —*Hebrews 11:1, GNT*

Even though this original experiment was a thought experiment, since then this principle has been applied in practical applications resulting from scientific research of similar quantum mechanics principles. So scientific research does not only back up the existence of God, who fulfills the hopeful expectations of the righteous, but also implies proof of the demonic principalities who fulfill hopeful expectations of evil, while the same principle also supplying scientific evidence concerning faith.

By the scriptural teachings behind what faith is, what prayers God does hear, and which ones he rejects, and how Satan comes immediately to snatch the word out of weak believers---the implications are all observers in the physical realm are being observed themselves by one force or another, standing by to deliver that expectation.

I guarantee you give a person two hats, one says Scientist and the other says Believer, and he explains this phenomenon with a scientific angle, a listening crowd won't question its validity but accept it as one of those quirky science facts. However, let the person switch hats and give a spiritual explanation for the same phenomenon, and many of the same listeners will think the person is full of baloney and with a mental screw loose to boot, or brainwashed by charming cultural backwards beliefs.

According to Roger Morneau, also in his same book, this is a big strategy the devil uses to his advantage: birthing false scientific theories to replace the truth of the spiritual reality, the goal being disqualifying the person who rejects the truth and upholds the mistruth, disqualified from eternal life. If you keep in mind this is a war, the evil side does whatever it takes, dirty, evil or cloaked in good to block people from eternal salvation.

Many people would rather accept this convoluted explanation of how observing affects the quantum mechanics of what is

Chapter 3: Demonic Principalities Are Entirely Real

observed, than how observing affects how a higher power caters to your observation, a good power to your blessing, an evil to malicious goals so it appears the observing is the driving force, when observing may merely act as the catalyst which triggers the true powers behind.

So the physicist Erin Schrödinger believed his quantum thought experiment showed the scientific phenomenon of the act of observing affecting what is observed. However, I say he didn't look past face value and get wider perspectives outside the box of approved theories, that he may have come across the phenomenon of the spiritual kingdoms, reacting to our observations to manipulate the environment for a desired end---good for our good, bad for our destruction.

All that aside, short of yourself seeing demons with your own eyes for you to believe in their reality, there are plenty of regular people who have seen demons and can testify to it, in <u>this</u> day and age, and many of them people who do not do drugs and do not drink, who were very much awake and in regular activities, and in such a group, people who have seen demonic activity jointly with others, giving further believability to the reality of the supernatural.

First thing of this is, if you believe in the Bible, then you should believe ALL of it, including the parts with demon possession, and the parts dealing with Hell, and Lake of Fire. Yet I am always surprised to encounter Christians who accept what makes them comfortable in the Bible and reject the rest as symbolic stories, even though they were told as facts straight from the mouth of the Savior.

Really, if you are a Bible-believing Christian, no one should have to 'prove' to you the existence of evil and the devil and demons. But you know what? Jesus really loves people and I believe he orchestrates some of these demon sightings to show by evidence that principalities of darkness are real, such as reported by filmmaker Darren Wilson in his interview with Sid Roth on his film *Furious Love* where God revealed to Darren the point of that film was to prove the existence of this supernatural war, that evil demonic spirits exist and the only way to win is through love, which is an interesting thing to consider when you read in the next chapter an *Exorcist* movie-like encounter I had where through love I overcame the encounter over 25 years before Darren Wilson's movie.

In fact, throughout history, it is evident Jesus orchestrates ongoing encounters with the demonic realm so despite Satan's underlying plan to stay out of site to make people come to the point to wonder if he ever was real, and in such, discard all of the reality of the kingdom of evil, and reject the need to follow any laws concerning such consequences, enough sightings and encounters continue to happen to reinforce the enemy is real, as is the battle between evil spirits and the heavenly good for human souls.

Okay, established, just by being a believer, you accept the Bible truths on the existence of the principalities of darkness. All the same, it is evident that God constantly arranges PR, as in Public Relations on this war to reveal the enemy on an ongoing basis because this is a dirty war by a dirty enemy.

God does so by setting up encounters for the sole sake to expose this demonic world as true. That is why sometimes people can find they have an appointment with evil, because that encounter will serve God a purpose to reveal the enemy, if not then, then later at God's appointed time, and help wake people up they are being played by the enemy.

Therefore besides the Bible, your loving God provides Show-and-Tell, kind of like randomly here and there switching on the spotlight in a dark forest so you see it is truly full of creatures lurking, which your night blindness can falsely lull you to believe are not there. By being alerted to them, you once more properly put your guard up so you don't get devoured.

The key to remember is God is all mighty, and has existence in total control. What occurs is part of his massive plan for the better good. The way God controlled Pharaoh's 'bad' behavior in Exodus which set the stage to show God's glory (Romans 9:17-18) is but one of many examples how God orchestrates events which may seem bad on the surface, as in Pharaoh's stubbornness and unyielding attitude to let the Israelites go, but which proved to impart important lessons as a result of that negative experience for the better of humanity, using a brutal dictator as a key player. In

Chapter 3: Demonic Principalities Are Entirely Real

Pharaoh's case, his evil behavior built the stage for God to show himself as an all-powerful God, the real God, the only God, and the importance of absolute obedience to him for the safety of their lives.

Because the world is big and it is full of people who never will even see a certain book or film God inspired to be made, God arranges multiple encounters as that, to reach as many people as possible through a chain of ongoing witnesses.

As one of those witnesses, I can testify that demons exist, having had several experiences in my lifetime.

In the next chapter I will cover some of those experiences in order that you can hear from another such person, who has actually witnessed the reality of demons firsthand, understanding that I am but one of many such witnesses, each of us living lives totally independent of one another, throughout the world, the world now, not the world back in Jesus' time to help scatter one of the schemes of the enemy that demon happenings only were confined to the days of Jesus, or were just concepts Christ spoke about, even though he was pretty literal when he talked about them.

> I have spoken to you of earthly things and you do not believe; how then will you believe if I speak of heavenly things?
> —*John 3:12, NIV*

***

Chapter 4

SOME OF MY DEMON ENCOUNTERS

> For they are spirits of demons, performing signs, which go out to the kings of the earth and of the whole world, to gather them to the battle of that great day of God Almighty.
> —*Revelation 16:14, NIV*

Being an eye-witness more than once, I speak with authority that this is not a fairy tail, evil is real, demons are real, and the warfare to destroy you is real.

When I look back, my having these experiences is not really a surprise considering how I had veered into the path of the paranormal only months after my open vision in 1972.

Had I had direction from a minister, following that experience, who understood visions from God, and gotten guidance on the right path of using the spiritual gifts imparted to me after that experience, I would have not been open to demonic influence and bought the lie these spiritual gifts were occult and psychic powers and for my own selfish personal agenda. At age 13, I had known nothing about spiritual gifts from the Holy Spirit: the only thing I had understood which gave people supernatural gifts was through what I had seen on television, which was paranormal powers.

At the school I had gone to they had not taught anything about spiritual gifts as a result of having received the Holy Spirit, yet from having watched Uri Geller on television I was well familiar with psychic powers and so thought that was what they were.

In addition they had also not taught things dealing with the paranormal in the vein of the occult were anything wrong. So here

I found myself with some spiritual gifts of some nature following the experience, and my example to understand them is what the world had to tell me, in other words, the enemy, because the prince of this world is Satan. In my neighborhood bookstore I found plenty of guides to lead me how to develop my natural psychic powers, not even considering Scriptures provided the right instructions, the ones that kept a person on the path to God and not to the demons.

Thus just months after, unguided as I was, I got hooked on study of the paranormal and started to meditate a lot, and was very proficient.

Wrongly believing the spiritual gifts I found myself with were psychic powers, I began soaking up all the paranormal titles I could get my hands on---Ruth Montgomery stuff, Edgar Cayce, and so on, beginning my journey as an aficionado of all things metaphysical.

I became so entrenched in the subject, that at only 14 years of age I had soaked up enough metaphysical information that my 9th grade teacher was so impressed with a class paper I wrote on the afterlife and metaphysical subjects that he wrote a personal note on my report that he had read it aloud to his wife and they both had gotten a lot from it. So you can see how deep I was into it, so fast, that I could impart intriguing information to adults at age 14.

However, totally on my own, and finding I had an inner 'knowing' of things, which I had not understood was a gift of the Spirit, not of my own, but a direction from the Holy Spirit, even where I sometimes got visions of future events, I listened to the false direction about what they were from the demonic with their strategy to have me spend my life doing their work and not the Lord's, getting drawn to paranormal subjects as a young teen, reading them voraciously, and believing this was what 'my' abilities were about.

One such example of my ignorant misuse of a gift of the Spirit at that time when 14 years of age, is as clear as yesterday to me when I wanted to impress my boyfriend, shown in this next photo with me that very year, by informing him how I had the power to see the future and I would prove it to him by telling him something personal of himself that would soon come to pass.

Chapter 4: Some Of My Demon Encounters

See it was just an innocent thing of a teen girl where I just wanted to impress a boy with what I could do.

But, as you can see, from the enemy influence to turn to the occult for answers, I was misinterpreting the closed visions that I was getting now and then when I was meditating that proved true, to be of my own paranormal power without a Spirit-filled prophet to lead me. That was a Friday when I had told that to my teen boyfriend attending the same junior high as I did. I had told him by the end of the weekend I would give him such an event.

That night I meditated, I got nothing. When he came to my house that Saturday, I had nothing to impart to him. I lay there in my bottom bunk bed that night trying really hard to get a future image, thinking that it was by my effort, but nothing happened that it got to the point I was going to make something up; after all I was 14 and trying to impress my cute boyfriend. Then suddenly, I got a vision in my mind like a mini movie.

I saw my boyfriend in my house, the subject of a monkey-in-the-middle game with my brothers. Next thing I saw was what seemed like hundreds of pieces of antique glass falling, then seeing my boyfriend looking down at his feet where glass was all around on the floor. That was the vision I had hoped for; yet in my unguided 14-year-old mind, I perceived these visions came of my own psychic powers, never thinking Holy Spirit, God, or devil.

So when my boyfriend came over the next day, as we sat on my living room sofa, I related him the future event I saw of him. He just laughed it off, not believing at all. Not less than 15 minutes passed later and it all took place, in a way I had not even put together myself.

My two younger brothers came in the living room, tossing a small football. Next thing I know my boyfriend had gotten up to play with them.

Their mini-football game went into the hallway and right away turned just like in my vision, with my brothers playing monkey-in-the-middle with him, tossing the football over him, to each other. I was soon to find out where all that antique glass would come from when one of my brother's pass he threw to fly over my boyfriend's head hit the overhead hall 1950s light fixture, busting it into small pieces which rained harmlessly down in front of him right at his feet, just as I had seen in that vision. Perhaps too shocked, he made no comment at all, and he ended up going home after that.

However, these psychic experiences as I saw them, were still a few years before I would actually encounter a principality of darkness, but the experiences which I continued to have, which seemed benign, continued to confirm, and got stronger in the reality of the supernatural, and supernatural forces and entities.

Like many who have erroneously been deceived on this path, one of pursuing the paranormal rather than pursuing the Lord for guidance, my early experiences were benign and fascinating as I continued in my teens to dabble in the paranormal, to what I perceived as many falsely do as a form of self-enhancement, to develop my ultimate power as a spiritual being, which was a demon lie to snare me in the sin of the occult.

> And the soul that turneth after such as have familiar spirits, and after wizards, to go a whoring after them, I will even set my face against that soul, and will cut him off from among his people.
> —*Leviticus 20:6, KJV*

I did so by studying telepathy, scrying, working on developing

Chapter 4: Some Of My Demon Encounters

my psychic powers, which are tools of wizards and also through which familiar spirits work, which are demon spirits who attend and obey a witch.

Of course I had no clue of those dark sides, but instead viewed these studies as personal spiritual development from a scientific metaphysical slant, which actually was instead a demonic propaganda to trick people they are rational paths to follow, concealing these are things of demons. In that ignorance, anything with a New Age slant, I wanted to know and absorb, fascinated by everything psychic. To me this was a rational, scientific pursuit of self-development, my untrained mind in the Scriptures having bought the enemy lies.

Through what I thought were my own efforts, I could often have visions of future events, and I got good at with operating under premonitions and could find places or people by what I had thought was my psychic sense, but now I know is my spiritual eyes.

One example was when, in late 1970s, one evening my father told me he had heard on the radio earlier that day an interview with a talented British psychic and medium named Freda Fell. He said she was there to give readings at a place in Hollywood, which was north of where we lived in Florida, about 25 miles.

Although he had gotten the name of the place, he had not caught any phone number or address. He had been so impressed with her interview; I was really moved to meet her while she was still in the area.

But all I had was a possible business name of Florida Society of Psychical Research, a city, Hollywood, and I knew the name of the visiting speaker supposed to be there, that was all. This was the days of no gps tracking devices or internet where you could type in names and get info, plus only directories one had was physical big phone books of just one's local area, not adjacent cities.

Because my desire was great to meet Freda Fell, I knew I could rely on my 'knowing' to locate this place and her, and went off the next morning to do so, just by that sense alone. I was entirely unfamiliar with Hollywood, but there was an undeniable 'knowing' within me that let me go from Miami by 'feel'.

Once approaching Hollywood some 25 miles later, I got the 'knowing' to head east on the exit onto Hollywood's main boulevard, and went for a few miles, when I suddenly had the 'knowing' to turn right on an upcoming road, South 20th Ave in the city, which was south, and didn't go too far when I got the impulse to stop at a payphone a couple blocks over. There had been other payphones on the way, but this was the one I knew to stop at.

This was back when payphones had physical phone directories attached by a chain you could look up phone numbers if they were published, a yellow book for businesses, white for residence or in smaller places both a yellow and white section in the same book.

Back then you only had your local city's phone books, not others. If you wanted to find out the address or number of a business in another city you had to have the city's phone book.

The other choice was to call that city's 411 information operator to locate it if it was listed in that local city's directory. But then you had to know the address or a nearby address for the operator to find it if you were not sure if the business name was right, and without gps or internet you had no way of being able to do that unless you had been there before. So the roadblocks to finding a place just on the name my father got off the radio were high if the name he got was not in its right order to locate in a phone book.

Opening that phone book, I looked up and was glad to find the Center listed as my father had heard. When I called the phone listed I was not just relieved someone answered, but when they asked where in Hollywood I was, and I told them my location, they answered I was right at the corner across the street from them!

When they told me the address, I realized it was the house I could see from where I stood, which further confirmed to me, I was coming to a place destined for me to be at, which specialized in psychic development and the paranormal, mediums and the like, again unguided from the teachings in the Bible about the schemes of the devil, this one a confidence game by the enemy to make me certain I was in the right place that by coming there supernaturally, the supernatural leading was right, and all good.

Chapter 4: Some Of My Demon Encounters

Paranormal Times in Apartment 5-110

During those early days I was an aficionado of the paranormal I didn't really encounter any hostile forces or anything straight out demonic, which again is part of the enemy's schemes, because if you are in the wrong, the enemy is happy to let you stay there, ignorantly in their clutches.

They stayed fun, fascinating and thought-provoking, to the point I was able to publish later on in 1989 some of my psychic experiences from that period of time when I was a teen just starting college and sharing a room with my friend from high school. The article appeared in *FATE* magazine, a magazine devoted to the paranormal, in their August 1989 issue as a full-length article I wrote entitled, "Paranormal Times in Apartment 5-110" with the hook subtitle lead of, "Welcoming ghosts to the new apartment wasn't such a good idea—because ghosts were all too ready to accept."

That article covered the more dramatic experiences I and my friend (see next picture of me and my friend from the photo of us in that 1989 *Fate* magazine article), from high school days, then become my roommate, had while living in that apartment, although by no means the sum-total of my experiences, these just relating to that particular year.

By that article it is clear, that like many people ignorant of the warfare between heaven and fallen spirits, I was clueless what I was dabbling in, didn't think anything worrisome about it and just looked at these things as fascinating fun.

I was unaware that The Spirit clearly says that in later times some will abandon the faith and follow deceiving spirits and things taught by demons, (1 Timothy 4:1 NIV) validating psychic encounters with paranormal as real, but not coming from the benign entities you think you are dealing with, but instead coming from crafty deceiving spirits able to deliver this information to the individual so it appears as coming from a dead relative, or a helpful spirit guide or your inner transcendent self.

All the same, it appeared that God had an angel on guard,

Author Vivian R. Cole (Left) with Lori Rice

looking out for us in this scenario from one of the mysterious experiences we jointly had in that apartment, in which each night, when we retired to our separate rooms, locked our doors, got in bed, someone would rattle our doorknob, as if testing if it were locked and we were safe.

For weeks we thought it was each of the other doing this, and frankly, we separately became annoyed with one another with this hen-pecking motherly security check, but then in a confrontation, finding out it was neither of us, it turned into a disturbing occurrence. That and the young woman's voice I heard when I was working on a diorama portraying a bombed church in the middle of a war, where only the crucifix miraculously survived, thoughtfully and slowly heard a female voice say behind my shoulder, as if digesting and 'getting' what I was doing, "Ohhhhh...," scaring me so much that I had to pull open all the curtains and windows, to let in comforting sounds and light to calm my wildly thumping heart.

However, the other experiences were not angelic like, but in the new age, occult arena. In other words, I wasn't very different from many people fascinated by the paranormal and gladly partook in various facets of it that were for entertainment purposes and not because we were devotees of it, but just college-age teens captivated and enjoying the thrills of the supernatural.

The problem with these activities is they seem harmless but they open doors of legal rights to the principalities of darkness through God-forbidden activities as mediums, psychics, summoning the dead, and turning to paranormal forces for your information.

> When you come into the land that the Lord your God is giving you, you shall not learn to follow the abominable practices of those nations. There shall not be found among you anyone who burns his son or his daughter as an offering, anyone who practices divination or tells fortunes or interprets omens, or a sorcerer or a charmer or a medium or a necromancer or one who inquires of the dead, for whoever does these things is an abomination to the Lord. And because of these abominations the Lord your God is driving them out before you. You shall be blameless before the Lord your God.
> —*Deuteronomy 18:9-14, ESV*

When you read this Scripture above, you must keep in mind that God is the same yesterday, today and tomorrow, and what he decreed an abomination to him yesterday, is still an abomination today, and will remain an abomination tomorrow.

I am the LORD, and I do not change. That is why you descendants of Jacob are not already destroyed.
—*Malachi 3:6, NLT*

Jesus Christ is the same yesterday, today, and forever.
—*Hebrews 13:8, NLT*

God is the same, Jesus is the same, and Jesus always is with what is in accord with the Father. And He who sent Me is with Me. The Father has not left Me alone, for I always do those things that please Him."
—*John 8:29, NKJV*

Therefore, you can be sure dabbling, even for entertainment in paranormal activities defiles you with God, whether it is like my friends and I often did, using a Ouija board for kicks, trying out scrying just because I saw it done on the family film Wizard of Oz, or learning how to read the Tarot in a sincere effort of what I perceived strengthening and developing my inner psychic abilities, and made me guilty of abominations as God decreed.

The immediate issue with that is when you break a law of God, demons obtain the legal right to harass you.

I will no longer talk much with you, for the ruler of this world is coming. He has no claim on me---
—*John 14:30, ESV*

By the word 'claim' in Verse 30, Jesus meant legal claim, as in legal right or legal hold through sin and since he was free of sin, free of the Original sin men are born in, and he was blameless with a stain-free righteous bloodline mankind does not have, Satan had no access to do anything to him.

He is the kind of high priest we need because he is holy and blameless, unstained by sin. He has now been set apart from sinners, and he has been given the highest place of honor in heaven.
—*Hebrews 7:26, NLT*

Chapter 4: Some Of My Demon Encounters

You can start small and so your demon troubles are 'small', but the pathway always leads further and deeper, and the demons which can plague you can be harder to get rid of, resistant to regular methods of prayer to banish.

Briefly, there are several ways demons have legal rights to you:

- Unsaved – you are an open doorway from Original sin, as sin gives the enemy a claim on you (1 Corinthians 15:22).
- Unsaved – breaking God's laws and not repenting, again because unrepentant sin gives the enemy a claim on you (John 5:14).
- Saved – temptations leading you to sin and you fail to repent (1 John 1:6).
- Saved – tolerance accepting displeasing things to God because just tolerating someone in a sin you are guilty of sharing that sin (2 John 1:11; 1 Timothy 5:22; Ephesians 5:11) with that person as by your silence to that sin you are giving your indirect approval.

These are not all, but these are heavy players to ways demons get legal rights to trouble you or downright possess you. To the demons it is all about dragging you down, and if they can't by your faith, they will then focus on making you as miserable as possible in the battlefield of earth.

Wed Devotee of the Occult & Demon Times Started

In my case, the tide turned to from 'harmless' fun, to demonic harassment when I married a man deep into the occult who had started his own religion, which held some New Age beliefs with earth Wicca and Kabala beliefs woven in.

It was my time in that relationship when I encountered demonic spirits as malicious spirits, not as fascinating paranormal experiences as they had kept themselves while I was in my 'science' paranormal stage and had not yet crossed into the threshold of occult magic.

My very first encounter was on the morning after my future husband and I had spent the entire night camping out at the old Biltmore Hotel in Miami, Florida on a ghost hunting chase with a handful of members from the club we belonged to, The Science Fiction and Fantasy Society. In this next picture, here I am pictured far right in the newspaper article written on that jaunt, shown with two of my friends from the club, as we got ready to spend our second night in this old hotel which was listed as the world's largest haunted house in a book by Richard Winer called *Haunted Houses*.

Club members prepare for spooky night
... from left, Barbara Clipper, Joe Kimbro, Vivian Pulido

Is old hotel haunted? They seek answers

By CRAIG MATSUDA
Herald Staff Writer

They were seven camped on the 13th floor of the deserted Biltmore Hotel and it was 2:30 a.m. The tape recorders were running, and so were these adult science fiction fans...

Science Fiction Fantasy Society thought.
They went home from their vigil tired and disappointed. Only later did they play the tapes they had made.
And that's when they discovered the sound.

Ever fascinated with anything paranormal, after reading Richard Winer's book and finding this local hotel was listed as the world's largest haunted house, I had presented to my friends in that club the idea of spending the night at the hotel with the premise we do some amateur paranormal investigation.

Since the timing of our outing was close to Halloween, the *Miami Herald*, which was our local newspaper, and one of our news stations, of which I can't remember now, did brief stories covering our jaunt. Although we were a Science Fiction and Fantasy Society, it seemed a natural extension of our interest to apply exploration of fantastic sci-fi ideas to the paranormal subjects, which we had started the month earlier by our first trip spending a night in a cemetery with a tape recorder, trying to capture anything paranormal, but only ended up riddled with mosquito bites.

You can see how it seems so innocent to get involved in the

Chapter 4: Some Of My Demon Encounters

paranormal and unknowingly open doors wide to the demonic principalities as we were inadvertently doing.

You don't have to join any cult or renounce your belief in Jesus to get caught in a treacherous web spun by the demonic in order to trap you into the danger of treading into paranormal activities that make you prey of demons.

We behaved responsibly; we obtained proper permissions for our excursions from the City of Coral Gables the hotel was part of, and participated only for the game of it, nothing further. Point of the matter is it doesn't matter how you enter in the demonic realm, the troubles and problems, and their agendas with you are the same, whether you are doing it on a lark, or you commit yourself to a witches group. This is why you should not be indifferent or complacent to participating in such activities.

The city must have thought it was also harmless fun, because they granted us permission to conduct our investigation on September 29, 1979 from 9 p.m. to 4 a.m. which was the day before my first demonic encounter through my connection with my soon-to-be husband, heavily into the occult, himself viewing his occult involvement as harmless New Age thinking.

In that first introductory encounter, it took place not at the hotel, but when I went afterwards to my future husband's house, and he left me alone, my first time alone in that house, while he went to work.

I was not alone in the house for long, when on my walk to his bedroom to sleep, something invisible yanked hard the hair on the back of my head, as hard as if you had a malicious elementary school age sibling sneaking in a dirty pull to your hair. Having already encountered experiences that I found scary, like that voice I heard while making that diorama in 1977 in Apartment 5-110, I made no reaction, ignoring it with as deadpan a face as I could, and locked myself in the bedroom, propping the wicker chair (shown below) he had so it faced the street in front, so I could be connected with the normal outdoors, despite feeling the presence of invisible hostile oppressive intelligences, and fell asleep.

In that same wicker chair I am seated in this next picture which I had put facing the front window, I fell asleep, and found myself having a strange dream.

When I fell asleep I found myself inside of a tent like those big circus tents, but just myself, and that tent was within another tent, and another, and so on. Above those tents on the outside were all kinds of demonic beings flying around, fluttering against the outer tent like moths batter against a bright light bulb in the dark.

You can be sure on his return I told my future husband what happened, first with the hair pulling, then with the dream. Soon as I told him the dream, he got a big smile on his face, not what I expected. With great satisfaction, he waved with his hand to look behind me, where I saw this altar I had seen he had there, not having thought anymore of it than I did my wizard and dragon statues I had at my house.

He said, "Every night I put a tent up around my house of protection at this altar." From his attitude, he was convinced his practice was working and made a barrier of protection.

But from what I saw in my dream, it looked more like it was

Chapter 4: Some Of My Demon Encounters

attracting evil, rather than repelling, but again at the time, age 21, I was green behind the ears on these things and not sure.

That marked my first encounter with clearly demonic entities, hostile and classic in appearance as those medieval artworks on deformed demons, which is what I had seen flying in the air outside those many tents (In the next photo see his altar at the far left; the banner above the altar bearing symbol of the religion he created---this same bedroom was where I'd had the tent dream

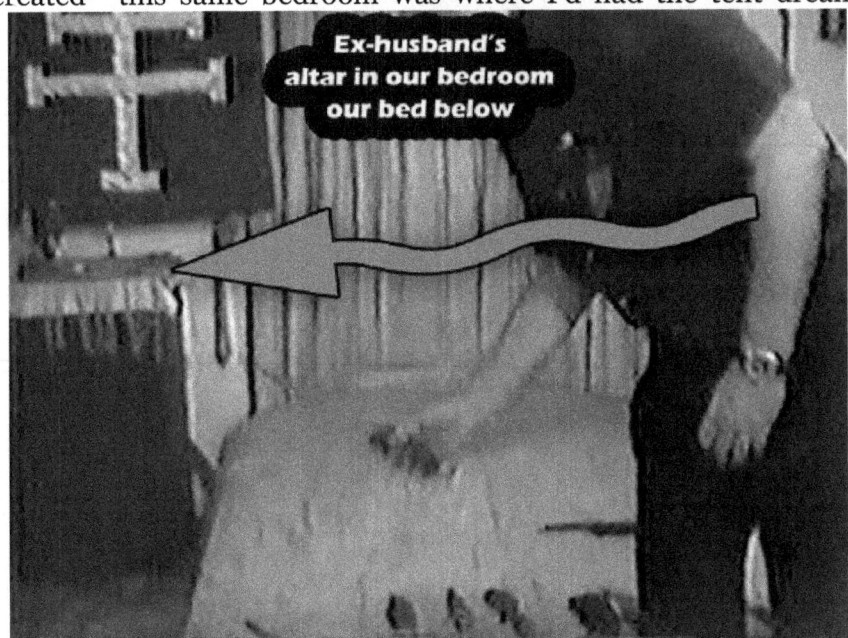
Ex-husband's altar in our bedroom our bed below

first time I'd slept there. It was outside that room in the adjacent hall where my hair had been yanked. Here at this altar he did incantations to spirits of north, south, east and west & nightly put up his 'tent' protection around his property just as I had seen a literal manifestation of some of those occult-created tents in that premonitory dream, which had introduced me that from this occult ritual it had turned his house into a demon attractant).

This experience also served as an example how God gave me warnings, gave me instructions, immediately taking me to a dream that revealed the entire dangerous occult scenario I had no clue of, in it's entirety: the man was deeply into occult magic to the point he was a burning light to demon spirits, drawing to him the very things he was confident his methods repelled, and being within these tents he had conjured through lifting incantations unwittingly to demons was to be in the middle of all this enemy garbage.

Did I get that? No, clueless, trusting a person's perception, instead of listening to the right source, revealing to me the threats in the dream.

Thus, this warning went over my head, and 3 short months later, in January 1980, I went through a New Age marriage ceremony with this man twenty-two years older than I, who was heavily into occult magic, divination, to the point he had created his own religion, and moved in with him into the community called Buena Vista.

That community was so close to the border of a place called Little Haiti, a community rift with crime, that we experienced the same crime, just 3 blocks south of Little Haiti. Where we had lived in Buena Vista at the time had a palpable oppressive air about it, very similar when you leave a safe part of town and journey into rough areas, and that is when my encounters with the demonic, uncloaked as it were, began happening.

This area was rough, as in bad crime and a lot of drug problems, with in fact our house being located in sight of a Fire Station on NE 2nd Avenue which later burned down and never was rebuilt, and in sight of a treatment center for drug abuse.

Now that area of town has improved somewhat with the growth of the Arts and Design District of Miami, but when I moved in there, the Arts and Design was just budding, and crime was so bad, it was hard to get police to come to the area.

To get an idea just how bad the crime was, the Crime Watch sign erected later as shown in this next photo, on the edge of my lawn, had been put precisely, unknown to the workers who erected the sign, in the exact spot I saw a man die on my lawn, his blood soaking into that very ground, shot in the head by robbers all because he ran from them, and didn't give up the zippered bank pouch he held that had only papers and no money.

Besides that rough edge from just crime, more important as far as this being a story of the warfare between good and evil, it also had an evil air about it that was detectable to me like smog is detectable, a kind of oppressive thickness to the air I could feel.

Chapter 4: Some Of My Demon Encounters

When entering and leaving the area, each time I felt distinct

differences that had nothing to do with the level of crime and toughness of the area, as my journeys into other equally tough areas in Miami, never gave me this distinctly evil oppressive sensation where it was like driving into a fog-covered area in hell and leaving a fog-covered area in hell where you could sense evil and oppression, palpable and weighing on you like a dense fog, a feeling you would have where evil reigns.

It is a very distinct feeling that is not normal to have and not related to how much crime an area has, nor how much gang graffiti there is, nor how run down buildings are, because those are people-created things, and that evil air I felt in that area was not due to people. It came from a demonic principality gripping that area, and though I did not know about demonic principalities, I knew it was demonically evil. I do not know if it came along with some voodoo going in that area, as only God knows, but I do know people, like my ex-husband, were actively practicing sorcery in that area and sorcery is only fueled by demons.

In essence I had moved into an area gripped in a demonic stronghold residing in intimate relationship with a person steeped in occult practices, the formula for demon ShowTime.

Just 3 years prior my now ex's mother had bought the house I had moved into with him, renting it out to him, herself living next door in a house she had purchased the decade before in 1969 when the neighborhood had been a decent residential area. But the neighborhood had started a decline into crime and poverty just a few years after, pushing many of the original homeowners out.

I say it was a New Age marriage ceremony because we had made a deal for how we would get married: the deal was that we first would be married his way, which was by a person from the social worker office he had supervised, whom he had ordained that same week as a priestess in his invented religion just to conduct our marriage. Then the deal had been that the next week we do it my way, which was a formal marriage in a church by a priest, just me, him and my brother.

But after his way, the next week when it came to follow through with my way, he refused, saying his way had been good enough; but his way involved a last minute 'ordination' of his office co-worker as a priestess in his religion, who was not a recognized notary, nor was his religion a recognized, formal religion, and involved only him as his church member in the state of Florida. So in essence, I found myself 'married' by a non-state recognized person to perform marriages, and moved in with a man who changed his mind after I had moved in to do it my way, through the church.

So it was really not a marriage, as later a couple of Catholic priests had told me after the 'marriage' was over, but more like we were living together, although I was too embarrassed to tell my family, and stayed, hoping he would change his mind to follow through with the marriage in a church, which never happened. Still, for ease of telling the story, I will still call him my ex-husband.

My ex-husband's mother was in her 70s and living with her was her mother who was over age 100, and they had no intentions of moving. Instead these two elderly women had adapted by putting iron bars enclosing their front porch with jail-like bars. I, myself, was 21 and my ex-husband was over age 40 so you can see I was naïve in dangers, naïve in life, and naïve in what I was

Chapter 4: Some Of My Demon Encounters

getting into neighborhood wise and spiritual wise.

Since there was no rent for a 2-bedroom house my ex-husband could find on his low social-worker supervisor income at the bargain price his mother gave him, under $200 a month, coupled with the fact his mother and elderly grandmother were right next door, he too, was set to stay in this neighborhood, no matter what crimes would come, and come they did that it was like living in the days of the Wild West, having to have guns loaded all the time and nearby to protect ourselves from all the attempted robberies, home invasions and kidnappings.

Getting back to the demonic evil air in that crime-filled area, thirty years later I would hear different Christian teachers describe the same thing, labeling it as demons in power over certain areas, strongholds holding the areas in evil grip, a demonic principality.

Living In A Demonic Stronghold

The Bible tells us there are demons ruling over the world, but this was the first time in my life I actually discerned such a phenomenon of a demon ruling over an area, a demonic principality, and it felt like a palpable evil dark oppression---I am talking back in the early 1980s before this seemed to become a popular and even sometimes solely-focused Christian ministry.

So without knowing about demonic strongholds, I experienced living 2 years in such an area, feeling the demonic oppression while in the location and feeling the distinct difference of getting out of its range, the difference between a spiritually 'clean' area, and one under a demonic principality.

> For we wrestle not against flesh and blood, but against principalities, against powers, against the rulers of the darkness of this world, against spiritual wickedness in high places.
> —*Ephesians 6:12, KJV*

Moreover, this led to my having several demonic encounters and struggles, more than once having waking encounters with such principalities of darkness.

In this next encounter I had during that time with the demonic was unusual in that it didn't happen suddenly, it seemed to be staged, almost like an appointment with the demonic principality, for a formal standoff of some kind.

Whether the plans of this principality to makes its way to me for a standoff was heard at the moment it was made by God, in advance before that principality actually followed through, or that it could be seen making its way to me for a formal standoff, or it was by permission from God to test me because I was living a double-hearted life, believing I was Christian yet I was doing all types of New Age activities along with my ex-husband, not seeing a conflict, I will never know.

But that this was a known event ahead of time, weeks ahead in fact, so I could be forewarned in that dream and prepared, is what I can attest to.

Looking back after all these years, it did seem like a Job Scripture devil thing, where the devil may have talked God into testing me in some measure as he convinced God to allow him to test Job, because it was so formal, like a controlled experience, in the way it occurred that that in itself was remarkable.

It was like God set strict boundaries the demonic principality could not cross in its encounter with me, as demonic principalities are not nice guys, they are full of hate. Even more amazing that I was not behaving right with God, but he still kept his hand of protection over me. Now that's mercy.

> The eyes of the Lord are in every place, Keeping watch on the evil and the good.
> —*Proverb 15:3, NKJV*

A good thing to take from this is even though I was married to a man heavy in the occult and had myself gotten way off the path since my God encounter in 8th grade, God had not only not abandoned me to my occult ways, he was still watching out for me all the same, and had not forsaken me, although I was certainly grieving him with my ignorant straying and abuse of my spiritual gifts.

Chapter 4: Some Of My Demon Encounters

No one will be able to stand up against you all the days of your life. As I was with Moses, so I will be with you; I will never leave you nor forsake you.
—*Joshua 1:5, NIV*

In the Bible, Jesus sent his disciples into different cities, where it seemed commonplace to encounter demons, not a rarity.

After these things the Lord appointed seventy others also, and sent them two by two before His face into every city and place where He Himself was about to go.
—*Luke 10:1, NKJV*

Then the seventy returned with joy, saying, "Lord, even the demons are subject to us in Your name."
—*Luke 10:17, NKJV*

Since each time back then I distinctly felt when coming and going into our section of Buena Vista that distinct oppressive demonic principality atmosphere, a part of town gripped by drugs, violence, very dangerous for anyone to be there, my encounter could have been with the very demonic principality in charge of that area. I say that because the demon I was face-to-face with wasn't any of the standard demons which had troubled me in my stay there as I lived with my divination-practicing spouse, but instead was like a formal, higher-up coming for a scheduled standoff as I had said.

No doubt the principality of darkness fueled those crimes that made living there risky business. So that just normal everyday trips from one's house were life-threatening events.

To illustrate that point, just to go to the grocery store, my ex-husband and I had to develop a routine where we kept our loaded handgun in our glove compartment as more than once when we were forced to stop at red-lights, thugs would come out trying to open our car door for whatever crime they had in mind.

In addition to that, the place where the encounter took place, had been in my mother-in-law's guest bedroom where we had been forced to temporarily stay while we had our own windows wired with an alarm system because we had just been victims of a home invasion, where we had been held at gunpoint, my ex-husband tied up while the guy robbed us, and the robber high off his head on drugs, who had then wanted to take me afterwards as hostage.

But by God's grace I had managed to convince him that would not have been a good idea as police might pull over seeing a white girl in just an over-sized shirt walking at 5 a.m. with a black man carrying a suspicious sack of goods. In his drug influence, he had found that good reasoning and he'd left our house with his stolen items.

All the same, as I had explained earlier, that evil stronghold sensation was a separate phenomenon apart from the classic tough part of town feeling, I had felt from day one coming and going into that area, before I had known about my future husband's divination rituals, as his house had often been the meeting place for another club those of us in the Science Fiction and Fantasy Club had belonged to, called the Society of Creative Anachronism.

Here I am in the next picture, photographed on the front porch of the Buena Vista house when I lived there those 2 years and dealt with a lot of demon activity, wearing around my neck an astrology Leo symbol in place of the Jesus figures and crosses I used to wear.

Before I get to the experience, let me share the warning dream I had gotten weeks before that April 1980, coming weeks before we had been victims of the home invasion by that drug-high robber with a loaded gun. The most important thing that dream did was put me on alert about expecting a demon invasion and be ready to defend myself.

Dr. Mark Virkler, president of Christian Leadership University and an author who has developed courses for Christians on hearing God's voice through their dreams, teaches about a God who still counsels through dreams today as He did to people in the Bible.

Here I was, 21-years-of age, strayed far from my Christian roots, living with a man who made his own pentagrams for protection, carried them in his wallet and also dug them in the ground on the property, and had designed a religion where his

Chapter 4: Some Of My Demon Encounters

symbol was a take of the cross, which can be seen partially in the photo a few pages earlier of his altar, where he had added some horizontal bars to a cross shape which represented transition to him, who actively engaged in tarot and magic, and admired Aleister Crowley, an English occultist who got kicks playing the role of a Satanist, one such book picturing Crowley's Satanist activities in an honored place in my ex-husband's book collection where I was introduced to Crowley.

Yet God never left me, coming to counsel me in a dream in

advance of an event, to prepare me, not only mentally, but arm me spiritually with the weaponry to overcome this pending confrontation with evil.

So I found myself getting counsel from God in a warning dream a little before March 1980. The dream itself while it went on had a warning feeling about it, like for the next 60 seconds this is an emergency drill.

In this dream, I found myself on the edge of a carnival

ground, near trailers for the carnival staff. I saw the ground suddenly open on the outskirts of the trailers. Demons, the size of capuchin monkeys, deformed and animal-like, started crawling out of this dark opening.

They crawled with intent to attack. I found I was standing on a stage near that opening, and a Bible happened to be there on a stand next to me.

I saw myself from a spectator vantage point like in a show-and-tell class, with my spectator viewpoint made for the purpose for me to watch and remember. I observed myself picking up the Bible and opening to a passage and reading it to overcome the demons pouring out of that hole. That worked to drive them back into the ground.

I awoke right after, taken aback at the dream, how it seemed like a powerful warning to observe, remember the Bible, not the physical book itself, but that its words, specifically speaking its words in a demonic assault, was the key to defeat, and not to forget the warning.

I took that dream to heart because it was so much like a strong warning, and I told my ex-husband that morning about the dream how it seemed like a true warning.

But the only Bible I had was an old King James that zippered closed that I had since I attended the elementary Catholic school where I had that End of World God encounter, and was buried somewhere in my possessions as I did not read it and had not read it for years. I had found the old English language too hard for me to make sense of to enjoy reading, and that Bible I did not bother digging out despite the dream. Yet I did take to heart the warning aspect, and stayed alert to such a possibility, because it came across like one of my dreams that were real warnings which I had to pay attention to in order to properly deal with some problem on the horizon.

A few weeks later as I reported above, a masked robber, high on drugs, broke into our house and robbed us at gunpoint, tied my ex-husband and planned to take me with him at gunpoint as a hostage to I do not know where until he was safe from our house to guarantee my ex-husband would not call police.

Fortunately, as I said, I was able to convince the man under

Chapter 4: Some Of My Demon Encounters

the obvious influence of drugs, it would not be wise to walk out in the street with me, and he had accepted what I had said and left with just the items he had decided to steal which he had stuffed into a pillowcase as we really did not possess much of value.

Well after the break in, my ex-husband and I were too unnerved to sleep in our own house, and we stayed over my ex's mother-in-law's house next door for the entire time it took for us to install our own alarm system that April in 1980. It was while staying at my mother-in-law's house for that period of a couple of weeks, that I had a classic *The Exorcist* film kind of encounter with a demon principality, midway into our stay.

I say *The Exorcist* movie type of encounter because in that film, the first in the series, there was a memorable scene in the beginning with two nearby dogs barking during the scene when Father Merrin confronts a large statue of the demon Pazuzu, the dogs barking as if alerting and signaling the dangerous presence of the demon, what dogs are wired to do, which is give an alert at danger by barking. Then one hears those same two dogs falling under the evil influence to violence, and fight each other off screen with vicious noises.

Having seen *The Exorcist* when it first came out, that scene stuck to me, dogs barking at an unseen demonic presence, announcing an evil dangerous presence was there, in same way dogs bark at any undetectable, but real threat, in alert and warning.

Little did I know that I would find myself encountering the same scene in April 1980, a dog barking in alert at a demonic presence a few years later, and be confronted personally by a demonic principality, for real, not in a movie, and having been forewarned in a dream weeks before what to do in that encounter.

In the early-morning hours that particular night, I found myself woken out of sleep from something really weird, which was odd in itself. My ex-husband and I were sleeping in the corner bedroom at the front of my mother-in-law's house. It was a regular house in Miami with a front yard, her house on the west corner of the block right on N.E. 2nd Avenue. This bedroom was on the east end of her house.

The odd thing that woke me was a dog was barking right

outside the bedroom window that faced the front yard. It wasn't that the dog was outside just barking, no.

This dog had come right up to the window, faced it, about two feet away, and purposefully barked in alert at the window, much the way if you had a family pet dog, and this dog was used to your letting it in and the dog could see you right there, yet you failed to follow through as normal and let it in.

Then your dog started barking at you to insist you notice it, and pay attention and come---like the old movies of *Lassie*, the adventures of a Collie dog, when Lassie would bark at her family to get their attention trouble was afoot which they needed to take urgent action on.

Only this dog was barking a warning alert bark, and it wasn't an ongoing barking, it was like it came up to our bedroom window just to bark a handful of times in announcing warning, almost like just in advance of this evil, enough to warn me, then skedaddle before this evil presence came and could harm it.

When I woke up it was just at the start of its barking, and somehow I knew this dog was barking to announce evil. Interestingly my ex-husband did not stir, even as I got out of bed and went over to the window to see if I could see this peculiar dog, and take a look at what kind of dog would come up to the window of a strange house to the dog when it is dark outside and just bark to get the attention of the people inside.

I have had dogs since I was a child and no dog I ever had ever had come up to any bedroom window deep into the night, when all is dark, all are sleeping, and bark to wake the people in that room, just never.

At that time with my ex-husband, we had no dogs, nor did my mother-in-law, and her front yard had no fence, and we had no cats, no pets whatsoever then, and this wasn't a case of a dog barking for or at a cat.

This was some dog strange to us, barking to get our attention in this room specifically, coming just right up to the house, just before the bedroom window, and bark like Lassie trying to get Timmy's attention the farm tractor brake has loosened and the runaway tractor is heading straight to Timmy's room as he sleeps in ignorance of the moments-away disaster. And secondly weird

Chapter 4: Some Of My Demon Encounters

was my getting the understanding the warning was about evil racing to me, not some tractor.

If you have had enough dogs, you understand basic dog-speak and you know when a dog is barking to get your attention, even if you never met the dog as there is a type of purposefulness to it of I'm out here and you need to listen to me now, it's urgent.

Immediately as I walked to the same NE bedroom window facing to the front yard shown in the next picture, all dark outside in the late night past midnight, hearing its purposeful barks, the scene from *The Exorcist* which I had seen 7 years ago, of the dogs barking at the presence of evil came to mind, as I got that unspoken information the warning was about evil making its way to the room my sleeping ex-husband and I were in.

Photo of actual outside of the bedroom where mystery warning dog barked. I put below a dog figure to show exactly where dog barked & at actual window, which was NE front. This was my mother-in-law's house, taken from the angle of my former front yard. Demon came into this bedroom from roof.

Though I looked out the window just at its last bark outside, having heard 4 barks from it in my process of getting out of bed and walking to that window, there was no dog in sight anywhere, none.

It could not have had time to run out of view, as I just parted the blinds on the end of its last bark, and by the laws of the scientific world of the closeness of the sound in relationship to the position of the source, this dog should have been right down below where I looked out, as I illustrated with the dog figure in the above picture. Yet there was nothing there, no dog, none, and the yard was clear of obstacles, that car in the 1986 film still image not there back in 1980, just the lawn, and that was even weirder to me than the barks.

All I could do was shrug it off, turn around and get back to bed, my ex-husband still asleep and tell him about it come the morning, or so I thought, now wide awake.

No more than the time for me to get back in bed, barely get under the cover, when I heard clunking sounds in the attic, things getting thumped about---this is Florida where there are no steps up to attics. It sounded like someone was picking up a heavy iron bed and dropping it, three times. Again, one of the *Exorcist* movies came to my mind when evil came in through the attic.

Then a black form materialized feet away from me in the corner of the room. As I was prepared by the previous dream, I was not thrown off.

A handful of times before in my life I had seen spirits of some kind or another, some of which I thought were souls of people, others seemed to be guardians, two of which other people had also seen with me at the same time I did. However, though they startled me, I never had any impression of evil.

However, I knew even at the sound of the dog's bark, a demon was present, and I knew when I saw that black form, an entity that was so black it could not be seen through, that it wasn't a hole, it was a being.

A shadow falls flat on the nearby surfaces, but this was hung in the air, several feet in size, in the corner, but around a foot away from the corner wall, which was the west-south corner of the room, the headboard of the bed at the south wall of the room.

This black entity was suspended in the air, a few inches from the floor, and was about the height of an adult person as far as several feet high but it was not a person shape but a more oval than round blob of a substance so black that it was almost like a black hole, yet it was not a hole, but a dense cloudlike entity, of which I had the undeniable knowledge it was a personality and an individual.

Not only that I had an absolute knowing it was not a person,

Chapter 4: Some Of My Demon Encounters

as in a former human now as a ghost, but in fact this was a demonic high-positioned being facing me. I had no Bible nearby, despite my previous month's dream and there were no Bibles in

The 21-year-old me the demonic principality had a face-off with in 1980, pictured here shortly after the encounter with one of 2 new puppies we got to be our watchdogs after the break-in.

view in my mother-in-law's house.

    Yet that dream had prepared me, and rather than experiencing fear, I projected feelings of love to this darker than black form, a love which I can say was like a mirror of a Christ-like love, just agape love where there was not even a toehold for fear to set in. For a few seconds I stared into his black void-like shape, sending this love, and he appeared to wither in purpose under this love, as if unconditional Christ-like love beamed directly to him, he had no weapon against, and I say him because I felt a male presence, and then he vanished.

Just like I wrote in chapter 3 on filmmaker Darren Wilson relating how the Lord had told him the way to win against evil is through love, it had been with love that I had overcome that demonic principality. However, I must add that as I had seen in my dream to use the Bible to overcome any demonic attack, the spoken word is also a powerful weapon that demolishes the enemy. Yet because I had failed to arm myself with a Bible where I could read Scriptures, it was like something switched on inside of me to have an automatic reaction to project love to this dark evil being, as if that information was divinely given to me.

Once the demon had disappeared, I totally panicked, shaking my ex-husband awake, who had slept through the whole encounter. I had to turn lights on and I was trembling and full of fear that lasted all the way to the morning, even though I had been composed during the confrontation which led me to believe God had taken me through the confrontation.

That had been my first and last face-to-face confrontation with that demonic principality, an entity so evil I understood he was blackness itself due to a total lack of God's light in him – what I saw was a core of what he was, his true emptiness of God in even the smallest microcosm, making him all evil to the core---yet Christ-like love he could not defeat.

I had distinctly felt this love deflate him, and it was a sad thing, almost like a prodigal son who you know never will come back because he is so lost, yet that connection that he once was loved and in that love, a love which he willfully rejected, enormously tragic, a self-created gulf because his inequity is so immeasurably vast. However, no more sadness than that because this principality was so bad to the core there was no safety in dropping my guard to entertain even slightly any changes possible in that hardcore corruption.

That wasn't to be my last demonic encounter, however, my most recent one in direct person, occurred just months ago in 2013 which I cover later on in this book because it deals with this

Chapter 4: Some Of My Demon Encounters

material.

So on top of the solid evidence in the Bible, I myself with my own eyes, have more than once dealt with demons and the demonic principalities.

Due to that nobody will ever, or could ever, convince me otherwise because I have had actual experiences nobody can take from me.

I didn't hear it second hand, I don't have to believe the integrity of so-and-so, but I personally had such encounters. I don't and didn't do drugs, nor have any alcohol issues, as I am a teetotaler, due to a sensitive stomach not tolerating alcohol, and had a clear mind.

Plus, as you can see, these were not due to near-death experiences and could not be blamed on a dying brain phenomenon, nor was I having surgery of any kind for these experiences to be explained as side effects to anesthesia, and a few of my experiences, of which I have not related all of them here, but do relate some more later on in this book, had been in broad daylight, and some seen jointly with others, both at night and in the day.

So the standard reasons the devil wants you to dismiss receiving such testimonies as true, do not exist here. However, there is nothing unusual about this as this is what was common in the days the apostles were spreading the news of the gospel.

Demons were out in the open then, fighting against us openly in this war, but now they are staying behind the scenes as a means to deceive the largest amount of people into thinking they are not real.

Through that false disbelief, they are looking to lead people to not take seriously the safety of their eternal destiny, so they become one of those many scoffers who are going to increase in the end times, not just in the unsaved, but in the Christian community, so Christians will turn on Christians and hate one another from these sharply differentiating belief systems, one strictly in accord with the Bible, and the others in accord with popular views.

Getting back to the state of my mind and health when I had these supernatural experiences, I want to point out that more important to the conditions I was in concerning my body and mind, is that I am not alone in having such encounters. There are enough other people with same drug-free, alcohol-free, sane credentials with demon encounters.

Having firsthand encounters with the demonic, and having heard directly from God in my 1972 open vision how evil humankind will become towards the end time when Christ returns, it grieves me especially to see today large numbers of children growing up in a public school system which leaves them deprived of the knowledge God himself is real, not even getting to get to the point in a normal growth process of faith that the demon world is real, and what that means for their personal eternities.

Soon the numbers of those who do not believe in anything more than what they can see in front of them, will outweigh the numbers who do believe. Yet it will not change the core truth: demons are real; demonic principalities are real; Satan is real, and the war between the dark evil and the righteous light is real, the light fighting to save us from the destruction the dark only wants for us.

If you have been a doubter, even though you know Jesus openly spoke about Satan and his kingdom, and instructions how to battle them, or even an outright disbeliever of that reality at all because some church leader or leaders have decreed it a concept rather than a literal truth, it's time to shatter that enemy deceit off your life while you can still do something about it, and be an overcomer, not a victim of the enemy. And that is what I am going to cover in the next chapters, starting on a briefing that entails what your mission is in this war, a mission I have dubbed "Operation Make It To Heaven."

***

Chapter 5

YOUR MISSION OPERATION MAKE IT TO HEAVEN

> Fight the good fight of the faith. Take hold of the eternal life to which you were called and about which you made the good confession in the presence of many witnesses.
> —*1 Timothy 6:12, ESV*

Whether you have been aware of it or not, from the foundation of the world you were enlisted for this mission, and it is a do-or-die mission.

When you accepted Jesus, you started on your mission "Operation Make It To Heaven," where you have been charged to wage the good warfare on the path leading to victory, to stand firm against an enemy seeking to knock you off the narrow way to your death.

No one has the time they think they have in these days, but yet, there is time, but the counter on that final grace has been started, and it is on its way to tick to the end.

If I can do anything with this book is to get across to you two things:

1) Instill in you the proper urgency to get right with the Lord.
2) Leave you with the certainty that the demonic principality is real, demons are real, and they hate us, and they are out to take as many of us they can to hell with unbelievably-horrific sadistic intentions.

This is not a drill; this is all real.

The key point on this mission to understand is if you fail to do your mission right, if you fail to succeed in the commands given to you by Jesus Christ, you will not be allowed entrance to the only place where you will have life.

Instead you will fall into the enemy's hands, into their camp. You will end up in the camp of the enemy, a land of brutality you have never seen the likes of. There is no camp, no torment or torture that has ever existed on earth nor ever will even if they were all rolled up into one concentrated experience that meets the level of brutality and torment experienced even an hour in the enemy camp.

Not All Commanders Mean What They Order Except Jesus

I learned that in 1976, while undergoing Basic Training in the Army, that when push comes to shove and an order is put to the test that order may not really be as grave as it seems, and could be optional, or even ignored, preferably, and definitely not to be taken literally, if a person is the origin of that order.

In this example of that point, I was at Ft. Jackson in South Carolina and at this particular training which was different than the normal drills in that high-ranking officers, captains and generals had come to observe our platoon, because the Basic Training I was participating in was the first group of women in an 18-month long study to see if women could perform like the men, if they received the same training.

So instead of women drill sergeants, we had male drill sergeants for the purpose their aim was to train us just as hard as they did the men, which from what I saw my first week there, for the men in another platoon, could be very rough, one drill sergeant screaming all kinds of insulting phrases at a male recruit in the meal line while making him drop and do lots of pushups.

Yet my experience in the lunch hall was quiet different as an 18-year-old young woman used to smiling at everybody and getting smiled back at, so even though the males were getting bullied, us female recruits were not, mainly I believe because the men drill sergeants supposed to be over us had always handled men and could not bring themselves to yell at young women the same way.

Chapter 5: Your Mission Operation Make It To Heaven

Because of that wiggle room I knew us females had, I enjoyed giving a smile at all the drill sergeants sitting in their row at the lunch hall when I would enter the mess hall, and it seemed they enjoyed it too as they would rib each other when I came in smiling at them all, the women and the men drill sergeants, seemingly all getting a kick to see me come in and smile. They would smile back, all of them, and they would smile back pleasantly. I believe it was because the boldness and joy of the Lord, erases all barriers of fear. Here I am pictured at Basic Training in 1976.

Such love has no fear, because perfect love expels all fear. If we are afraid, it is for fear of punishment, and this shows that we have not fully experienced his perfect love.
—1 John 4:18, NIV

Thus, I never saw such harsh treatment as were given to the male recruits, even allowed to carry my camera around as I did during Basic Training, taking pictures as if I was on a fun vacation, in order to send them to my little brother who was crazy about military things, and I got myself a few funny pictures as a result with the drill sergeants hamming it up also in my little joke photos I would take about my basic training experience to give my family laughs.

In this picture above, I got the drill sergeant to point as if he ordered me to where the Army assigned me to sleep, which I was telling my family as a joke was the top shelf of my locker as shown, which you can see was definitely <u>not</u> the way a male recruit would have been treated.

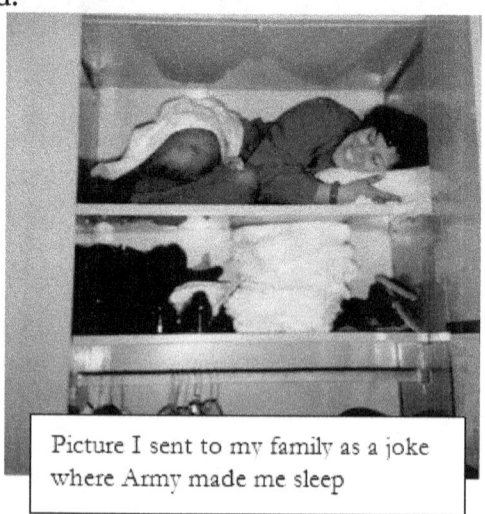

Picture I sent to my family as a joke where Army made me sleep

Chapter 5: Your Mission Operation Make It To Heaven

Thus this is the background story behind this example I am leading into when my platoon was on a special march when we were visited by higher up officers, to observe us, due to that special program we were in and where I learned that not all commanders literally mean what they order.

The scene took place at Ft. Jackson, South Carolina training camp, and we had been on a march in the woods, dressed in fatigues, carrying our backpacks.

Me, on a similar march ⬇

We were stopped for an explanatory briefing of the upcoming exercise: gas would be detonated further up the trail, and we were to don our issued gas masks. As we were being talked through it, we were led through the steps to don our masks.

However, I found that the strap on the bottom of my mask was broken, so the mask hung on my face. On top of that I was getting through a cold so my breathing also was compromised a bit by that, though not so I couldn't participate.

I pointed out to my sergeant my mask strap was broken, but he waved it off like it was okay.

He told us that we were going to be observed by these high

ranking officers, and then he said in a strong order, glaring menacingly, "If *any* of you mess up to make the platoon look bad in front of these officers, just keep on running!"

Still I had thought I would be given a replacement mask from the other sergeants around, but no.

So we were marched ahead. As we had been told, further up on either side of the dirt road, gas was set off, and white clouds engulfed us.

I put on my mask, but it just hung there. When I breathed, I was breathing in gas. The next thing I knew I was running.

I was told later on that I cleared a bush as high as myself and this with my backpack on. I know I ran, and that I ran with the survival momentum to rush to fresh air, running into the woods off to my right. Sometime in that run, I became aware I was being chased.

"Pulider!" a man yelled behind me, mispronouncing my father's last name, who I knew from the voice was my sergeant. "Pulider!"

I kept running on automatic deeper into the woods. After a few minutes he yelled again, unable to catch up to me, "Why do you keep running!?"

"Because you said if we mess up to keep on running!" I yelled

Chapter 5: Your Mission Operation Make It To Heaven

back, still running on auto obedience to what he had threateningly ordered minutes before.

"Don't run no more!" he said, and so I stopped.

Okay, see? If he had not said that prior, I am sure I might have cleared the bush, but stopped when out of the danger of the gas.

But since I had been told this as an order before, and it was an order in retrospect but it ended up really not literally, as even though I had pointed out to him and a couple of others my mask strap was broken, and the gas ended up being, well, gas you can't breath in calmly and keep marching, his barked command ended up not the all-out-costs literal command it had seemed.

In fact, it seemed he never really meant that literally in the first place, and never imagined someone would then take it to heart and just keep on. However, that one ended up with no harm, and a comical edge, as it got a few laughs later on even from the higher ups there.

But the orders from our leader, Jesus Christ, to obey his commandments, to follow the will of the Father, to endure to the end he strictly means, because how we perform on this mission equates to our life or death, and Jesus does not play with our lives; he died to save our lives. So what he told us to do in the Bible was not an if-and-or choice or to entertain free-food seeking crowds with interesting antidotes, but imparted to us to save our lives, that if we don't follow what he instructed that we endanger our own eternal lives as a result.

As an 18-year-old I didn't know I wouldn't be court-martialed for that gasmask failure induced AWOL and I had felt once I had messed it up for the platoon in front of the officers, I just had to do just as my drill sergeant had commanded to 'keep on running'.

That ended up a funny incident, but the consequences if we don't obey Jesus instructions given in love, are deadly because we will be too filthy to enter heaven, we will be strangers to him, and for those reasons entry to heaven won't happen, very serious consequences with no funny side to it at all.

Jesus didn't tell us about how to avoid hell to scare us, he told us about hell to save us.

Which brings me to the next point in your mission debriefing here: in order to allow you to get the proper perspective in every respect of the stakes involved in your accomplishing and performing and sticking to the operation to make it to heaven you need a 360 degree total and complete understanding of the consequences on both sides, to understand in full the criteria by which you will be allowed or blocked from entrance to heaven. When you understand everything that Jesus said is true, it actually becomes simple to get that 360 degree total understanding.

This, though, has proved to be a big stumbling block for a lot of people: which is taking the time to read and understand in full everything Jesus taught, including what his apostles added later, and what the Old Testament added before, because Jesus as the Messiah is a fulfillment of the prophecy of the Old Testament and he did not abolish what is there, but fulfilled it.

Many people rely on their preacher to preach to them about the values and they don't ever crack open a Bible, or they piece meal the Bible and they don't read the whole thing and it doesn't sink into them. They disregard some things or their preacher will have them disregard some Scriptures as not relevant to them today. They don't have a balanced view of God and Jesus and so they are living the way they like, they are disregarding the parts of the Bible that are essential, the instructions and teachings of Jesus that are essential for them to do.

The Gift of Salvation

First off let me make clear: Salvation is a gift, yes. You don't earn it; it has been given to you. However, you can trample that gift, you can reject it, you can be clueless how to make use of it so it actually is never activated, or you can take it and disregard it, after it has been given to you.

There are many people who have gone through the steps to get the gift who are in ignorance how to make use of that gift so they receive the inheritance offered. That is why God said,

> My people are destroyed for lack of knowledge. Because you have rejected knowledge, I also will reject you from being priest for Me; because you have forgotten the law of

Chapter 5: Your Mission Operation Make It To Heaven

your God, I also will forget your children.
—Hosea 4:6, NKJV

Notice God said **my** people, meaning people who were his, not strangers or unsaved.

The gift Jesus gives us in salvation is like being given a complimentary pass to a closed-door elite club that requires the pass, requires personal admittance at the gate by the giver when you get there and show the pass, which will only happen if you develop a relationship with the giver to be recognized at that time and let in, and requires a type of etiquette and dress code to attend.

> But when the king came in to look at the guests, he saw there a man who had no wedding garment. And he said to him, 'Friend, how did you get in here without a wedding garment?' And he was speechless. Then the king said to the attendants, 'Bind him hand and foot and cast him into the outer darkness. In that place there will be weeping and gnashing of teeth.' For many are called, but few are chosen.
> —Matthew 22:11-14, ESV

So the pass alone won't cut it if you disregard the rest of the requirements to make use of the gift to enter. You can't show up drunk at heaven's gate, with a guy or gal on each arm, and show the pass to get in. Since you would fail to meet the dress code of inner cleanliness, and by your lawless behavior show yourself to be a stranger to the gatekeeper, you will be rejected, your pass refused.

> ...A person is a slave to whatever he gives in to. People can know our Lord and Savior Jesus Christ and escape the world's filth. But if they get involved in this filth again and give in to it, they are worse off than they were before. It would have been better for them never to have known the way of life that God approves of than to know it and

turn their backs on the holy life God told them to live.
—*2 Peter 2:19-21, GW*

Unlike some people are falsely led to believe, possessing the pass does not gift you with an auto-cleanser that instantly wipes away filth as you commit it, so you remain 'spotless', in essence giving you a free card to live as you please without consequences.

This is a typical doctrine of demon example, which is a demon-inspired doctrine that adds or subtracts from the actual Bible truth, which in this case subtracts that we must be holy or pure to enter heaven.

The Scripture, "Make every effort to live in peace with all men and to be holy; without holiness no one will see the Lord" (Hebrew 12:14 NIV) is not just an impressive saying nor is it symbolic, but it is literal, on a basic level because since everything in heaven is holy, nothing can profane it, nothing can come in that is corrupt and sinful. By the words 'make every effort' to be holy, the Verse shows that it requires our effort to live holy, and is not something that is automatically given to us, which is what the other Scripture telling us to 'put on Christ' means, which is that we are to put on the mind of Christ, in that we are to imitate him in every way he would handle what we are going through in our personal lives, every day renew our minds so we are living like him, and not still like the former worldly persons we were who dealt with everything that came our way according to the world's standards.

> But put on the Lord Jesus Christ, and make no provision for the flesh, to gratify its desires.
> —*Romans 13:13, ESV*

The enemy wants you to think this is no more than a familiar saying that does not mean what it says, as that would make everyone have to live like monks and that would be impractical with modern life, and thus does not require following.

But the Bible makes clear "Don't you know that friendship with the world is hatred toward God? Anyone who chooses to be a friend of the world becomes an enemy of God" (James 4:4 NIV). In that Scripture is a fountain of information to be aware of that

Chapter 5: Your Mission Operation Make It To Heaven

relates it is not about not changing yourself to meet the approval of the world, it is not about going with the worldly flow; it is instead conforming to what God wants 100%, him the only one important to please.

Don't Skip Instructions

In relation to the success of your mission Operation Make It To Heaven, the Bible can be compared to a book of instructions that have instructions numbered 1 through 28 with photos in-between and samples of A through Z, and maybe you belong to a denomination that covers instructions 1, 9 to 15, 23 to 28 and skips on 2 to 8 and 15 to 22.

The problem is when you build on those partial instructions since it is being grounded on not the full foundation of the true teachings, it is going to fall apart at the first stress and you will not get into heaven because you did not do the full instructions.

As any instructions you have to follow it entirely, to get the thing built right, you can't just pick what you like and ignore the rest. You can't just be taught to do one particular step and that it is okay to skip the rest. If you do, what you are going to get from that, it might look like something, but it is not built correct and it will be rejected and be burned with fire.

So if you stick to the full instructions, beginning with building your faith on the solid rock, your faith will prove genuine and able to weather all forces, and achieving by that solidly-constructed faith the successful completion of your mission, gaining entrance into heaven, your soul eternally saved.

To succeed in your mission it is imperative you know that the instructions Jesus gave in his teachings are not just beloved points to repeat, they are literal facts to follow, literal facts that are critical to do and being told literally about the scenario that you need to perform in order to succeed getting your mission right to make it to heaven.

You are dealing with an enemy with long experience deceiving people to their camp, and you are like predictable putty in their diabolical hands if you let yourself be led by the popular beliefs and do not take the time to learn the full truth yourself from the direct source, which is the Bible.

It is like learning to drive on the popular sayings of what makes a good driver and never bothering to read the driver manual yourself and learning what the laws are in full yourself, and expecting to succeed at the driver's written exam and driving test.

No one would have to tell you, if you are a licensed driver that is a foolish attitude, because even if you pay attention to all the popular beliefs on what makes a good driver, still you are missing out on various laws and techniques you need to know.

It goes the same for passing the qualifications of getting entrance to heaven through Jesus: in the Bible, Jesus set qualifications he expects adherence to for a believer to be recognized by him as worthy and allowed in to his kingdom---qualifications which compared to the statutes and judgments given through Moses, are a yoke easy to bear, yet it is a yoke, a yoke in the cross you must carry on your mission according to his teachings.

The yoke is easy in that your mission is to perform these specific teachings, to live entirely according to them, showing you pass the test of a true convert, one according to the heart, who is a doer of the teachings and not just a talker who is all talk and no walk revealing them to actually have an inner character that is anti-kingdom, does not belong there, can not mesh there, and is instead a character belonging to the prince of the world's domain.

Thus, it is not that you are being judged how you perform your mission, but that you are being put through fire to see if the nature of your core, which on the outward may profess Christianity, when tested in the fire, actually reveals you are indeed a true believer, pure, in line with purity of heaven, and a child of it.

When you put a metal in fire, it can't fake what it is, it will reveal what it truly is, and thus your life on earth here is your testing in the fire, what are your proving to be to the Lord: a true believer to your core, or possessing impurities which reveal you don't belong in heaven.

So that the tested genuineness of your faith—more

Chapter 5: Your Mission Operation Make It To Heaven

precious than gold that perishes though it is tested by fire—may be found to result in praise and glory and honor at the revelation of Jesus Christ.
—*1 Peter 1:7, ESV*

Therefore, since the promise of entering his rest still stands, let us be careful that none of you be found to have fallen short of it.
—*Hebrews 4:1, NIV*

Here is the grace of the Lord: if you follow his teachings, he will work with you to bring you to that purity level, existing in you to aid you there. It is easy but complex at the same time in that we really can't meet that purity on our own, but Christ gave us clear instructions that when you follow them, the Father and He will be the perfection in you to obtain to that purity.

However, if you don't stick to his teachings, the Father and he will not be in you, no matter how faithfully you attend church, no matter how many devils you may cast out or miracles you may perform.

Not everyone who says to Me, 'Lord, Lord,' shall enter the kingdom of heaven, but he who does the will of My Father in heaven. Many will say to Me in that day, 'Lord, Lord, have we not prophesied in Your name, cast out demons in Your name, and done many wonders in Your name?' And then I will declare to them, 'I never knew you; depart from Me, you who practice lawlessness!'
—*Matthew 7:21, NKJV*

No relationship with a church will get you to heaven; the relationship you have to build on is a direct one with Jesus.

It doesn't matter how advanced you are in your Christian walk Satan's army is working hard to derail you from your mission that it is a constant struggle to stand firm. That is why it is essential to have the right mindset and perspective your life is a mission to get to heaven, a military mission, as you are in a fight against an enemy scheming fulltime to make you fail.

Don't undermine the right mindset, as this is a key Biblical strategy that will lead you to succeed on your mission.

> Since therefore Christ suffered in the flesh, arm yourselves with the same way of thinking, for whoever has suffered in the flesh has ceased from sin, so as to live for the rest of the time in the flesh no longer for human passions but for the will of God.
> —*1Peter 4:1-2, ESV*

Because you are on a mission and it is the core reason you were created to make it to heaven, you need to develop the mindset and the attitude to win, to stand firm, to be successful at what you were created for.

Therefore, this mission is as challenging as Lord Jesus so put:

> Small is the gate and narrow the road that leads to life, and only a few find it.
> —*Matthew 7:14, NIV*

A few, you read that, a <u>few</u>. If the Lord himself specifies a few only find it, that is more than food for thought; it is a warning flag.

If only a few find it, it stands to reason that not everyone who believes in Jesus enters heaven. If that were so, Jesus would have said 'a lot find it,' or 'many find it.' Instead he said, "Only a *few* find it."

Your mission is to be one of those few, the ones that find that small, small gate on this really narrow road. If you continue to hold out against the enemy wiles, and stand firm in your faith, you can do it, following the commands of Jesus in order to accomplish that.

***

Chapter 6

FINAL GRACE TIMER NEARING LAST TICK

> His grace made us right with God. So now we have received the hope of eternal life as God's children.
> —*Titus 3:7, NIRV*

There are a couple of prophetic dreams I've had in line with the subject of this book that could be significant for you to pay attention to and take revelation from them for yourself, on what you do with the information presented within the pages of this book concerning getting your house set in order so you are ready to face the Lord and succeed in your mission to make it to heaven.

Before I get to those two prophetic dreams in this chapter, I am going to give you as evidence, several prophetic dreams I had of future events that came true 100%, in order to establish to you I dream dreams that do come true, and when I have these dreams, I recognize them at the time as different from normal dreams and they are predicting future events.

The selection of these dreams also serve to show I have had such prophetic dreams that were years ahead of the eventual occurrence, and obvious to me at the time those dreams were much further future events, and in addition, events I had no way of influencing to come about.

Some of these dreams are known to my family, as in my parents and siblings, as I listed them in the life story my mother asked each of her five children to write in the year 1998, in order to include in the family album she had put together with the intent to give each of her kids an album of our family tree.

It was a really big album full of photos going back to our grandparents and great grandparents, such as my grandfather on my father's side, a war veteran from Columbia in South America, who was a prisoner of war in the revolutionary war between the Conservative Party and the Liberal party, and later joined the Venezuelan army, rose to Colonel and later became aide-de-camp to Venezuelan President Cipriano Castro. Then on my mother's side, photos of my great grandfather, an infantry captain from Spain, who was brother of the Mariana Islands governor in 1893-95, while the Marianas was a Spanish colony (making me the great-grand-niece of the Governor of the Philippines back then), interesting family tree stuff my mother wanted to pass on to us 'kids' while she could.

Though I am of Spanish heritage, due to the doctor's advice when I was age 6 to my mother to pick one language for me to learn, since trying to teach me both English and Spanish had led to me to start stuttering, my mother chose English being Miami, Florida was our home. Thus, I can't speak a lick of Spanish and actually have a southern twang sometimes when I talk.

Okay, I can say 'french fries' pretty good, which is 'papas fritas' from my teen years working at Burger King in Miami (me at the right in the next photo, pictured at the rear of the Burger King with my best friend from high school, where both of us had learned to say 'papas fritas' in 1974, wearing the Burger King uniforms from that decade as we worked part time after school to earn money to go on our school's choir performance tour in Spain), but even when I do, I say it with a distinct Southern twang.

To get an idea how poor I speak Spanish, native Spanish people pretty much laugh at me when I try to speak the language, sure I am a 'gringa' which is a female native speaker of English, but being raised with 'Cubanos' I understand everything being

Chapter 6: Final Grace Timer Nearing Last Tick

said, though. I like to joke I was born in the southern part of Cuba, which is why I have a southern accent.

However, my mother flew to Cuba just to have me born there (I like to joke to complicate my life with a Cuban birth certificate) and after I was two months of age, returned to the States (I like to joke on a banana boat). But my parents, though, are both Spanish, my father from Brazil neck of the woods, my momma from Cuba, and both sides stemming back to Spain.

Besides some of those dreams, in that life story, besides a couple of my military antics, I also included some other supernatural events I'd had, which of those events, a couple more I will include later on in this book in the pertinent chapters where they serve to illustrate particular schemes of the enemy.

As an aside, when you live such experiences, they don't stay under the cover, and generally, you are known as having had some of these experiences to some of the people in your life, which I say to you so that your belief can be further built up that the supernatural is real, and the enemy is real.

When you have such experiences, you really aren't the same, and you really can't separate them from your life, even if the events make you a family oddball, which I was because everyone else had normal stories in the 'life stories' they gave to my mom for our family album, giving 1 or 2 pages of childhood impressions, and school to work accomplishments, and here my story was a 30-page long tale of adventures including some of my supernatural experiences because those were significant events in my life.

In other words, I have a paper trail going back in time, that backs up theses events, and I don't just come out of the blue, claiming such experiences. But since I am a non-celebrity, these experiences have only stayed within my immediate family, with the exception of the ones I published in *FATE* magazine in 1989, and the one the *Miami Herald* covered in brief, when on our first campout at the historic Biltmore hotel, then closed to the public, we did get on tape a paranormal voice during the night we spent there at that historic hotel purported to be haunted which led the city officials to let us stay there a second night in October 1979 as I touched on in chapter 4, where you see an image of that *Miami Herald* article.

Dream 1, 1972

In eighth grade, the same year I had my vision with God, I had a dream I was on a honeymoon with my husband. We were at some lodge, but the problem was his mother kept getting in our way.

She looked like a witch. She was old and mean and she disliked me! She kept ruining our marriage. Here I was 13 years old and dreaming about being on a honeymoon with a husband with a meddling mother-in-law, definitely not the dream subject for a young teen, in a day when shows like *Divorce Court* where decades away from common daily television shows. I don't remember every dream I have, but I do this one because when I had it the dream had a weight to it like it was a future glimpse.

Eight years later I entered that relationship with the man I wrote about in chapter 4, steeped into the occult, and as I mentioned, he lived next to his mother, who was in her seventies when I moved in with him.

What I didn't know when I got married to him through his co-worker he had ordained as a minister in his invented religion, because I was young and naïve and thought people in love didn't ask each other questions about mortgages and such, was my husband rented the house from his mother. As I mentioned earlier in chapter 4, she charged him less than $200 a month to keep him living next to her, a monetary cost-saving enticement to him that did end up being a problem in our relationship.

At first she seemed nice enough, but I should have suspected something wrong when he asked his mother if he should marry me, and he told me he decided yes because she said why not. After we 'married' many times she would call him to ask him to change a light bulb or some other chore at any time of day or night, even 2 a.m. She would invite only him over for breakfast, or a cup of coffee, as if I didn't exist. I thought she had liked me all the same while we were living together, but I learned in the end her great jealousy of me.

As I also covered in chapter 4, due to high crime we were in constant danger in that neighborhood. It was just in the first three months after we married that robber broke into our house while we slept, terrorizing us.

Even though his peace of mind had been shattered, my ex refused to move. He chose to continue to live next to his mother, whose entire house was covered with bars, rather than keep us safe.

Then, a month later, that man was shot and killed on our front lawn where that Crime-Watch sign I gave a picture of in that chapter was later erected. Still my ex wouldn't move. Then two weeks later another man tried to break into our house, armed with a gun! As I detailed before, we got used to driving around with a gun in our hand to ward off the thugs that would try to pull us out of the car at stoplights. Still he refused to move from beside his mother and lose the cheap rent he paid.

In the end he told me his mother didn't want me living in her house any more and she had arranged for him to stay at her friend's house so he could divorce me.

He confessed his mother didn't want him married to me anymore, even though he still wanted to be with me!

Here I was watching unfurl that same scene of my 1972 dream with the meddling mother-in-law. While all the time I had been living next store to her, the witch-part I had seen in my dream, had been kept hidden from me, but now that woman that looked like a witch in that dream was finally surfacing for me to see myself.

We 'dated' afterwards for five years until I tired of it and broke it off. Because we still dated she hated me more, and I was to see the witch when in the beginning following our divorce she threw my mail on the lawn a couple of times, saying terrible things to me because he had given me the keys to the house after she'd had the locks changed.

My ex had to talk to her and tell her even though he had divorced me, he still wanted to see me, and she had to live with that, and here he was a man in his forties having to say such a thing to his mother, as if he was 9-years-old. It was only then that I understood why people made such horror stories about mother-in-laws. Yet it had all been a fulfillment of my prophetic dream at age 13, showing this was something that was going to happen to me.

In fact, that brings me to the next prophetic dream where I received the information, that although I had no romantic involvement with my ex at the time, at a period he was in a relationship with a live-in girlfriend that was 5-years-strong, I was destined to be in such a romance, shown this by experiencing a future time, at a colorful unmistakable day when that romance would be in full bloom.

Which brings me to:

Dream 2 1979

In the summer of 1979 I had another predictive dream, this one a positive one that showed me I would be together with my ex a month before we had any romantic involvement. With the hallmark of a typical prophetic dream I get, the dream had a power and clarity that made it seem to be a transmission from the future.

As I mentioned in chapter 4, at the time I belonged to the Society for Creative Anachronism (SCA), which was a club where medieval buffs met dressed in period costumes, trying to replicate the customs back in the country of their chosen personas.

SCA Group pictured here at a meeting outside of our house where I experienced several demonic encounters. Behind us, you can see the window to bedroom where my ex-husband's occult altar was.

I was either of two: Raissa la Mondresh de Gascony, France or Yawarakai-san from Japan. The club met at Greynolds Park in North Miami sometimes, but most of the times my ex and his then live-in girlfriend of five years, hosted the Sunday meetings at his house next to his mother's house.

Anyone wearing or talking mundane modern things were fined a small fee to discourage breaking the medieval atmosphere everyone worked hard to create at our weekly gatherings. This was before the yearly Renaissance Fair at Viscaya, which my ex and I helped to organize later when we were married. But, at the time of my dream we had nothing to do with one another, except club business.

At the beginning to what would be this prophetic dream, I had been dreaming some nondescript dream, which also is the trademark of many of my prophetic dreams, when suddenly the ordinary dream was interrupted.

I found myself walking through a tunnel of snakes, and when I came out I was walking in a field. I was dressed in my medieval Raissa costume, a blue gown.

Up ahead a few yards stood a small group of people gathered about, looking at the ground.

When I came up to them, I saw they stared at a hole in the ground covered with a small grill. Inside lay a snake. I then walked on to a large tent where people from my SCA club sat and talked.

I took a seat at one of the benches. My ex's girlfriend at the time of my dream, sat behind me. My now ex came in looking for his lady, for he was about to fight and he wanted to dedicate the fight to her.

To my surprise, he passed the woman I knew as his long-live-in girlfriend and came up to me as if I were his lady!

I was shocked, but the woman I knew as his girlfriend seemed okay about it, as if it was normal. He bowed to me and kissed my hand. I was still bewildered, aware this was a dream, yet all the members of the club there acted as if everything was as it should be, so I handed him a ribbon to carry with him in battle. Then I woke.

I wrote the dream down, unaware at the time that his girlfriend was away in California and they were going to break up shortly.

To my surprise a month later we did begin to date. At that

time I told him that I had had a dream that seemed a premonition, but I would share it with him if it came true. I kept it sealed in an envelope and carried it in my purse. Well, four months later it did indeed come true!

I found myself going with my SCA group to a tournament somewhere in the middle of Florida at a campground. As always I had the letter on me, but little did I know this was the weekend I would share it with him.

By then, it was old history I was his girlfriend. The group stayed in tents and we dressed in our costumes.

The day of the tournament, I found myself walking from the public showers where I had dressed in my costume to watch him battle. I crossed the field to go where the main tent was where he would battle outside.

Imagine my surprise as I spotted ahead, as in my dream 4 months ago, a small group of people gathered about staring into the ground.

When I came up to them I was further amazed to find also like in my dream a snake in a shallow hole in the ground covered with a grill! That snake in my dream had not been a symbolism, but it would be a literal snake I would see precisely as shown in my dream, a highly unmistakable, verifiable fact to confirm the validity of the dream. Turns out someone had brought their pet snake with them and thought to temporarily store the snake in this hole, never knowing they would be fulfilling a key confirmation of my prophetic dream!

My ex, holding bull shield, in battle in his front yard.

That was when I

knew I was reliving my dream.

I smiled as I walked to the tent, excited to share this with him.

Of course when I got to the tent as in my dream he waited to dedicate the fight to me, and it was okay with everyone there.

The only difference was his now former girlfriend did not attend the tournament, because she had stayed behind in California. However, as in the dream, it was fine with her, and she knew that I was now his girlfriend.

As soon as he fought the tournament I got my letter and gave it to him! For the first time he read what my premonition dream was about as amazed as I.

Which brings me to the following prophetic dream, which happened shortly after his mother had gotten him to separate from me, in order to divorce me, though it had backfired on her because he had still kept dating me several years after until I didn't want to keep on in that way.

Dream 3, 1982

Two or three weeks after my ex and I separated in 1982 I had an odd dream, the same kind of odd that told me it was a precognitive dream.

The soul of a man appeared to me in my mother's house where I stayed. He floated in the air and looked formless. He told me he was my future husband, and he came to show me he existed.

I think he appeared to me because I was so distraught from my recent divorce and the why of how it happened, that my ex's mother had orchestrated it, and to let me know another future existed for me with another man.

I didn't know what to think of the dream, because at the time I didn't want another husband. I told my girlfriend in the Biltmore hotel picture in chapter 4 about it, not sure what to make of it.

But during the years it played through my mind. I would wonder who he was and how we would meet, especially since there seemed to be no opportunity to meet anyone as I did not like to frequent bars and my social circle was limited, plus, I was always busy working on my efforts to write fantasy novels.

Nine years later, more information would be given to me, very specific now, taking this future husband from a formless soul, to our future house, and a glimpse into our daily routine.

Which brings me to:

Dream 4, 1991

In 1991 I had another dream about my future husband, this one he appeared as a definite person.

I was in the living room of the house my future husband and I would live in. In the setting of the dream it was a normal part of our lives that we each took turns selecting restaurants to eat at and this time it was mine.

It was mid-afternoon and we had just taken a nap, though not in "our" bedroom. I saw myself picking up the yellow pages and searching for a restaurant. I was happy.

The man was a senior citizen, important to remember as I was 33 years of age at the time of the dream.

In another scene in the same dream we were entering a restaurant to join friends of his. They were seniors who liked me and accepted me. That scene was to show me I was an accepted part of his group of friends.

At the next scene I was in our open garage, spending time with his granddaughter. Our yard was flooding. We lived in an area that experienced floods. The flood was a passing event that didn't cause damage to the house, but played to show me that I lived in a real flood zone.

Well in December 1998, when I was forty, I was to find myself exactly in that situation, living in the house with the living room I saw myself browsing through the yellow pages seven years earlier, which I would do in that house, looking for restaurants to eat in a neighborhood new to us, having lived in the house only a few month.

We each had our own room at opposite ends of the house, which answered the mystery why we were napping in what was not 'our' joint bedroom, and my husband, Al, was a senior citizen, seventy-one years of age.

Like in my prophetic dream, he also had one grandchild, a girl like in my dream. Lastly, like most South Floridians we lived in a flood zone, but more importantly we had a long lake right in our backyard, which made the flood part of my dream more significant as the flooding was more of a problem than anywhere I ever lived in Florida because of the lake.

And the garage I saw myself in during my dream of 1992 was exactly like our single-car garage!

Plus, by that time, I had gone to a formal luncheon with his senior friends from a poetry group at a local Red Lobster restaurant, the only young-un there under age sixty, and very accepted in the group as his wife, just as I had dreamed.

I had met my late husband at a writer's group a year and a half before, at a time when neither of us had dated for over four years, making the unfolding of the prophetic dream down to the very detail more amazing.

Now to two dreams, labeled dream 5 and dream 6, leading up to the first of the two prophetic dreams, dream 7 and dream 8. These next two prophetic dreams are not those dreams, but leading up in succession to the 1st , (dream 7) put here so you can see two times I had dreams with the person involved in dream 7, who is now deceased, that were prophetic and proved 100% true, dream 6 when the person was deceased, and it proved true, which is important to establish the truth of after-life communication I had with that person that was verified as total truth.

Dream 5, 1984

It was Wednesday, May 2nd in 1984, and I was asleep dreaming, when my brother who in reality was away on Army desert maneuvers and could not be reached by phone, came into my dream, same as some of my other prophetic dreams in that I was having a regular dream-dream when it was interrupted by the precognitive element.

My brother told me he came to see me because he had suddenly had a change of heart and decided to go ahead with his wedding plans. He told me to tell my mother this, and he wanted me to convey this message. At the time I did not know he had no plans to not marry his fiancé, his girlfriend since high school.

I said to him, "Well, how do I know it's really you and you're not just a dream I'm having?" I added, "How can you prove to me this?"

He seemed startled and put off by this, not expecting me to say that at all.

I continued, "Why don't you tell me something you have told mom in the past two months so when I tell her I will have proof that it's you, something that I wouldn't know about."

This seemed to go across like a dead fish in his face. Whether he told me something or not, I can't recall because when I woke my dogs had distracted me in their need to go outside, and when I tried to recollect that part, it was lost to me.

However, I did remember he told me further on in that dream that the reason he told me in this medium, was because he wasn't able to write me a letter and he couldn't telephone me, and, of course, this was such important news he wanted us to know, especially my mother, because he knew this would please everyone concerned.

I had the impression in the dream it was quite close to the actual time he had experienced this change of heart.

The prior circumstances I had no knowledge of was that he had written his fiancé a letter essentially 'dumping' her the weekend before and had refused to talk to her by phone, saying he didn't know her or she him, and that he didn't love her anymore, and with him out in the desert, she couldn't even reach him.

Now, unbeknownst to me, my brother had then telephoned his fiancée from the desert two days prior, having gotten access to a phone, which was unexpected because he was not going to call her until he returned from the desert maneuver the following month, which was June.

Their conversation had been non-plus.

But this Wednesday he had phoned her again unexpectedly to tell her that he was going to go ahead and marry her in August as they had originally planned.

I found out from my mother about his calls to her the next night after my dream.

I had told my mom 'the dream' because I had felt it was a true precognitive experience and had told my ex about it in length who

Chapter 6: Final Grace Timer Nearing Last Tick

I was still with at the time, and my mother not so much in length that very Wednesday the dream had happened, before anyone had heard from my brother.

Some time after, my brother had called my soon-to-be sister-in-law and recommitted to their marrying, and it was after my mother had gotten this update from my future sister-in-law that she told me about my brother's calls to my future sister-in-law on Monday and Wednesday.

Here the first prophetic dream involving my sister-in-law that proved 100% true, the person who is the subject of my prophetic dreams 6 & 7.

Dream 6, 1987

On July 26th, of 1987, a Sunday morning when I was asleep and having an average, non-memorable dream that I can't even recollect of what, that dream suddenly froze like a film paused, the whole scene, everything, just frozen.

From the right of my dream stage, in walked my sister-in-law, twenty-two-years of age at the time.

Last time I had seen her, before she had left to join my brother at his post overseas at Germany, she had been her fit, cute little self, all of 4 foot, 11, trim and spunky.

Yet, her real life had taken a nightmare turn the month before this dream, as pregnant with an ectopic pregnancy, though she had tried to convince the Army doctor she was pregnant from home pregnancy tests she had taken, she had been ignored, turned away, until her tube had ruptured.

She had then been rushed by ambulance to the dispensary which then had referred her to a German hospital at Mutlangen.

To combat the trauma, fluids had been forced into her body during surgery but her lungs became filled with excessive fluids. As a normal procedure they then collapsed her lungs, but she developed an infection resistant to treatment.

Her condition sharply declined and she had then been airlifted to Uhm hospital, where the best intensive care equipment in Germany was, where she had been for weeks in an induced coma to help her heal.

At the time of my dream it was day 56 of her ordeal she had been caught in that fight for her young twenty-two year old life as the German doctors did all they medically could.

All that time I was in Miami, Florida, living with my parents after the separation with my ex and had not seen my sister-in-law, nor been told anything how her body had changed in that fight.

Since the last time I had seen her in reality she had been healthy and fit, I was not prepared for the sister-in-law I saw walk into my dream and her appearance shocked me. Her body was bloated, monstrously swollen, like a victim of gout.

This was the first time I had dreamt of her in several months. She didn't look like she was twenty-two, she looked like an old lady.

The first thing I said in a half warning smile to her was, "Don't tell me you've died."

Solemnly she told me she was coming back to Miami.

We embraced and sat talking like two schoolgirls a couple of minutes as her outward appearance returned to the beautiful sister-in-law I knew and loved.

My alarm went off, waking me. I looked at the time, 8:59 a.m. There is a six hour lapse between Miami and Germany, so I noted the time overseas and that in Germany it would be 2:59 a.m.

The dream was so vivid like other prophetic dreams that I wrote it down.

It felt more like she had really visited me than a dream. From that feeling of reality, I was elated from our visit despite its sad implications.

Soon as I got to the kitchen for breakfast, I shared it with my mother, who brushed it off as a good omen my sister-in-law would live a very long life.

Five hours later my brother called from Germany. The hospital had called him late at night because my sister-in-law's condition suddenly nose-dived, after a week of hopeful improvement.

Seems the stress was too much on her young heart, and at 2:56 a.m. German time, which was 3 minutes before my dream took place, my sister-in-law passed on in my brother's arms.

Here is a picture of my sister-in-law, posing with my father

Chapter 6: Final Grace Timer Nearing Last Tick

months before she would meet a tragic end.

My sister-in-law posing with my father months before her death.

A week later my sister-in-law did indeed return to Miami, in a casket to be buried.

At the open casket service, I suddenly understood why the sister-in-law that had walked into my dream was so horribly monstrous: the stress her athletic twenty-two-year-old body endured from the fluids fed her to combat the respiratory distress syndrome, had aged her fifty years, so much that a photo of her smiling and radiant in her cap and gown after graduating from Miami Charter College was placed in the casket for a reminder to all of her so recently-lost beauty.

Sad as it was, this was a prophetic dream that shows that when my sister-in-law came to me after her death to relate a message that it proved entirely true.

Now, finally, the dream, the 7th dream, with her that should be food for thought for you on the information I am telling you to get your house in order for the day of God's wrath.

Dream 7 1992

It wasn't a long dream, it actually was very short, but as other dreams, I was having a regular non-descript dream, when like an emergency broadcast single interruption test for the next sixty seconds, the regular dream stopped.

Then I saw a sky, a blue sky and clouds and I saw my sister-in-law descend from those clouds. I was thrilled to see her, she looked great.

She only came to say a very short sentence to me before she started to go right up again to what I knew was heaven.

She said, "You are one of the fifty."

I understood it had something to do with 50 as in number of people, and on earth, alive, having something to do with something of God.

However, I was too interested to ask her how heaven was as she started to float up that I didn't think to ask her what that meant.

Instead trying to find out how it was in heaven, I asked her, "Is there corn in the cob in heaven?" very stupid, I know, but that is what blurted out of me as she was just moving away too fast.

She nodded yes.

I asked as she was halfway up, "Do you eat it?"

She nodded as she was hurrying up and was then gone, my three-second window to ask questions gone. It was like she was only allowed to say that, like she really wanted to deliver me this info, and then had to go back.

I didn't know what to make of that at the time as I was just not doing anything for God. In fact, what I was still doing was wild oats sowing that kept me far from God.

Yet, I tucked that away, because it had that prophetic dream situation to it, and it had felt exactly the same as when she had come to tell me she was coming to Miami minutes after she had passed.

As you can see, though, that God is a detailed planner and whatever it is, he doesn't leave it up to one person; he has a network in place that makes sure all his plans succeed.

Later on when I had started a business selling rosaries, I had wondered if that was what she had meant, one of fifty people doing rosaries on the Internet as I had set up several sites on the subject, but was not sure.

However, after I got revelation that led me out of the Catholic faith and out of Marian activity entirely, I knew that couldn't have been it. It was only after I had two more experiences that I understood it has something to do with this information and the passing season of grace, which brings me to the last dream, the 2nd of the two dreams I said at the beginning of this chapter were the two prophetic dreams for you to be aware of that could very well pertain to your mission to be found ready to enter heaven.

Dream 8, 2011

In this dream on December 31, 2011, I found myself in a hall, sitting in one of 3 chairs, a man sitting in the chair to the right of me.

This man was some kind of scholar, like a tenured emeritus scholar, with Jewish features.

His hair was distinctive too, Einstein-ish hair, in that it was frizzy, controlled frizzy, except instead of white, it was dark brown with varying gray and not as out and frizzy as Einstein's hair, partly from the weight of the length which came almost to his shoulder pad area, the kind of hair you expect on an intellectual noble-prize winning man.

From the aura I got from him, he seemed wealthy and rich, like he was enormously successful scholar, top in his field.

I got the impression he had come to be with me. He held my right hand. It was the manner in which he held it that was incredible. He held my hand like I was a very precious artifact only of which he recognized how enormously precious, yet it was matter of fact.

We got up from the chairs and we were walking out to a parking lot.

I wanted to know who he was, yet because it was so nice how he was holding my hand, I let him lead me like everything was okay even though I didn't know who he was and he just appeared out of the crowd purposefully to come to me to sit and hold my hand, me the subject of his visit.

We came to what was his car.

I wanted to ask him a question. If I had not wanted to ask him a question, I understood he would have gone.

He conceded to it and opened the passenger door for me and I went in, yet found myself not seated in the front passenger side, but the back right hand seat.

All this time I was holding my little short-hair dachshund, who is my pet in reality, like Dorothy held Toto through the Wizard of Oz, being girlish and childish, holding onto my doggie, something this man had no issue with or even any kind of reaction to, as if that was all fine, understanding me to the core, that inside I really was child-like and girlish and totally accepting me as I was, which was a non-issue to him, whoever he was.

As I sat in the backseat holding my dog and I waited for him to go around the car, he went in the driver's side, shut the door. Then he turned back to me.

I asked him who he was, the burning question on my mind.

He said, "I specialize in seasons, the *passing* of seasons," stressing the word 'passing', looking at me like I was that season in passing.

The way he said the word 'seasons' was not like the regular seasons of nature, like seasons of the weather, seasons of biological things, but crucial passing seasons that were extremely momentous and important in divine significance.

Somehow, according to the way he treated me through the way he had held my hand, and the way he looked at me then, he conveyed I was a super key piece, key enough to get him treating me that way, a timing of which he was a scholar of, and he was now himself at a place and space in this phenomenon where he got involved as if the momentous divine season was now officially in progress.

How I was so important I don't know. It is almost as if the me there with him, like the me here now typing this, didn't realize yet my role and had not yet done what I was going to do, but of which he had full knowledge of and of which was absolutely undoubtedly a crucial piece, something that was his specialty to work with to the successful passing of each momentous season, of which he

Chapter 6: Final Grace Timer Nearing Last Tick

alone had the full knowledge to understand and monitor.

At first I was glad for the answer, and at the same time found it interesting.

Then I felt a sudden feeling of panic, a panic at the thought to be temporary, to soon have no importance to him, and be yesterday's news and that I would no longer be an issue at one point. At that time my alarm went off.

Even though the alarm interrupted the dream, I found myself reasoning with myself as I got out of bed, to get over the panic I hated, that the apostles' seasons passed, and they did not become forgotten no ones, they have their secure eternal place in heaven and their teachings still yet continue to have relevant super impact. Reflecting that gave me some calm though I had not started writing this book until months later.

When I'd had this dream it was before I knew I would have a Christian album out and that I would be working on this book, and before the enemy would visit me in March 2013 nine weeks later which I write about in chapter 10, with plans to do me in to stop something they *really* are super distressed about.

Friend, I tell you this, because I want you to be like the faithful servant Jesus spoke of in the parable, the servant who is awake and ready for his master's coming whenever that will be. Now I am afraid, really, that what this passing season is, is the passing season of grace. What this means is the reality shown to me in 1972 that God's day of wrath is coming is on the horizon, and the season that the Lord is extending for grace is already in effect and it is passing, and that is grace for repentance, grace to walk right with him, to be found walking right when he comes, and ready to go.

From my background of prophetic dreams, I wouldn't take this information lightly. I would take it to heart to get right with the Lord, while the window for grace is yet available.

I will be honest with you, it makes me afraid. I am afraid to see grace pass, I am afraid to see grace shut and no longer available for people. That will be a very bad day.

My salvation has depended on grace, time and again, I tried the Lord from my oats sowing, but that grace, praise God, was available.

There is coming a time as said in the Bible, that it will end, for the Lord's Day of Wrath will come, and what is essential to know is God's word never returns void. He said the terrible day of the Lord will come and so it shall whether any of us like it or not.

While I love the idea of the Marriage Supper of The Lamb (Revelation 19:9), and I wrote a song about how much I look forward to that party titled "Only One Party," what I don't look forward to is the end of grace and the terrible day of the Lord. If anything I would like that delayed; I do not want to rush people to hell, people who would benefit from all the time they can get to get right with God and repent.

In this vein, I want to say, I am finding people on the Internet, making videos and having discussions in longing and deep desire for the day of the Lord, wanting it to be as soon as possible, yearning for it, and gaining for themselves followers in this desire and developing the same passion in them as if this is pleasing to God.

However, in Amos 5, the Lord gives a warning to someone who desires such a thing, that it is foolishness to desire such a thing, showing that the one who does has no idea of the terror for which they are desiring to finally come to the world.

> Woe to you who desire the day of the LORD! Why would you have the day of the LORD? It is darkness, and not light, as if a man fled from a lion, and a bear met him, or went into the house and leaned his hand against the wall, and a serpent bit him. Is not the day of the LORD darkness, and not light, and gloom with no brightness in it?
>
> —Amos 5:18-20, ESV

While it is good to be confident in your salvation, Paul warns in 1 Corinthians 10:1-12 against such sureness which if held against the measure God will bring on the day of the Lord may prove a false confidence.

Moreover, brethren, I do not want you to be unaware that

Chapter 6: Final Grace Timer Nearing Last Tick

all our fathers were under the cloud, all passed through the sea, all were baptized into Moses in the cloud and in the sea, all ate the same spiritual food, and all drank the same spiritual drink. For they drank of that spiritual Rock that followed them, and that Rock was Christ. But with most of them God was not well pleased, for their bodies were scattered in the wilderness. Now these things became our examples..., and they were written for our admonition, upon whom the ends of the ages have come. Therefore let him who thinks he stands take heed lest he fall.

—1 Corinthians 10:1-12, NKJV

***

Born In A War Between Dark And Light

Chapter 7

DEMON DOCTRINES COMING TO A CHURCH NEAR YOU

Now the Spirit expressly says that in latter times some will depart from the faith, giving heed to deceiving spirits and doctrines of demons.
—*1 Timothy 4:1, NKJV*

Grab some popcorn. Get some Milk Duds for soon, if not already, coming to a church near you, are the scariest, chilling demon doctrines as predicted by Christ. Don't delay because there will be a sold-out crowd on this enemy feature. Starring in the production are some of those considering themselves Christians ready to meet Jesus in eternity, but are under an evil delusion from a demon doctrine or two or three. You haven't seen deluded characters until you have seen these, so bring your hanky; it is going to be tearful.

The drama increases whenever the scene will feature one with a strong delusion, as it is very difficult to convince them of the truth, and they will not hear or receive anything else contrary to their delusion, no matter how many supporting Scriptures they are shown. Such people never see themselves as the one in error, but everyone else in error. This is called a strong delusion (2 Thessalonians 2:11) and one based on what it is, a demon doctrine, given by the Spirit of error.

Hollywood producers can't script this scale of misfortune that has already hit many Christians all over the world. If it were only a movie, we could cry a little bit, boo at the bad guys, clap when it is over, and walk away.

Unfortunately demon doctrines is not the title of a movie that we can soon forget, but demon doctrines are the way many

Christians are going to stumble in the end times and fall away from the faith.

For the people led astray into these, they will not realize, as part of the delusion, they are in deep trouble if they do not snap out of the scripturally-wrong thinking, before the day of the Lord or their appointed time to die, whichever comes first.

The reason being is demon doctrines give people the wrong idea some kind of sin is acceptable to God and requires no repentance, luring them to live a life of iniquitous acts God abhors and die in them, having lost forever the opportunity of grace from repentance.

In the event this term is new to you, a demon doctrine is Scripture that is twisted wrongly, giving a spirit of error to what it means.

The spirit of error is actually a spirit, who is from the Father of lies, the devil (John 8:44). This means such Scriptural errors come from the demonic for the purpose of leading people to their destruction. Thus anything that is not in line with the Bible is instead in line with Satan's Bible, and one of his doctrines.

From the Scriptures we get this revelation, learning there is a Spirit of Truth, who is from God and is the Holy Spirit, and a Spirit of error, who is from the devil and is an ungodly spirit.

> We are of God. He who knows God hears us; he who is not of God does not hear us. By this we know the spirit of truth and the spirit of error.
> —*1 John 4:6, NKJV*

> But when he, the Spirit of truth, comes, he will guide you into all the truth. He will not speak on his own; he will speak only what he hears, and he will tell you what is yet to come.
> —*John 16:13, NIV*

This chapter covers what a demon doctrine is for two reasons:

1) When I cover the ones I do later on you have the scriptural understanding of what that is and the enemy cannot get you to

Chapter 7: Demon Doctrines Coming To A Church Near You

turn from the term 'demon doctrine' like it is some kind of gothic horror novel invention, and keep you from receiving the truth.

2) Because it is important to not be bound under a last day, last time delusion, when that day of the Lord comes upon one unexpectedly, it is crucial to be certain to clean your house, to examine yourself diligently now while there is yet a certain amount of time to discern whether or not you might be holding or be under a demon doctrine.

The only way you can be diligent against something is to know what it is, to not only know what it is but to see it coming no matter how crafty it is concealed. A demon doctrine can come upon you like a stealth intruder. It can be camouflaged to appear in all righteousness, and yet be blasphemous against the way of truth, filled with false words delivered by those in condemnation. This is a warfare thing, another form of attack.

At this time of the war, we are all at the point where we are still in the boat of our everyday, normal life as humanity believes life to be, but a small leak has recently appeared in this boat and the process to sinking begun, though unsure when and the time left, whether years or months.

Though uncertain how long before it gets too close to too late to save yourself, it behooves you to now search all over your boat and cast out all the things that are going to take you down in order to stand buoyant until your Savior arrives to lift you out before that boat goes into destruction. Now is the time to start throwing everything away, not casually because the time is not that long.

You must start casting all these deadly weights away from you, and rid yourself of these deadly weights against you by the enemy. One of these can be a demon doctrine.

It is especially difficult to guard against them because at this time of the approach of the day of the Lord, there are a lot of people within the Christian community who have the false idea they are a part of the Body of Christ, but they are actually apostles of demon doctrines.

So falling for one can be easier to do because they are coming from the mouths of people who clearly love Jesus, who are within the Body of Christ as far as physical presence, have the false idea they are in the right, while they are in grip of the Spirit of error through a demon doctrine, and thereby they are false apostles of these ways of lawlessness.

We are in the last days where there are false teachers among all of us who are bringing in these destructive heresies as Peter said in 2 Peter 2. These false apostles are going to lead astray many Christians through doctrines of demons.

> And then many will fall away and betray one another and hate one another. And many false prophets will arise and lead many astray.
> —Matthew 24:10-11, ESV

It is important you know that the Greek σκανδαλισθήσονται πολλοὶ translates in English to the words 'will fall away many' as this shows that Christians will fall from the faith; while the King James just says many will be 'offended' which paints a whole other picture.

Folks, this is more than just being 'offended'; offended means taking offense at something, but 'falling away' means leaving something, and in this Verse means leaving the true faith. You need to know that Christians will be falling away, as they are doing now, from the faith because of these demon doctrines. That is why it is ultra urgent you not only understand about demon doctrines, that you know they are going to proliferate in these end times, but you know how to overcome them.

Literally you may find yourself a lone survivor among Christians lead astray by these doctrines, and find yourself hated on by them and the focus of their attacks as Verse 10 states will occur. These are not physical attacks, but verbal arguments hell-bent to prove your conviction to the full Scriptures as wrong. In other words, a full, all-out war as we are in.

That is why it is important you are prepped, and you understand these confrontations, and know when to walk away when you recognize seared consciousnesses and don't let the enemy drain your energy just for the debilitating effect on you with the goal if they can't convert you to practice lawlessness, to

Chapter 7: Demon Doctrines Coming To A Church Near You

then cripple you by snaring you in vain fights so you are not a threat putting the truth out to those yet saved who will still hear and understand.

These false apostles will lead many into lives of sin, taking their souls from eternal life to certain death (James 5:19-20). One of the hallmarks of such false apostles is they follow their own sensuality because they are in the doctrinal error these things are not sin, that they are covered by Christ, that the war of the flesh is acceptable to Jesus and he does not, as a result of that mercy, require self control or any measure like that, ignoring quite a lot of Scriptures stating otherwise. In addition greed for monetary gain will rule their ministry, driving them to exploit Christians with false doctrines.

> And many will follow their sensuality, and because of them the way of truth will be blasphemed. And in their greed they will exploit you with false words. Their condemnation from long ago is not idle, and their destruction is not asleep.
> *—2 Peter 2:2-3, ESV*

In other words they have bought into the lies and deception, twisted things to their own error and their own destruction. Being that they have an apparent love of Christ and a love of what Christ has obtained for all, and that they hang out in Christian environments, they often pass under the radar as a 'true' believer, yet by their way of not following Jesus teachings in full, which shows they don't have God and they don't have Jesus, they really are not true believers, often to their whole ignorance as a result of that doctrinal error.

Because they blend in as a regular believer in the common crowd, that is how true Christians will be at risk to be also equally fooled into such snares, because they will not be expecting that kind of delivery of demon doctrines from someone who does not consider themselves a false apostle, and is not acting like any kind of apostle as you would see that role, but acts only as one who is fervently upholding a particular incorrect doctrine, not even believing it is a false doctrine because it is made up of parts of

Scriptures, yet twisted incorrectly in teaching.

On top of that, often they many times have a great fervor to enlighten others of this 'true' way, and make it their mission to 'correct' those thinking otherwise, putting more time into spreading that falsehood than many true Christians do spreading the teachings of Jesus.

Through this fervor they may produce voluminous writings supporting a doctrinal error, but do not fall for this warfare strategy that sheer volume on a subject alone lends it credibility, nor fall for the trick that through the tactic of repeating that 'good news' in a lengthy doctrine makes the doctrine right, because it does not.

Around twenty-five years ago I remember in my interest of the occult, picking up at a local occult bookshop this exceptionally-long paperback book, black cover, something like 2000 pages, which claimed to be written by a godhead or entity behind the true reality of existence.

The structure of thoughts was not that of a madman, but orderly, well-written, interesting information, almost encyclopedic, and it appeared there were some kinds of devotees behind this belief-system. This intelligence called itself something like Ra or 'One' and went into what reality really was about, with that intelligence the real master behind it, giving explanations of all of existence, in a way almost a spin-off of the Bible, but twisting it to put this intelligence as the true mastermind behind it.

However, being a writer myself, I did not find it convincing, knowing the human capability for creative thought process to set up a universe reality, from my interest and love of writing science fiction and fantasy stories back then.

What was missing for me was the absolute lack of any proof: one huge book does not a truth make, as it can all be the flight of fancy of one mind. Whereas the books in the Bible are built around thousands of eye-witnesses to the marvels of God in the Old Testament, and the evidence given by Jesus in fulfilling scriptural prophecy and also eye-witness accounts of his divinity, starting with the appearance of an angel shining with the glory of God who appeared to shepherds living out in the fields, announcing to them the good tidings of a Savior born that day, who was Christ the

Chapter 7: Demon Doctrines Coming To A Church Near You

Lord, directing them where they could find him, to glorify and praise God.

Though on a vastly smaller scale, on my own book here I provide you photos and newspaper evidence to some of my experiences, and others of them experiences I jointly had with someone else.

When I had picked up that book, I had already encountered in my interest in Sci-Fi certain people convinced of a reality if the information presented was complex enough without any proof of any kind other than the written material.

As far as that book by that 'intelligence', I can tell you it could have been ten thousand pages and it would not have made that doctrine true, yet, clearly that there were some followers, some people had bought into the message by the sheer volume of it having some kind of authority of truth.

It is on the level with a magician trick by the way a magician presents something as having truth, such as levitation, but in reality, it is all illusion of a truth the magician places his future earnings on the public will buy. However, the magician behind a voluminous demon doctrine is Satan and not the person imparting the doctrine, who is entirely deluded to believe it is total truth.

If volume is a strategy you face, you have to always know that you cannot put blinders on to other Scriptures and just claim one slant is it. Do not be deceived by a super long treatise on something. Satan has spent centuries producing volumes of such doctrines and never has what he produced ever changed the truth.

As the days pass, such false apostles will increase in numbers, that by numbers only to some weak in Bible knowledge, they will seem right. They will use usernames inspired by the Spirit of error to further convince, such as Understanding, or Truth, or Knowledgeable. From their common interest to 'correct' those 'mistaken' Christians teaching obedience, self control and the requirement to be slaves to righteousness, they will gravitate to the same blogs, videos and forums, and their demon doctrines will stay like seducing billboards in posts and comments, such as this first example of a demon doctrine.

7-2 Demon Doctrine: After Cross No Guilt

In this doctrine, the Spirit of error deceives through mixing the Scriptures concerning Christ's sacrifice wiping away sins and that all people are sinners and they sin. This doctrine teaches that through the blood of Jesus the believer is cleansed internally once for all and that 'parental forgiveness' that is, needing to ask for forgiveness of those sins to our parent, who is God, Our Father, is not needed because that would imply the guilt of a believer, and well, such guilt negates the full forgiveness of Christ at the cross, and goes against what this doctrine states which is after the cross, John and Paul say all sins are forgiven, meaning no guilt exists after the cross.

Thus, this implies if after we become Christians we murder, rob or destroy, we do so guilt-free. For example; if we murder our neighbor, we do so guilt free, or if we rob a bank, we do so guilt free, or if we destroy the reputations of those we dislike, we do so guilt free. In accordance to this doctrine, we can discard all morale and ethical compass, and toss civilized behavior out the window with our new found freedom in Christ.

Most importantly, it implies no repentance at any point is required, because if repentance is not required for present and future sins, certainly repentance is not required for past sins. This doctrine stands that at the cross all sins for all times are forgiven equates to no guilt from that point on, which equates to no repentance necessary as that cancels out the sacrifice of Jesus.

Do you see how it weaves in a hyper inflating of an attribute of Jesus to convince of its rightness because who would want to be the one accused of canceling out the sacrifice of the Lord?

What it fails to focus on is that it makes a liar of Jesus.

It makes all his teachings one must repent (Luke 13:2-5), the teachings of a liar. It makes all his warnings it is better to cut off parts of your body than land in hell (Matthew 5:29-30), the warnings of a liar. It makes all his teachings that he will refuse entrance into heaven to those who preached about him, delivered people from demons but who practiced evil (Matthew 7:21-23), the teachings of a liar.

Jesus came specifically to destroy the works of the devil (1

John 3:8), and to call him a liar on these things is to be not for him, but against him (Luke 11:23). You cannot accept one thing Jesus did, over other things Jesus did. You must take the whole of it and stand your faith on it.

Moreover, these claims are done on partial doctrines. Just because it claims John and Paul state all sins are forgiven after the cross, it is an out of context statement, twisting what they said into false doctrine.

On John, it ignores he refuted that angle that all sins are forgiven meaning we are all guiltless when if any sins are committed and repentance is not needed here. Here John is saying a person lies they are a believer if they walk in darkness and do not practice the truth.

> If we say we have fellowship with him while we walk in darkness, we lie and do not practice the truth.
> —1 John 1:6, ESV

And John further disproves this claim he stated repentance is not needed because all sins from the cross were forgiven, when he wrote here how believers take care of any sins they may commit after they have accepted Christ.

> My dear children, I write this to you so that you will not sin. But if anybody does sin, we have one who speaks to the Father in our defense--Jesus Christ, the Righteous One. He is the atoning sacrifice for our sins, and not only for ours but also for the sins of the whole world.
> —1-John, 2:1-2, NIV

If all sins do not require repentance, and our present and future sins also were covered at the cross to the point though we 'sin' we are guiltless and thus do not need to repent, then it makes John a liar to give instructions to Christians that if they do sin, because John was writing to Christians and not unbelievers, telling them not to sin, but if they did, what recourse there was for that, which was to "confess them and he would be faithful and just to forgive us our sins" instructions which he wrote so that if any

Christian did commit a sin after having their past sins forgiven, they could count on the grace that if they confess those sins, Jesus as our advocate to the Father would forgive us, and cleanse us!

Clearly this shows a condition 'if' we confess, showing that confession is required. So this no need to ask for parental forgiveness already is a mistruth. Also, this Scripture from John shows that new sins require confessing, and to our Advocate.

How this doctrine twists is to take the truth that Jesus died once as a sacrifice and that his blood is good against all sins of which Jesus stated requires repentance for that cleansing, and omits the need for confession and repentance, which opens the support to believe no need for guilt, which then means no need to confess and repent.

However, Scriptures instruct otherwise. If the devil can trick you to think you do not need to confess and repent of your sins, you are going to die in your sins. They will not be forgiven and you will not make it to heaven.

The interesting thing is forgiveness of our sins is easy: if you do sin again, you can have confidence you have an advocate with God, who is Jesus. It is so easy: you just confess, and repent to the Lord, and ask him to cleanse you with that same blood he spilled only once, which stands active and alive as from the moment it spilled at his death, and he will take that blood and cleanse you. This doctrine is to deceive you from believing you need this and keep you from coming to the Lord to be cleansed. If you willfully keep on sinning, though, you will not get that forgiveness as your repentance is not sincere.

> If we deliberately keep on sinning after we have received the knowledge of the truth, no sacrifice for sins is left, but only a fearful expectation of judgment and of raging fire that will consume the enemies of God.
> —*Hebrews 10:26-27, NIV*

This also shows this doctrine is wrong claiming all sins were wiped out at the cross means that once we accept Jesus we do not need to ask for forgiveness because such repentance would 'cancel out' the sacrifice of Jesus. Again, see how it tries to make you feel

Chapter 7: Demon Doctrines Coming To A Church Near You

bad on something which actually is right to do? Oh my gosh, better not ask for forgiveness or I will be blaspheming the sacrifice of Jesus....but that is a demonic twist, a lie to get you to believe it. This Scripture here is main springboard of this doctrine:

> Nor did he enter heaven to offer himself again and again, the way the high priest enters the Most Holy Place every year with blood that is not his own. Then Christ would have had to suffer many times since the creation of the world. But now he has appeared once for all at the end of the ages to do away with sin by the sacrifice of himself.
> —*Hebrews 9:25-26, NIV*

With these two used as reinforcements:

> ...so Christ was sacrificed once to take away the sins of many people; and he will appear a second time, not to bear sin, but to bring salvation to those who are waiting for him.
> —*Hebrews 9:28, NIV*

> If we claim to be without sin, we deceive ourselves and the truth is not in us.
> —*1 John 1:8, NIV*

These are twisted to mean that the sins Jesus wipes away are past, present and future sins of EACH person who accepts him as savior, twisting the meaning 'everyone sins' to mean 'everyone continues to sin' and if anyone denies 'continuing to' sin, they are a liar.

Let's give applause to the Spirit of error for that clever twist which unstable and weak in the Scripture accepts to mean lawlessness is unavoidable, it can't be stopped, is normal and is all right with God as long as you accept Jesus as your savior. So the difference between an unsaved adulterer, or unsaved murderer, and a saved adulterer and a saved murderer is the later holds in their pocket a membership card that reads "Jesus is my Lord."

If you ask such a deceived person to show you where in the

Scripture it is stated that each person's future sins are forgiven without confessing and repenting, they will come up empty handed. However, since they are in an enemy delusion, most of the time what they will do is just repeat to you the main Scripture this doctrine is woven on as if repeating it will override the Scriptures showing the error.

This one actually is an easy one to cleave in half with the Sword of Truth, because there is a Scripture that specifically states what time-zone of infractions you commit Jesus sacrifice removes when you accept him as Savior.

> For this very reason, make every effort to add to your faith goodness; and to goodness, knowledge; and to knowledge, self-control; and to self-control, perseverance; and to perseverance, godliness; and to godliness, brotherly kindness; and to brotherly kindness, love. For if you possess these qualities in increasing measure, they will keep you from being ineffective and unproductive in your knowledge of our Lord Jesus Christ. But if anyone does not have them, he is nearsighted and blind, and has forgotten that he has been cleansed from his past sins.
> —2 Peter 1:5-9, NIV

So you see that the sacrifice of Jesus buys for every believer at the time of repentance cleansing from that person's past sins. Please let that sink in, the word 'past' alone is what is stated one is not to forget one has been cleansed from.

As I showed earlier in this chapter, 1 John 2:1-2 gives a Christian instructions concerning that if anyone does sin, though they should not willfully sin, what are the steps to cover that, because obviously the new sins are not automatically covered and required John to tell such a person what to do, which was to know Jesus is the propitiation for not only those of the whole world, meaning those outside of the faith, but also for those in the faith who do commit sins, and to thus follow what he wrote just prior in 1 John 1:8-9, which is to confess to Jesus and if they do those things they will receive forgiveness.

Chapter 7: Demon Doctrines Coming To A Church Near You

This makes a no-brainer demon doctrine whacker, provided you have this link in your Armor of God in place gotten by "receiving with meekness the implanted word able to save your souls" (James 1:21 ESV) and ever increasing your efforts to "supplement your faith and virtue with godly knowledge" done by steadfast hearing and reading of the Bible.

First off, realize that any time you are confronted with receiving deliverance from God in any measure, Satan tries to keep you from receiving that truth. The first way Satan will try is to stir rebellion in you so you simply close your ears to the message which can save you.

> He who is of God hears God's words; therefore you do not hear, because you are not of God."
> —*John 8:47, NKJV*

If you will let the enemy do this to you, you will follow his lead to refuse to watch or read or listen to someone speaking a word based on Scripture that can free you from an enemy stronghold. I have seen this in action by people posting in forums they refused to watch a talk show through with a pastor or evangelist who was giving a Holy Spirit-filled message, as if this turning away from the message was good and showed the message they never heard through as bad and not of God.

However, not listening through to the person preaching on that message before passing judgment is a sign of influence of the Spirit of error, because anyone truly of God will give ear through the power of the Holy Spirit in them working to convict all in the world of their sins (John 16:8) while mercy yet exists, and if the words spoken are all sound doctrine from the Bible, should acknowledge the issues said come from the Lord.

> If anyone thinks that he is a prophet, or spiritual, he should acknowledge that the things I am writing to you are a command of the Lord.
> —*1 Corinthians 14:37, ESV*

Such refusal to listen through the Scriptures show this is a flag of someone who is under the grip of the enemy, that the person will not hear the message of God.

> For this purpose I was born and for this purpose I have come into the world--to bear witness to the truth. Everyone who is of the truth listens to my voice.
> —*John 18:37, ESV*

And if they listen, they will not understand.

> In them is fulfilled the prophecy of Isaiah: "You will be ever hearing but never understanding; you will be ever seeing but never perceiving."
> —*Matthew 13:14, NIV*

Thus, if you find yourself on the receiving end of a spoken word on a matter which if it proves true by the word, convicts you of sin, I urge you to resist the enemy influence to get you to close your ears to that message and turn away, before you hear the whole thing through. Understand also, that message, though you may vehemently feel otherwise, if it is true, will act as a seed of grace planted in you, and though it may take some time, will lead you out of bondage to that sin, as the Holy Spirit works to open your eyes to the truth through putting you in the path of those who belong to Christ in order to reach your ears with Scriptures pointing you to your straying or error so you may repent.

> Look at what is before your eyes. If anyone is confident that he is Christ's, let him remind himself that just as he is Christ's, so also are we.
> —*2 Corinthians 10:7, ESV*

I can point to several places in my own life where I was not ready to receive such words from other people also in the Body of Christ as I felt I was, and rebelled against them in my spirit, feeling the person or people were mistaken, only to find myself bit by bit being led by the Spirit of Truth as I studied the Bible, and sought to draw nearer to the Lord, to conviction of the truth of those words given to me while I was in the thick of such sins yet thinking I was saved while involved in things not of God some of the processes taking years to sink into me the Scriptures I had heard did apply to what I was practicing then.

The problem anyone reading this has if they are caught up in the deception of any demon doctrine is they don't have the years I had to reach that point because the signs of the time are heralding the soon coming of the day of the Lord, and that is part of what this book is about to help such people get accelerated deliverance they would ordinarily have across a normal lifetime.

If the strategy to get you to turn away from the message does not work, Satan will see if you will be deceived to combat receiving the truth by stirring in your mind doctrines of demons familiar to you which seem righteous by giving a false glory to the Lord. By false, I mean one that is not a true glory, but evil flattery meant to convince you to harden your heart through over-magnifying one attribute of God, such as the demon doctrine that Christ's sacrifice covers a person's past, present and future sins, so no matter what sin a person commits, the blood of Jesus auto wipes it away, making it impossible for a 'believer' to be held accountable for murder, adultery, covetous, idolatry and any other sin.

The way this example demon doctrine over-magnifies God's grace over the rest of his attributes is through hyper-inflating his mercy so it dominates above his attribute of his holy severity in order to convince you it is contradictory for him to be a holy righteous judge. This leaves you deceived in a false belief a believer never needs to repent again over any new sin, which is a twisting of Scriptures that promotes lawlessness, lawlessness being sin (1 John 3:4), and ignores the Scriptures which counter that, such as 1 John 3:9-10 and Hebrews 10:26-29 which proves a believer's future sins are not covered by that believer's initial washing away of his sins, but counted as separate new transgressions requiring a new atonement.

You have to just stop in a sober moment and reason what that is saying, and you will see it is depravity. The core root of it is depravity. The Bible has something to say about depraved thinking and it is a state where someone prefers perverse thoughts over what is right which God just gives them over to such twisted thinking if that person insists thinking that way (Romans 1:28).

Although this particular demon doctrine is talking about the sacrifice of Jesus it is presenting it in a way that equates to depravity, depraved thinking, the only kind of reasoning that people after downing 10 shots of Tequila would find sound, even by our human standards, not even the holy God's standards.

When you take it to where it can go, where it does go, you see it is depraved, because there is no limit to it when you put that condition that asking for forgiveness is not needed, there is no limit. It doesn't just stop at 'little' sins like helping yourself to a fruit off the fruit stand without paying for it; it goes to the level of all types of unconscionable sins that you don't need to repent of because it would cancel out the sacrifice.

If you don't need to repent because you will cancel out the sacrifice of Jesus, then you can commit without any guilt of condemnation from God any number of the heinous crimes people commit which can shock even the jaded, if you accept its reasoning all guilt was removed at the cross. That reasoning, that depraved mind of reasoning, which is diabolical, goes to every level of sin.

To think it stops somewhere is not to follow its full reasoning, which is what the demons hope you will not do, that you will instead limit it somehow and that is really how they plan they can pull a fast one on you which is you just stay stuck on that motto 'don't cancel out the sacrifice of Jesus' and so never repent, and you never think for yourself exactly what that is when you are doing that.

Jesus did not come from his glorious heavenly throne to give carte blanche to every type of sin that the Father wiped out cities and nations for, which Jesus abhors as well. That is the thinking of 10 shots of Tequila, which is warped reasoning, that is depraved, that is what depraved means from an example everyone understands: 10-shots Tequila reasoning.

Such is this train of thought in this demonic doctrine that at the cross all past, present and future sins were forgiven for every person without repentance needed ever again, and to do so is to cancel out the sacrifice of Jesus.

It is like a killer saying to his intended victim, "Don't let that arsenic laced milk go to waste because the price of milk is high,"

Chapter 7: Demon Doctrines Coming To A Church Near You

and so the victim agrees and drinks it. If you haven't progressed to darkness and you are not in darkness, you can stop and think for yourself and consider the full consequences of what is being said, determining though the advice seems reasonable, it is yet warped and unsound.

This is called the devil pulling the wool over your eyes. If you have embraced this one, pull it off and reject it. Stop being the laughing stock of hell for following that and buying into that demon doctrine. Don't forget the laughing stock of hell part doesn't just end there. They are rubbing their hands together in glee in expectancy of your arrival where their idea of fun and games concerning you just begins.

Don't mindlessly follow the others in deception. Stop and think it through. Think for yourself, examining the Scriptures and see exactly what this doctrine is saying, what it really means, and make your own decision based on what the whole Scriptures say.

Everything that someone tells you is biblical in these days, you have to check for yourself and see if it is true, which includes comparing it to the whole Scriptures around it.

It is dangerous enemy ground to just take someone's word for it, no matter what the Christian pedigree they claim or can show, whether they are the daughter or son of any famous preacher, or a preacher themselves, or communicated directly by the Lord. You, alone, will have to pay for any error on your part, no matter if someone else misleads you.

You wouldn't take one of those rare $10,000 bills yet known to exist, without checking it is real or fraud; this same kind of caution you must take to every doctrine someone tries to introduce to you or that you wonder is true because it sounds too 'good' or not from what you know.

Also, doctrines you now practice which you have previously entertained as sound, now is the time to take out that counterfeit detector called Scriptures and run it across each and every one of those doctrines to see if any show as fraud or if they each hold up according to Jesus teachings.

If you find any show counterfeit, you have to get rid of that phony stuff, not make use of it, and refuse to accept that item no matter from which hands delivered it, no matter what spiritual genetics they stated or displayed as theirs.

The irony of this particular demon doctrine is if you follow it, you actually do trounce on the sacrifice of Jesus at the cross.

You trounce on the cross of Jesus because everything he came down to do, the very reason he came and he suffered all that abuse, the thorns and the horrific beatings, and painful death, you do cancel it out by rejecting what he really came to do when you follow this doctrine.

- o When you follow this doctrine you reject that he came so that his blood will wash away sins if you are repentant (Luke 24:27).
- o When you follow this doctrine you reject that he came to warn people about how it is imperative to get rid of anything in your life that causes you to sin even if you need to cut it off (Matthew 5:29).
- o When you follow this doctrine you reject that he came to make clear that workers of evil whose past sins his blood washed, if they do not repent, they will not enter heaven (Matthew 7:21).
- o When you follow this doctrine you reject that he came to destroy the work of the devil by teaching the truth to destroy the enemy lies that are leading people to hell (John 18:27).

He did not come to wipe away sins without the need to turn from them (1 John 1:9). He taught and had the other apostles teach, you must turn, repent and turn from your sins and do deeds in line with repentance (Acts 26:20). He did not come so heaven can be flooded with the unrepentant citizens of Sodom and Gomorrah and the violence of the world of Noah (Matthew 13:41-42). That is what is called a demonic lie. It is a lie.

The apostle James summed up powerfully that any believer who strays from the truth is set to pay the ultimate price for the sins that believer will commit as a result of straying, which is destruction of his or her soul.

Brethren, if anyone among you wanders from the truth,

> and someone turns him back, let him know that he who turns a sinner from the error of his way will save a soul from death and cover a multitude of sins.
> —*James 5:19-20, NKJV*

By the word 'brethren' James is addressing Christians, which is whom he was addressing in this book. So James is telling Christian brothers that if anyone *among* them, i.e. Christians, wanders from the truth, which is the truth of the teachings of Jesus, that whoever turns that wayward Christian back to the truth, will have saved that person's soul from death and cover a multitude of sins, which means all the many sins that wayward Christian committed from the moment he/she strayed and lived according to the world, committing sins.

This shows that if a Christian disregards the teaching of Christ to 'sin no more' (John 5:14) and does sin, that those new sins extol the **same** wages of any sin the unsaved commits, which is death.

> For the wages of sin is death.
> —*Romans 6:23, KJV*

So don't be tricked and deceived by the enemy to actually trounce on the gift of the cross and to treat Jesus like a liar, all the things he warned and taught about, the way to follow him. He said few are those who find the way to heaven. Demonic lies as these are really what are blocking people from heaven.

If you are a believer, or you were a believer at one point, and you choose to continue to do evil and sin, you are in darkness and you do not have God in you.

> By this it is evident who are the children of God, and who are the children of the devil: whoever does not practice righteousness is not of God, nor is the one who does not love his brother.
> —*1 John 3:10, ESV*

Practice means to do something regularly or habitually. Thus if you are not regularly righteous, or habitually righteous, you are not of God, but are a child of the devil.

To practice righteousness means you do lawful things (good) rather than lawless things (sin). Children of the devil have no entrance to heaven.

You can claim to be a Christian and in the light, but if you practice sin, you still are in darkness, such as the sin of hating a brother.

> Anyone who claims to be in the light but hates a brother or sister is still in the darkness.
> —*1 John 2:9, NIV*

If the enemy has deceived you to believe that to ask for forgiveness, repent and sin no more is canceling out the cross of Jesus that is the biggest joke on you by the demonic principality.

You need to reject that bad joke on you and come to the truth, and turn and repent, and follow the Jesus way, which is all the things he taught and not a demon doctrine which takes parts of Scriptures and twists them in error to lead to destruction.

The most difficult issue to overcome with a demon doctrine is because of its craftiness spun to seem correct on partial scriptural truth; it can put a strong delusion on a Christian, and grip that person firmly in an enemy stronghold that keeps the person from breaking out from that delusion.

That is why it is really important to see if you are embracing any doctrines of demon which has you gripped in a delusion that some sort of sin is not sin, and you are in some serious spiritual trouble if you do not snap out of it.

The trouble is always the same: loss of salvation. Which gives me a good lead into the next example of a demon doctrine because of course you can be sure there is a spirit of error going on in that subject, 'loss of salvation'.

7-3 Demon Doctrine: Once Saved, Always Saved

Pretty catchy phrase, huh? Yeah, the devil wants you to bumper-sticker phrase yourself to hell.

Yet, one hack of the Sword of Truth with this Scripture, cleaves that falsehood in half:

> Watch out that you do not lose what you have worked for, but that you may be rewarded fully. Anyone who runs ahead and does not continue in the teaching of Christ does not have God; whoever continues in the teaching has both the Father and the Son.
> —*2 John 1:8-9, NKJV*

Thus if you do not continue following the teachings of Christ, you lose the salvation you have worked for.

The key words to focus here are 'lose' and 'worked for' and 'does not continue' and 'whoever continues', showing that salvation requires continued work, that you must continue in it, signifying that when you initially receive Jesus free gift, that it then requires that you continue in his teachings, and this takes practice to not sin (1 John 2:10) and abiding in him (John 8:31), and that failure to not continue will result in the loss of salvation. Is it no surprise Scripture says only the holy will see God (Hebrews 12:14)?

But, understand, there are dozens of more hacks like this from the Sword of Truth which can obliterate that demon doctrine as it deserves to be.

Such as this one here where Paul is speaking about the measures he regularly undergoes against his body to prevent losing his salvation from the law of flesh waging war (Romans 7:23-25) against his inner being set only on things of God.

> But I discipline my body and bring it into subjection, lest, when I have preached to others, I myself should become disqualified.
> —*1 Corinthians 9:27, NKJV*

Think about this: This is an apostle speaking about his own potential disqualification from heaven after having preached to all the people his books in the Bible show he reached, a disqualification possible if he failed to discipline his body and keep it under control against sinning.

There we see two things: again that future sins are not covered, and being saved once, does not mean being saved always if you do not keep obedient to Christ's teachings.

If this has been a doctrine you are basing your right standing with Jesus, and yet, after the Scriptures I have presented, you are still finding it difficult to let go, here is a question to consider:

If an original apostle who authored many books in the Bible understood he could become disqualified from salvation if he practiced sin, what gives you the idea you are any different? What makes you believe you have special exoneration Paul himself did not have, nor the other apostles who gave similar testimony they were at this risk?

The Bible explains through Scriptures I have related above that what is giving you this idea your future lawlessness is overlooked is the Spirit of error. Therefore, if this is you, you have bought into a demon doctrine of which you can see shares some similarity to the first example I related above of Past, Present & Future Sins, yet is a doctrine of itself.

The warfare we wage revolves heavily around one of information: counterintelligence, espionage, and enemy propaganda which the demonic works to feed us and see if we take the bait to destruction. Thus, doctrines of demons are standard heavy artillery wielded by Satan's demonic army.

When you understand a demon doctrine is a falsehood imparted by a spirit feeding erroneous interpretations in order to snare to destruction, you know to take care around it and do not fall for it. Cleverly devised by a spirit that leads to error, it can come across sound, but be a total falsehood, an intentional demonic scheme.

Demon doctrines are delivered in the same method that a lying spirit used to deceive King Ahab in the Old Testament (1 Kings 22:22), which is through other people, some purposefully feeding those error-leading doctrines, while others falling for the deception of the spirit of error and embracing the error as truth, despite warnings from the Spirit of Truth within to reject the falsehood.

Although demon doctrines have been getting taught to

believers since the early Church, two of which Christ referred to in Revelation 2 as teachings of Balaam, and teachings of the Nicolaitans, which were specific false doctrines taught by those two parties, what is different today is the large scale of believers these doctrines are influencing.

Any person, who is not careful to guard their mind and arm themselves with the full counsel of God and keep it foremost in their mind, may come to follow teachings not in line with the Bible.

All of these come from demonic sources springing from the spirit of error.

What is interesting, and how the waters can be muddied to fool even learned scholars of the Bible, is such doctrines are often woven expertly with known truths which gets them to buy the demonic doctrine hook, line and sinker. Then the spirit of ego gets involved which stirs them to not yield out of pride to any trying to point out where they have gone astray, to the point they may call such instructors as the ones from demonic sources.

We wage warfare against ancient opponents who by their long experience, not so much superior intelligence, but by their veteran status in the battle, have gained and use highly crafty methods of deceit, which can leave even brilliant Bible scholars to be deceived if they grow slack against what they know are Biblical truths.

Just so you understand, it can be common for denominations upholding some demon doctrines to be firm on sound doctrine at the same time, which is part of the deviousness of the enemy work and a common strategy used in many kinds of combat because it causes a confidence that the whole terrain is good, and get one to overlook a flag signaling a hidden deathtrap, and falsely reason that if sound doctrine is there, then so must all that the denomination give be also sound, a deadly attitude to take.

As the day of the Lord comes nearer, you have to be on guard for demon doctrines because they are only going to strengthen in their power and in their variety, because as they are already, these doctrines are going to not only continue to come, but the numbers of powerful leaders in the Body of Christ promoting these doctrines are going to exponentially increase where it will reach a point where those doctrines will appear the truths, and the Truth, a demon doctrine.

How will this be achieved, is the way it has started in the last few decades, which is through the massive influence of those deceived powerful leaders to convince tremendous numbers to believe these doctrines, and then those numbers turning around and spreading those doctrines using mediums that spread their false beliefs around the world.

These will be and are trusted spiritual leaders who are scholars of the Bible, know God's truth, yet still allow the enemy to plant these doctrines in their heart, and then teaching them to the believers under their leadership.

Because one sin like that, opens the doorway for a demonic right, then the spirit of ego will take residence in them, and keep them intractable to refute these demon doctrines. Because they are coming from that position of respected and honored leaders, in order for you to not be caught up in that leader's error, you must think for yourself, turning to the Bible to see what it says.

If a clash exists in the information, with that person saying one thing and the Bible relating another, and you have to make a choice what to believe, the right choice a hundred percent of the time is to choose the Bible, and not that beloved, dedicated evangelist or preacher or Bible study teacher pushing the kingdom of God whom you like, you believe in, and you trust.

You can be entirely confident that no person shall ever override God's word. But be sure you are on the overall whole Scriptures when you do it, and not some partial Scripture whose meaning is not its ultimate message when taken out of context, and leads to error. This can be tricky when you are a newcomer to reading the Bible, but gets easier as your knowledge grows.

This you easily accomplish by putting on the Armor of God and wielding the Sword of Truth as Paul instructed here.

> Put on the full armor of God so that you can take your stand against the devil's schemes...and the sword of the Spirit, which is the word of God.
> —*Ephesians 6:11-17, NIV*

That is the method to not be fooled by any demon doctrine

Chapter 7: Demon Doctrines Coming To A Church Near You

and taken off the path to heaven.

The deceit of the enemy is ruthless, and this is where you have to stand firm against their wiles, as this will be a key weapon the demonic uses to derail millions and millions of believers from qualifying for entry to heaven. That is why it is crucial you have the fundamental training to know them and resist them.

That said let's go on to another example of a demon doctrine, highly popular today in many congregations.

7-4 Demon Doctrine: Living By Pharisees' Righteousness

The demonic spirit of greed has successfully inspired a lot of churches to zealously follow the righteousness of the Pharisees in the belief they are following the righteousness of Jesus. Jesus warned your righteousness must exceed that of the Pharisees to make it to heaven.

> For I tell you, unless your righteousness exceeds that of the scribes and Pharisees, you will never enter the kingdom of heaven.
> —*Matthew 5:20, ESV*

Satan knowing this has devised clever schemes based on partial doctrine to snare believers into imitating the Pharisees righteousness rather than Jesus, entire congregations, slating those people to end up in hell.

The interesting thing about it is through the demon of greed the enemy gets the same churches, leaders, pastors and people who reject the 10 commandments and the Law of Moses, claiming it is outdated to zealously lift and uphold partial doctrine of the laws of Moses that suits their self gain, and leads to them building treasure on earth and realizing all kinds of personal gain for themselves, a hallmark of the Pharisees righteousness which is hypocrisy.

> ... He began to say to His disciples first of all, "Beware of the leaven of the Pharisees, which is hypocrisy."
> —*Luke 12:1, NKJV*

The primary law promoted by some preachers and evangelists is presented under the Malachi 3:10 "Bring the whole tithe into the storehouse, that there may be food in my house. Test me in this," says the LORD Almighty, "and see if I will not throw open the floodgates of heaven and pour out so much blessing that you will not have room enough for it" (NIV) which is the decree of God to tithe given to Moses.

And from that the teaching that one is under a curse if they fail to tithe, that God considers that robbing him, which actually amounts to breaking the commandment "Thou shall not steal."

> Will a man rob God? Yet you rob me. But you ask, 'How do we rob you?' In tithes and offerings. You are under a curse--the whole nation of you--because you are robbing me.
>
> —*Malachi 3:8-9, NIV*

Yet they are building the foundation of their teaching on Scriptures where God begins by the statement in Malachi 3:6, "I the LORD do not change."

So if the tithing stands true, and the blessings stand true and the curses stand true, so do all of the blessings and curses on the other laws detailed in Leviticus and Deuteronomy that do not deal with food, days, seasons or atonement as Jesus is our high priest who atones for us, and Jesus declared all foods clean.

To instruct that the curses and blessings on tithing still stand, and following the laws of tithing unleashes God's blessings, and leading believers to proper tithing according to the law, is to make that believer accountable to all the law because "You shall therefore keep my statutes and my rules: if a person does them, he shall live by them: I am the Lord." (Leviticus 8:5 ESV)

Yet out of the same mouths of these Christian teachers of tithing according to Malachi 3:10 come denial that we are under the law and accountable to the law with the argument that to follow the letter of the law is to be bound to all the law. Hypocrisy, plain and simple.

As it is clear, when it leads Christians to their own building of

Chapter 7: Demon Doctrines Coming To A Church Near You

their symbolic phylacteries and storehouses, these same false apostles will zealously honor, uphold and promote a particular Old Testament statute or the part of one that supports their tithing point as pertinent and necessary to follow, stating in that vein all the promises which reinforce what suits their tithing message in the Old Testament hold true, and at those times standing behind the Scripture that God is the same yesterday, today and tomorrow.

This is by no means an anti-tithing message; what it is, is an anti-righteousness of Pharisee message, which is an anti-hypocrisy message illustrated through the most popular example, which is based on supporting the tithing statutes in Leviticus and Deuteronomy, in the vein presented by God in Malachi 3, yet making, even in some cases, all the commandments void and outdated, not just the statutes and rules, giving a classic example of the righteousness of Pharisees practiced by many Christian ministries today.

When it does not deal with the tithing issue or other issues they want to support, their viper tongues will then lie that the other words of God which do not broaden their phylacteries are outdated, that we are not under the law, and to follow the law is to become accountable to follow all of it, yet hypocritically leading believers into observing the rules of tithing or otherwise that suit their agenda, according to the letter of the rule given by God through Moses.

In the New Covenant way tithing is important as you are producing good fruit to the Kingdom when you tithe to spread the good news of Jesus, which requires sustaining God's ministries. In fact, giving financial support to spread the gospel is commanded by the Lord in that those who proclaim the gospel should get their living from the gospel. (1 Corinthians 9:13-14).

Which means they do not hold a side job but are sustained by the congregation or those they evangelize to or teach to from the offerings received. Thus any believer able to give out of a ten percent portion who does not support their ministry, under the false belief tithing is not commanded by Jesus, is under deceit and stands to be judged as a poor servant not doing his or her duty to sustain God's ministers.

In addition all who do work to further the gospel, whether

traveling musicians or speakers to your local church and the like ought to be supported in like because doing so, in line with the New Covenant, is to become fellow workers for the truth through our financial support to them.

Thus, if you refuse to give and can, you will prove not to be a fellow worker for the truth.

> Dear friend, you are doing a good work for God when you take care of the traveling teachers who are passing through, even though they are strangers to you. They have told the church here of your friendship and your loving deeds. You do well to send them on their way in a manner that pleases God. For they are traveling for the Lord and accept nothing from those who are not Christians. So we ourselves should support them so that we may become partners with them for the truth.
> —*3 John 1:5-8, NLT*

As you can see from Verse 8 above in 3 John (last sentence) that giving financial support, which is the same as receiving them in that receiving them you house them, you feed them, and you send them on their way with provisions, is considered producing good fruit for advancing the Kingdom of Christ same as any other work that promotes the Kingdom whether writing Christian books, or producing artwork that builds up faith of believers or convicts of sin to unsaved, or handing out Christian tracts, because as we all know it takes money for the beautiful feet that travel spreading the gospel to travel to each and every place.

Just as it takes money for your church to stay open and minister to the congregation under its care. In that vein you will be counted a worthless worker if you have the means and you do not tithe.

When I say you have the means that you have above your crucial needs to tithe; and if you do not, you support the ministry in how you can, whether volunteering to maintain the building in some way, even so keeping in mind the widow and her mite giving (Mark 12:42-44), that if you do give out of your needs any amount, which any would be a sacrifice taking from any of your needs, in order to be obedient in supporting the preaching of the truth, God will record that and you will be blessed.

How can you determine if you or your church is practicing the righteousness of the Pharisees that is prevalent today in many churches, and as a creed of many evangelist and Christian leaders, which counts as valid some of God's rules and dismisses the rest?

No doubt you need to be able to figure this out and not participate in this any further if this is true, since your righteousness must be above the Pharisee righteousness in order to enter heaven.

The righteousness of the Pharisee leads to hell. The righteousness of Jesus leads to heaven. Therefore it's essential you determine what righteousness you are serving: the righteousness of Satan or the righteousness of Jesus?

By your mindset and by the fruit you're bearing you will know the answer. If you find you have been serving the righteousness of the Pharisee you need to align yourself with the righteousness of Jesus and learn how to follow his righteousness and achieve it.

The righteousness of Jesus while it involves adhering to the law through his commandments, which includes tithing, it puts emphasis on what all was considered weightier matters of the law to God which are judgment, mercy, and faithfulness (Matthew 23:23). Don't let the enemy mislead you through the righteousness of the Pharisee message of prosperity which focuses on the world and the things of the flesh to deceive you and take you to hell.

If you find you are serving the Pharisee message you need to repent of being conformed to this world through the focus of a love of the world and the love of the things of the world and be transformed by the renewal of your mind as Paul wrote about in Romans 12:2 and begin to put the principles of the Jesus righteousness into practice so you can bear the fruit that matters, build the treasure that matters, and increase the kingdom of our master and bear fruit for the kingdom of God and not your own kingdom.

What is the giving that's being emphasized in Pharisee righteousness version of fulfilling the 10 Commandments?

You will only see bringing the tithes to a Christian ministry.

You will not see anything about tithing to the needy within your community, which are the stranger, the orphan and the widow.

> When you reap your harvest in your field, and forget a sheaf in the field, you shall not go back to get it; it shall be for the stranger, the fatherless, and the widow, that the Lord your God may bless you in all the work of your hands. When you beat your olive trees, you shall not go over the boughs again; it shall be for the stranger, the fatherless, and the widow. When you gather the grapes of your vineyard, you shall not glean it afterward; it shall be for the stranger, the fatherless, and the widow.
> —*Deuteronomy 24:19-21, NKJV*

You will only see the emphasis of not stealing tithe from God. You won't see the emphasis of not stealing tithes from the temporary foreigner, the fatherless, and the widow.

> When you have finished setting aside a tenth of all your produce in the third year, the year of the tithe, you shall give it to the Levite, the alien, the fatherless and the widow, so that they may eat in your towns and be satisfied. Then say to the LORD your God: "I have removed from my house the sacred portion and have given it to the Levite, the alien, the fatherless and the widow, according to all you commanded. I have not turned aside from your commands nor have I forgotten any of them.
> —*Deuteronomy 26:12-13, NIV*

You will only see an emphasis on obedience to the commandments for prosperity to build up treasure on earth, to gain earthly rewards. You won't see an emphasis on obedience to the commandments in order to enter heaven.

> Lay not up for yourselves treasures upon earth, where moth and rust doth corrupt, and where thieves break through and steal: But lay up for yourselves treasures in

Chapter 7: Demon Doctrines Coming To A Church Near You

heaven, where neither moth nor rust doth corrupt , and where thieves do not break through nor steal : For where your treasure is , there will your heart be also.
—*Matthew 6:19-21, KJV*

The blessings taught in the Pharisee righteousness come only from tithing to a ministry; yet, the Bible says blessings come from God in all the work of one's hands if one takes care to tithe specifically to the temporary alien in your gate, the orphan and the widow.

At the end of every three years you shall bring out all the tithe of your produce in the same year and lay it up within your towns. And the Levite, because he has no portion or inheritance with you, and the sojourner, the fatherless, and the widow, who are within your towns, shall come and eat and be filled, that the LORD your God may bless you in all the work of your hands that you do.
—*Deuteronomy 14:28-29, ESV*

It is not only every 3 years, but also from every time you 'reap' your harvest (paycheck) that you do not comb through every cent to make use of for yourself, but that you set it aside for the stranger, orphan and the widow as Deuteronomy 24 shows that when you collect your harvest (money) together, don't take everything that remains for yourself to the last bit, but leave it for the disadvantaged stranger, fatherless and widow.

As you can see from Deuteronomy 24 given above below the first bulleted giving emphasized by Pharisee righteousness, this group receives regularly not ten percent as the tithe is for the priests, but they get the excess that remains each time from your harvest, these purposefully you are commanded to set aside and give to the poor foreigner, the orphan, or the widow in your gate.

Yet, the Pharisee righteousness has buried this so far over time in performing the enemy work, that faithful believers who would want to do God's will, are entirely ignorant this is part of the Father's will as Pharisee righteousness highlights only that which broadens their own phylacteries, and have proven they care not for the widow as they devour their houses to build theirs (Mark 12:40). The Pharisee heart only gives to 'recognized' charities in the community and ignores giving to any orphan, stranger or widow directly within their town, which is a hypocritical heart without mercy.

The Pharisee way exacts a toll, providing only to those needy who can receive the gift in a formal show, whether television, radio station, in front of the church congregation, or any other formal gathering where as many eyes can see in order to be seen giving to the needy to get honor from men.

> So when you give to the needy, do not announce it with trumpets, as the hypocrites do in the synagogues and on the streets, to be honored by men. I tell you the truth, they have received their reward in full.
> —Matthew 6:2, NIV

The Jesus way puts no burden on the needy to receive the monetary gift, and only gives to the needy in private in total secrecy with the giver only looking to reap God's blessing and reward for that true Christ-like charity.

> But when you give to the needy, do not let your left hand know what your right hand is doing, so that your giving may be in secret. Then your Father, who sees what is done in secret, will reward you.
> —Matthew 6:3-4, NIV

The Pharisee way is not the message of Jesus. When you follow Jesus, his message is not obedience to achieve personal prosperity. The fruit of following Jesus leads to salvation.

The ministry of Jesus emphasizes not personal prosperity but personal austerity (Matthew 19:21).

Jesus continually repeated his way is to deny yourself (Matthew 16:24), his way is to be the servant to others, not serve yourself (Matthew 20:26), his way is to build treasure in heaven and not treasure on earth (Matthew 6:20).

Continually Jesus was emphasizing when asked how to follow

Chapter 7: Demon Doctrines Coming To A Church Near You

him he would tell those people to sell what they had, give what they had to the poor, leave and follow him with nothing but what they had on their backs, trust in him and obey him.

Jesus words, the new covenant, are not based on a prosperity that you accumulate or you acquire on earth. The way of Jesus involves giving things up, giving them away, sharing with those who do not have what you may have one or more of. And if you have more than one earthly possession to just voluntarily give them away. Jesus emphasized it is difficult for a rich man to enter heaven.

His emphasis had to do that the property of a rich man would own the rich man and the rich person would put those possessions and the pursuit of them and the pursuit of money above God.

What kind of obedience to the commandments of God exists in your church, if at all? Is it one whose fruit leads to increasing your personal wealth on earth, improving your health, getting all kinds of 'give me' and needs fulfilled by the Pharisee way, which is the tithing way?

Are you being instructed in the way of the Pharisees or are you being instructed in the way of Jesus? The answer to this is clearly concluded by the fruit that such a method results in.

The Pharisee way involves establishing the tradition of a man over that of God. It involves observing a way that involves setting aside some of God's commands which are more important to observe and should have been done, and in some cases more importantly to have been done over the tradition of men.

The way of the Pharisee appears to be righteous and it appears to adhere to the commands of God but the end fruit only leads to prosperity message, the prosperity that appeals to men that involves self gain, that involves financial wealth, that involves improved relationships, that involves improved health, and that sets aside and never touches salvation. The focus primarily and always is obedience to God for an outpouring of worldly blessings that involve the body, blessings that involve the storehouse of Earth earthly treasurers and all those things. If that is the case you have to question what god, when the commands of God are absent in the method and when the traditions of man are upheld over the traditions of God, is the one providing the prosperity?

Do you know Satan does counterfeit works that mimic they are of God but which lead to death? Churches that put prosperity message as the end fruit, the money central to the faith, central to what's important while ignoring the weightier matters of the law are synagogues of Satan.

The unfortunate scenario in such a synagogue of Satan is that often the congregation has no idea that you can participate in an organization that is in every outwardly appearance looking as a righteous institution of the righteousness of God in Jesus and is Christian but in fact the underlying power is not God but is Satan and the blessings that are coming are from the hands of demons.

When you understand the enemy, you are able to realize their sophistication and their motivation in their warfare to snare people to hell. Satan is an expert on the Bible. Satan understands the definition of a sheep that really belongs to Jesus, the one that Jesus recognizes the sheep, the one who Jesus would not disown and not reject as being a worker of lawlessness.

Satan understands the Scripture you cannot serve money and serve God (Matthew 6:24). Satan understands the Scripture what is the point of gaining the riches of the world for a man to lose his soul (Mark 8:36). Satan understands the Scriptures to not build treasure in the world that can be robbed by the robber himself but which is the treasure that matters in heaven (Matthew 6:19-20). Through the sin of greed Satan has gotten the legal claim (John 14:30) to infiltrate some churches to deceive the people on the road to hell through the prosperity message.

Certain congregations have bought the false doctrine that tithing puts one in favor with God and meets the righteous requirements that please God and makes them right before God and approved by God, that they are in right standing with God and thus their salvation is secured.

These are false apostles leading churches around the message of prosperity which are synagogues of Satan shown by their entirely leaving aside the weightier matters of the law which are the weighty matters of the law of spirit: judgment, mercy, and faith. In fact the new covenant of Jesus elevates these matters to paramount level above everything. It reinforces they're weighty and then raises them to an entirely new plateau. But the Pharisee

Chapter 7: Demon Doctrines Coming To A Church Near You

message elevates tithing as the primary key to God's acceptance and right standing leaving everything else to fall in place as a result.

The focus of the Pharisee message always involves prosperity, self prosperity. The measure of the success is always measured against the increased prosperity a church member experiences as a result of faithfulness to everything involving tithing. The Commandments are molded around defining tithing as the solution. The spotlight is always shined on tithing, and all the weightier matter of the law, i.e. mercy and love to a brother are ignored. Always the giving leads to the coffers of the church, or the individual teaching that method.

Any stumbling blocks that arise during the member's life is always explained to some lack of tithing of some form or another, and the solution always involves more tithing.

This is a doctrine of demons the Pharisee message which ignores the entire word of God and focuses on certain wants. They give a false assurance of right standing with God and salvation in Christ. They are agents of Satan, his soldiers which man various idols and various methods of demon doctrines whose job it is to fulfill the prayers, the desires of the individual in that method in order to keep them deceived and locked in the deception and their eyes off of the truth that leads into salvation. You have to question: what is the source of the miracles, what is the source of the prosperity you are receiving?

The answer lies in the fruit of what that teaching has led you to and has led other members to. Has it led you to set your mind on the Spirit?

> For those who live according to the flesh set their minds on the things of the flesh, but those who live according to the Spirit set their minds on the things of the Spirit.
> —*Romans 8:5, ESV*

Or has it led you to set your mind on the things in the world?

> Do not love the world or anything in the world. If anyone loves the world, the love of the Father is not in him. For

everything in the world--the cravings of sinful man, the lust of his eyes and the boasting of what he has and does--comes not from the Father but from the world.
—*1 John 2:15-16, NIV*

Has it led you to set your mind on increasing your bank account? Has it led you to set your mind on an attractive spouse? Has it led you to set your mind on a brand-new car? Or maybe a trim figure, or a better job, or a job promotion, or your house paid off, or car paid off? All these goals are things of the flesh and are worldly.

What is the difference between using the righteousness of a Pharisee to meet a prayer need, and the righteousness of Jesus?

Here's an example: Say you want to be married, and you want a godly spouse. If you seek first his kingdom as Jesus instructs, which is the righteousness of Jesus, you can stand on his word that all your needs God will fill accordingly; thus, when you pray this to the Lord he hears you the first time and slates the answering of that prayer to his divine timing.

One prayer to the Lord to send you a spouse walking in his way and the Lord will do so in his timing. It is when a person wants to do this according to the righteousness of the Pharisee which is to say to his or her timing, that there comes a clash.

When you are too impatient for God and want to do it your way, your time, Satan is all too glad to meet your prayer and send you a worldly spouse as a result of which will lead you to suffer from that clash of the spouse not handpicked by the Lord for you. Thus it is not necessary to keep focusing on this goal, as if your works of the focus alone will bring it into fruition. If you seek God's kingdom first, as Jesus instructs, as is true in everything you have need of, if you put that prayer out to the Lord, and you continue to daily seek His kingdom first, in his timing he will meet that need of yours, a divine timing, a timing and fruit thereof of that timing you can count on to be the true one, that truly blesses.

God does not need you to grease his wheel of provision continually putting extra tithes in his hands like he is a corrupt official in order to speed up his timing to your liking, nor does he need you to steer from the backseat in anyway once you put that prayer to him. Part of the process is your faithfully seeking his kingdom and your trusting in him in full as your savior, your deliverer and your God. The Lord is faithful; the Lord makes an elephant's memory seem addled---he never forgets and he is the Master of multi-tasking.

Therefore when out of impatience you want to set the date when God meets your need and take the first offer that crosses your plate, even if the offer is way off your walk with God, then that source of the miracle or prosperity is Satan. If in the impatience to force God's timing you have taken it on yourself or outside advice to set your mind on the worldly goal, and grease the wheel with more tithes as if the first was not enough and God is holding out answering to see how much he can get you to give, then that marks it a Pharisee message.

This is a book about getting right with God despite the war with darkness increasing towards Armageddon. Since the Lord established by his word that a Pharisee righteousness, which is a message of hypocrisy, never leads to the kingdom of heaven, then you need to gain knowledge how to spot any righteousness that is a Pharisee righteousness.

Primarily that righteousness is a hypocritical righteousness: hypocrites in the word of God, hypocrites in the way of Truth, hypocrites in how to follow Jesus, hypocrites in what you need to get to heaven. The hypocrisy is in whatever they tell you on any of these things in how the word of God is overridden or outdated or rendered void, replaced, usurped or wiped-out by their own self-serving definition or tradition.

It's important to understand like all whom the Pharisee message corrupts and destroys, initially those followers started as converts of the faith, then the bearer of the Pharisee message after the person was initially a convert, molded that person from the mindset that focuses on the worldly goods to become as much a son of hell as the deliverer of the Pharisee message.

It's important to understand the bearer of a Pharisee message can appear all righteousness outwardly, can be convinced of their righteous standing with the Lord in their state of a seared consciousness, and have no idea they're actually false apostles. They can be earnest in their belief, yet by the fruit born by their message will be shown to be doing the work of Satan whether they realize it or not rather than the Lord's.

> For to set the mind on the flesh is death...For the mind that is set on the flesh is hostile to God, for it does not submit to God's law; indeed, it cannot. Those who are in the flesh cannot please God.
> —*Romans 8:6-8, ESV*

The giving Jesus emphasizes is the giving to others. The mindset Jesus teaches is one of denial and giving up worldly goods and following him and obeying him in his word. Don't be deceived by the Pharisee message which bears deceitful rewards when adhered to which leaves you serving money over God, which leaves you with serving the god of your belly over God.

God knows the intent of every heart. God will discern the motive behind your tithing. Was it for obedience or was it to serve the god of your belly and for your own increase and not out of a love of God? When you bring your tithes to the church, did you drive by the homeless on the street and harden your heart and not reach out in compassion like the Good Samaritan, if you had it on you to give?

Is your tithing only to further your kingdom, your worldly treasure and not used to meet the need of the needy you meet in your everyday travel, real people you encounter, not the poster-poor the approved charity of your choice bring to your attention by campaign letters which serve as tax write-offs (the god of your belly) or resume builders to further your personal cause (idol of self) or are your pet causes (sin of partiality)?

If you recognize your giving is the latter here, then I must ask what rebellion do you allow Satan to put in you to harden your heart against genuinely following the command of Jesus to love your brother and love your neighbor? These are the more weightier class of people to aid, whom should not be left aside and put second to the poster poor, meaning those in remote areas to you who are in a class of poor always needing help and those in remote areas who need crises aid.

While those are to be aided, you need to include aiding real

Chapter 7: Demon Doctrines Coming To A Church Near You

people in your daily life you encounter or you know of who are in need in some way, who are Christian brothers, who are orphans, who are widows, who are foreigners, whether need for worldly goods or need for human company and help as the lonely, the sick, imprisoned, these more weightier in judging the love you show according to the word of Jesus and determining if you are righteous to enter heaven.

These people are the ones that you cross path with in one form or another: the ones you drive by, the ones you step around in front of stores, the shabby dressed ones in the pew seats you get nothing from talking to, the ones you look away from in your neighborhood bearing more work than they can handle, the ones in your circle of people friends or family you know sit alone from age or illness or poverty not fun or convenient to give help to, all these ones reaching their inner hands out to you for real, in silent desperation, the ones in which Jesus is within, reaching his hand out too.

When you give testimony to God's blessing you as a result of your diligent tithing, did it involve tithing to the needy in your town, did it involve giving any clothes you may have to someone on the street in shabby clothes, or did it only involve giving clothes to a 501(c) charity that you were certain you can deduct from your tax, showing the god you serve is the god of self?

You need to pursue the righteousness of Jesus and not the righteousness of the Pharisees. The righteousness of the Pharisees overlooks commands of God and serves their own self interests and bears fruit that builds up their storehouse on earth and lead to hell.

The righteousness of Jesus adheres to the commands of God, makes you slaves to doing good to the will of God and obligates you to the commands of Christ to love your neighbor as yourself and to love God with all your heart, mind and strength, building up your storehouse of treasure in heaven.

Next let's look at another cleverly devised demon doctrine which makes you seem that once you accept Jesus you are living right with God and do not need to be told what is right or learn what is right, pretty much making it unnecessary to read a Bible again.

7-5 Demon Doctrine: How God's Law Is Put On Hearts

Many believers are in deceit from this scheme of Satan concerning the 10 Commandments and how they are all observed in the New Covenant. The scheme involves the Scripture from Jeremiah 31:33 "I will put my law within them and I will write it on their hearts."

In this particular enemy scheme, which you can see by now there are many, the enemy has inspired misunderstanding of how that is fulfilled, a scheme that is in full play today past the plotting stage, and some denominations are basing their Christian walk by this demon doctrine, treading on the path that all demon doctrines lead to which ends in a straight drop to the abyss.

As every scheme of the enemy concerning schemes Satan has set with Scriptures, the scheme is built or its success stands on partial doctrine teaching a different truth and its difference being that it excludes essential Scriptures that present the entire truth necessary to follow and the entire explanation behind that particular Scripture.

Without that understanding and just stopping at the partial doctrine a believer will be in deceit, will be unable to please God, and will be clueless there is a process involved that leads to a transformation required in order that God will put his law within them and write it on their hearts.

Often a person who is under that deceit knows of the Scripture, and has the belief that the law is written on their heart from the time they accepted Jesus and somehow they are fulfilling it.

When they continue to live according to the flesh, and when they continue to do acts contrary to the commands of Jesus that fulfill the law, they may have a sense of conviction they committed some wrong that separates them from God in that moment, but they can brush it off under the false confidence, "Well, God's law is written on my heart and even though I know I just stole something I still somehow am meeting the law because of this incident in Jeremiah that happened when I became a believer, even though my heart really doesn't feel changed and even though, I have to be

Chapter 7: Demon Doctrines Coming To A Church Near You

honest, I'm not really meeting the law but it must be so anyways, right?"

And so they blissfully, although slightly troubled from this conflict, continue on their path or so they believe, leading to heaven, not bothered about coveting what their neighbor has, looking at someone else's spouse with adulterous eyes, disrespecting their parents, using the name of God in vain and so on, in deceit that because God said so in Jeremiah that his laws are put within them and written on their hearts that they somehow through this unknown thing are satisfying it even though by their fruit they are not, shrugging at the conflict but at the same time fine with it if that is the way God called it, since once in, always in salvation, right?

This is the kind of Christian who is going to approach the door of heaven in confidence under that promise and when he or she knocks on the door is going to be floored to hear the Lord say as he said he would in Luke 13, "Depart from me, you worker of evil. I do not know you."

And that person will counter, "Lord, Lord, I took communion, I drank your blood! Lord, I preached your word, Lord, I cast out demons!"

And the Lord will answer, "I do not know you, you worker of lawlessness. Depart into the outer darkness!"

As that person lands in hell, he or she is going to be over and again saying, "But his laws were written on my heart, his laws were put in me, that's what the Bible says!"

Maybe after some long time in the grips of the torment of hell, they may understand that nagging feeling they had every time they obviously weren't in line with the 10 Commandments yet shrugged it off because of how they had interpreted what that Jeremiah Verse meant, that they had been deceived, finally what Jesus had told them at heaven's gate sinking in to them that they had been required literally to not be lawless, that it took them actually obeying the commandments, and what Jeremiah had said was not some kind of phenomenon that automatically overrode their disobedience, somehow cloaking them magically and wiping away any failures to keep the Law.

John, Paul, James, Peter, and Jesus talk about the process

that leads to the state where God's laws are indelibly etched within a believer's heart. It becomes clear when you read what they had to say that there is a process behind getting to the point where God's law is part of you. This is the information that Satan through this scheme works to conceal which is very easy when a lot of people are not familiar with the Bible and they don't come to those points. They are just accepting the repeated popular Scriptures to stand alone, not realizing there are all too often a lot more to them and not just as they sound alone.

If you don't go through the process you're not going to get to that state where the law of God is integrally part of your inner heart. One of the things of a Christian walk is to make sure that you have come to the knowledge of Jesus and that you know him and it requires that you examine yourself and test yourself, because it's easy to be deceived.

In 1 John 2 he describes that the way that we know we have come to know him is if we keep his commandments that whoever says I know him but doesn't keep his commandments, is a liar and that truth is not in him. So a litmus test that you actually know Jesus and you will not hear from him "Depart from me, evil doer, I do not know you" is that you keep his word and you know you're in him.

> And by this we know that we have come to know him, if we keep his commandments. Whoever says "I know him" but does not keep his commandments is a liar, and the truth is not in him, but whoever keeps his word, in him truly the love of God is perfected. By this we may know that we are in him: whoever says he abides in him ought to walk in the same way in which he walked.
> —*1 John 2:3-6, ESV*

He further on goes to say that the person who abides in Jesus ought to walk the same way he walked. It's not like may decide to, might every now and then, but should walk the way he did. Thus if you don't walk the way he did, then you're not abiding in Jesus.

It can be possible to start a Christian walk and be proven not to be a Christian as John goes on to further talk about a group of people who did start the Christian walk but proved not to be Christians because they didn't continue in the walk. They left and it was plain by their leaving the faith that they were not Christians to begin with. So when they started out, they started out believing they were, but then they left which means they didn't adhere to the teachings, they didn't remain with them, they simply didn't continue with them that was how it was defined.

So that indicates and reinforces that by going through the process of being Christian and knowing that these particular people had to have been baptized, and had to have professed in Jesus but that initial step and that initial journey of theirs obviously did not result in these people having the Law of God written on their hearts because if it did they wouldn't have gone away. That would have been a permanent transformation. But they were like the parable of the seed that they were Christians to begin with but when they were tested they fell away (Matthew 13:20-21).

The enemy wants to conceal from you that you can start as a Christian but if you don't stick to it, if you give up on it, if you don't continue, you will prove not to be a Christian at that point. This example about proving to be a Christian can be further shown in the example of Timothy here, how he proved obedient.

> I hope in the Lord Jesus to send Timothy to you soon, so that I too may be cheered by news of you. For I have no one like him, who will be genuinely concerned for your welfare. For they all seek their own interests, not those of Jesus Christ. But you know Timothy's proven worth, how as a son with a father he has served with me in the gospel.
> —*2 Philippians 2:19-22, ESV*

Paul wrote about how he was sending Timothy, that there was no one like him who would be generally concerned for their welfare because they all seek their own interests not those of Jesus Christ. But Timothy apparently sought the interest of Jesus Christ and he was genuinely proving himself to bear fruit of a Christian. Paul went on to reinforce that saying 'But you know Timothy's proven worth' so he proved himself obedient in all things.

> For to this end I also wrote, that I might put you to the test, whether you are obedient in all things.
> —*2 Corinthians 2:9, NKJV*

In 2 Corinthians 13:5 Paul said that to examine if you're really in the faith, to test yourself if Jesus is in you because it's possible when you test yourself you fail the test. Paul was talking to other Christians whom he was making known it could be possible they think they have Jesus in them, but could prove to fail the criteria Jesus abided in them, which reinforces that God's laws are not instantly inscribed in all the hearts of those who confess Jesus as their savior and involves something else than just accepting him as your Lord.

There are more than a couple places where the apostles show the start of the process that when you accept Christ you are at the infant stage along the path of salvation, and that like a newborn infant in 1 Peter 2, Peter wrote to desire pure spiritual milk which is the word so that you can grow up into salvation.

You only grow up into something that has a process. He said that you may grow up into salvation, stating that salvation wasn't automatic they had to mature to achieve salvation that starting as infants they were not yet grown up into.

If they were not yet grown up into salvation, and it required going through the growing stages, and they were behaving in ways contrary to the law at that point, then it is evident that at the initial stage in the early stages of a Christian walk the Law of God as declared in Jeremiah 31 is not imparted at that point of infancy, or else they would have been automatically behaving in ways according to the Law.

In this particular deceit, the enemy wants you to believe that when you are initially saved the laws are written on your heart and it is an automatic process no matter what it seems that you're doing and lead you astray that way so you don't feel any need to learn about the laws of Christ.

But as long as you are behaving worldly and behaving as a person of the flesh which is through behavior that is against the law of Christ and as a consequence against the Commandments, you haven't reached the maturity point yet where you have the

Chapter 7: Demon Doctrines Coming To A Church Near You

mind of Christ, where you abide in Jesus. You haven't yet come to the point where you're abiding in Jesus when the laws of God become part of your heart.

In Galatians 4:19 Paul gave more revelation on this when he was addressing the Galatians that he was anguishing over them in their birthing process to become Christians.

Obviously they were baptized, obviously they had accepted Jesus but they were still in the birthing process like babies emerging from the womb, not certain if they would live or not, all tension hanging in that process if they would even survive, as Paul was fretting like a distressed father that they were not stillborn, that he had not labored in vain until Christ was formed in them.

> ...my little children, for whom I am again in the anguish of childbirth until Christ is formed in you!
> —*Galatians 4:19, ESV*

Here is revelation that you are a believer, you accept Jesus, you start the process and you are an infant at the beginning shown by your continuing to exhibit behavior of the world and behavior that is not of Christ, and in that time Christ is not abiding in you because you're not abiding in Christ.

But as you learn and grow in the process to put off your old self, you actually practice it, as saying it is not enough. It is a daily commitment where you each day commit to putting on the mind of Christ, putting on Jesus like a suit, and being Jesus that whole time and being like Jesus and imitating Christ, and walking in righteousness and doing good and learning about God and learning about Christ because part of the process is to gain full knowledge of Christ and what it means to walk like him and what it means to follow him and you are like a toddler learning to walk, at various times falling, until it is like second nature to you and you are doing it, walking like Christ.

That is the knowledge that you are being nurtured by. It is the spiritual milk that will lead you to the maturity of Christ.

This is illustrated in here where Paul is saying,

> But you have not so learned Christ, if indeed you have heard Him and have been taught by Him, as the truth is in Jesus: that you put off, concerning your former conduct, the old man which grows corrupt according to the deceitful lusts, and be renewed in the spirit of your mind.
> —*Ephesians 4:20, NKJV*

So part of this deceit is that Satan wants you to stop on the Scriptures that we are not tutored under the law, that we do not receive any tutorship under the law and for that to then leave an infant believer to believe they don't require any learning that Christ will teach them and they don't have to learn anything, falsely believing Jeremiah 31:33 means this will be divinely assigned to them.

But that does not jive with what Paul said above in Ephesians 4 that the truth is learned through teachings from Jesus and involve putting off one's former corrupt behavior, meaning the laws are not on the heart automatically and require studying the teachings of Jesus and then following his instruction to shuck off your old sinful self, and have an attitude change by renewing the spirit of your mind to be like Christ's. This involves following instructions, not automatic knowledge as you would have if God's laws were put in your heart the moment you were saved or baptized.

Also in Ephesians 4:13 Paul reveals that part of the process is for you to come to the unity in your faith and knowledge of Jesus where you have grown up to the point of salvation, you have grown up to the point Christ is fully formed in you through that education you received and you're now measuring up to the full complete standard of Christ, and that's where you do have a tutor, you have a tutor of the word of Jesus.

> This will continue until we all come to such unity in our faith and knowledge of God's Son that we will be mature in the Lord, measuring up to the full and complete standard of Christ.
> —*Ephesians 4:13, NLT*

You're not tutored by the law, you are tutored by the standard of Christ, to become Christ, to imitate Christ, to do this every day as a day-by-day commitment as Paul says in 2 Corinthians 4 that day by day you are in a process where your inner self is being renewed.

> So we do not lose heart. Though our outer self is wasting away, our inner self is being renewed day by day.
> —*2 Corinthians 4:16, ESV*

In that process, in that day-by-day renewal, you put off your old conduct and you put on the new conduct which is behavior in righteousness and holiness as is said in Ephesians 4.

> ...and be renewed in the spirit of your mind, and that you put on the new man which was created according to God, in true righteousness and holiness.
> —*Ephesians 4:23-24, NKJV*

This day-by-day renewal signifies a daily conscious commitment to put on Jesus like an actor puts a character on for a play only it is not just for three plays scenes but from the moment you rise out of bed and the moment you get back in for your next sleep.

So you live, eat and breath as if you are Jesus living through you to every situation in your life. By that day by day process you become more and more like that character until he is an integral part of you.

If you have ever taken on an acting role, you know that the more you 'play' that character, the more you are that character until that character and you are inseparable to the point you find yourself thinking like the character.

This is how you start following Jesus. You are the lead actor in your play and your master role is the Master. While at first you might not do very good, but you will get better at it as you do. It is as the Bible proverb teaches, As a man thinks so he becomes.

So as you think Jesus, and live Jesus in your day to day life, in that thinking Jesus you will become Jesus if you continue long enough in his footsteps, and this character emulation, this imitation of Christ is a daily conscious choice to put on Christ and in that putting his character on, your inner character is being renewed, transformed.

In 1 John 2, John goes on to say if what you have heard in the beginning continues in you, lives in you, and you follow this, you will abide in the Son and the Father, and you will get eternal life that way if what you heard <u>keeps</u> abiding in you.

> Let what you heard from the beginning abide in you. If what you heard from the beginning abides in you, then you too will abide in the Son and in the Father. And this is the promise that he made to us--eternal life.
> *—1 John 2:24-25, ESV*

Still John goes on to instruct in 1 John 2 to abide in Jesus so that you, a believer, won't shrink from him when he comes, meaning you cannot abide in him and find yourself shrinking when he comes although you are a believer, which reinforces that the laws were not written on your heart when you were first a believer or there would be no concern that you could shrink from him in shame because it would have been part of you to have been righteous to have kept all of his Commandments perfectly and be living according to the spirit and not to the flesh.

> And now, little children, abide in him, so that when he appears we may have confidence and not shrink from him in shame at his coming. If you know that he is righteous, you may be sure that everyone who practices righteousness has been born of him.
> *—1 John 2:28-29 ESV*

That the laws of God are not written on your heart is further illustrated in Romans 12:2 when Paul gives the instructions don't conform anymore to the pattern of the world, but be transformed by the renewing of your mind.

Chapter 7: Demon Doctrines Coming To A Church Near You

> Do not conform any longer to the pattern of this world, but be transformed by the renewing of your mind. Then you will be able to test and approve what God's will is--his good, pleasing and perfect will.
> —*Romans 12:2, NIV*

Paul goes on to say in Romans 8:13 that if you live according to the flesh you will die but if by the Spirit you put to death the deeds of the body you will live and he's speaking to Christian brothers, warning them that if they don't live according to the Spirit they will die.

> For if you live according to the flesh you will die, but if by the Spirit you put to death the deeds of the body, you will live.
> —*Romans 8:13, ESV*

Such warnings would be redundant and totally unnecessary if God's laws had been written on the new believers' hearts. It is clear the Christians Paul had been addressing were not counted in the group Jeremiah spoke of in 31:34 who had no need to be taught to know the Lord. Instead these were in some process that involved going from infancy in the faith whereby they were nurtured and grew solely on spiritual milk, until they had grown up into salvation to the point where Christ was formed in them and then at that point Christ was in them as in Romans 8:10.

> But if Christ is in you, although the body is dead because of sin, the Spirit is life because of righteousness.
> —*Romans 8:10, ESV*

Because if Christ is not fully formed in you, then he's not in you. If he's just partway there, you haven't achieved the transformation process and are yet imperiled you won't make it, that you won't grow up into salvation.

The Bible provides such examples where people started the walk with the apostles and they were staying stuck in the 'infant' stage as here in 1 Corinthians, still worldly:

> But I, brothers, could not address you as spiritual people, but as people of the flesh, as infants in Christ. I fed you with milk, not solid food, for you were not ready for it. And even now you are not yet ready, for you are still of the flesh. For while there is jealousy and strife among you, are you not of the flesh and behaving only in a human way?
> —*1 Corinthians 3:1-3, ESV*

By their continued worldly behavior, they were showing that they were yet in the infant process and Christ was not in them at that point because if you are still in the flesh as Paul told those brothers in 1 Corinthians 3, they were yet hostile to God as Paul writes about in Romans 8:7 and being hostile they did not submit to God's law.

> For the mind that is set on the flesh is hostile to God, for it does not submit to God's law; indeed, it cannot. Those who are in the flesh cannot please God.
> —*Romans 8:7-8, ESV*

If they were not submitting to God's law because they were hostile to God's law, they obviously did not yet reach the stage in the process where God's laws were indelibly part of them because they were hostile to those laws, and being in the flesh they could not and did not and were not submitting to God's law and indeed could not as Paul so said.

As long as they were staying in that stage which they were staying much longer than Paul expected, they could not please God and they were showing yet that the Spirit of Christ did not yet dwell in them, that they were still in the flesh.

They were still at the point in Romans 8:9 where they did not have the Spirit of Christ because they were yet in the flesh.

> You, however, are not in the flesh but in the Spirit, if in fact the Spirit of God dwells in you. Anyone who does not have the Spirit of Christ does not belong to him.

Chapter 7: Demon Doctrines Coming To A Church Near You

—Romans 8:9, ESV

They were still at the point where Paul was yet concerned because they were not holding fast that his labor might be in vain as he addressed the Philippians in Philippians 2:16.

> Do all things without complaining and disputing, that you may become blameless and harmless, children of God without fault in the midst of a crooked and perverse generation, among whom you shine as lights in the world, holding fast the word of life, so that I may rejoice in the day of Christ that I have not run in vain or labored in vain.
> *—Philippians 2:14-16, NKJV*

In addition when you have reached the state that Christ is formed in you, as Paul had reached the state, and you test yourself and you see that Christ is in you and the laws of God are within your heart and you automatically, by keeping to the Commandments of Jesus, fulfill the commands of God's morale laws through the Spirit and not by letter of the law, you still run the risk of becoming disqualified from salvation if you fail to remain standing firm in the Lord as in 1 Thessalonians 3:8.

> But Timothy has just now come to us from you and has brought good news about your faith and love. He has told us that you always have pleasant memories of us and that you long to see us, just as we also long to see you. Therefore, brothers, in all our distress and persecution we were encouraged about you because of your faith. For now we really live, since you are standing firm in the Lord.
> *—1 Thessalonians 3:6-8, NIV*

Paul wrote about this in 1 Corinthians 9:27.

> But I discipline my body and bring it into subjection, lest, when I have preached to others, I myself should become

disqualified.
—*1 Corinthians 9:24-27, NKJV*

Here Jesus also talks about this as he addressed the Church in Philadelphia.

> I know your works. See, I have set before you an open door, and no one can shut it; for you have a little strength, have kept My word, and have not denied My name. ... Because you have kept My command to persevere, I also will keep you from the hour of trial which shall come upon the whole world, to test those who dwell on the earth. ...Hold fast what you have, that no one may take your crown. He who overcomes, I will make him a pillar in the temple of My God, and he shall go out no more.
> —*Revelation 3:8-12, NKJV*

Although Jesus approved of the Church in Philadelphia because this church kept his word, and was keeping his command to persevere, even then, however, he was telling the church to hold fast so no one can take the church's crown.

What is that crown, but life, eternal life as James so stated:

> Blessed is the man who perseveres under trial, because when he has stood the test, he will receive the crown of life that God has promised to those who love him.
> —*James 1:12, NIV*

Jesus went further to say he who overcomes, the Lord will make a pillar in the temple of God, showing that even when Christ is formed in you, if you don't persevere in keeping his words and obeying him and everyday committing to the renewal of your mind to walk like him, to put him on and to be him once you have gained the knowledge how to imitate Christ and have full knowledge of what it is to imitate Christ, you still are going to have an uphill struggle that's going to be like successfully conquering something difficult, a struggle only an overcomer can achieve, a warrior, a fighter against tough odds.

That's not easy street. When you overcome you are going against difficult odds, you're like a salmon going up stream, you're going to have to keep at it and have patience because it is going to lead you through a tough trial, thus that is why the apostles warned to continue to abide in Jesus, continue to keep his commandments, continue to keep his word, to stand firm.

Standing firm implies holding up against difficult forces. You don't need to stand firm where there's no opposition to you. You only stand firm were there is some kind of difficulty where you are instructed to stand firm, you are told to stand firm in the Lord.

Therefore even when Christ is formed in you and at that point God has written his laws on your heart, if you don't continue abiding in him, if you don't renounce your faith in him as Jesus says in Revelation 2, if you don't turn from God as Jeremiah wrote about 32:40, keeping the fear of God in your heart for your own good to not turn from the Lord, and turn from the way, then you will prove worthy, you will achieve the crown Christ promises to the one who endures.

> I know where you live--where Satan has his throne. Yet you remain true to my name. You did not renounce your faith in me, even in the days of Antipas, my faithful witness, who was put to death in your city--where Satan lives.
> —*Revelation 2:13, NIV*

> I will make with them an everlasting covenant, that I will not turn away from doing good to them. And I will put the fear of me in their hearts, that they may not turn from me.
> —*Jeremiah 32:40, ESV*

So even when you reach the stage where the laws will be written on your heart when Christ is fully formed in you, it still requires a daily commitment from you to persevere.

At no point is it going to mean that you are hands free, that it requires nothing on your part, that you no longer have to adhere or think about any thing and it's automatic that you get to heaven. That's an enemy scheme. Like I said this particular scheme has several threads of schemes going in it and these are lies of the enemy that you will need to stand firm against.

This is where this is part of the standing firm the Lord is commanding you to do.

Stand firm against the schemes of the enemy and the schemes are complex and the schemes are well-crafted to deceive even the elect. When you are armed with the Sword of Truth you can keep from falling to such deceits that leave you with the wrong idea and keep you from the right daily mindset to properly follow Christ.

7-6 Demon Doctrine: Deceive You Are His Sheep

The purpose of this doctrine is to leave people with false assurance they are counted as one of Christ's sheep who hear his voice. This doctrine imparts that when people go through the routine of becoming a Christian they are automatically part of one of the folds of sheep Jesus talks about that are his, which no one will be able to snatch them away.

> My sheep hear my voice, and I know them, and they follow me: And I give unto them eternal life; and they shall never perish, neither shall any man pluck them out of my hand. My Father, which gave them me, is greater than all; and no man is able to pluck them out of my Father's hand.
> —*John 10:27-29, KJV*

Satan wants to conceal from people that unless you have the hallmarks that clearly mark which are his sheep, you will be found not part of his flock, and not permitted entry to his pasture, and instead go into Satan's tremendous flock.

> And when he putteth forth his own sheep, he goeth before them, and the sheep follow him: for they know his voice. And a stranger will they not follow, but will flee from him: for they know not the voice of strangers.

Chapter 7: Demon Doctrines Coming To A Church Near You

—John 10:4-5, KJV

Only the sheep who responds in recognition and obedience to his voice, and he knows the sheep as his, is the one determined to be a true sheep. That is the only sheep, then, that will not be permitted to be snatched away, and any other sheep will be blocked entry, or thrown out if found in the pasture and the shepherd will not waver from this criteria.

So the warning here is just because you think you are a sheep in his flock, does not make you one, and just because a pastor or church tells you that you are, does not make it true either.

The shepherd has his *own* criteria to identify those who are his real sheep, and that is how the gatekeepers to his pasture and he himself will determine if you are. Jesus is not going to go by a pastor's word, or your own concept, but only by his own test which he has specified what that is in his teachings, which reveals if you really are or not, and that involves how you did or did not respond to his voice.

> I am the good shepherd, and know my sheep, and am known of mine. As the Father knoweth me, even so know I the Father: and I lay down my life for the sheep. And other sheep I have, which are not of this fold: them also I must bring, and they shall hear my voice; and there shall be one fold, and one shepherd.
>
> *—John 10:14-16, KJV*

Jesus knows his own sheep, those sheep being those who hear his voice, and always respond to it, always listen to it, listening meaning to pay attention to and follow, and always follow his lead. Someone who does not pay attention to and follow all of Jesus' words, is not part of his flock, and so is not under the unwavering protection from death in the Father's hands.

Anyone who is not listening to Jesus word to love one another and shows hatred to a Christian brother, marks him or herself as not of Jesus fold, and stands in peril to perish, and get snatched out of the proximity of the Lord by the enemy, who is Satan, who is always seeking to snatch out of any heart the word of God, but loses out doing this against true believers where the word stays rooted deep in rich soil.

In order to be proven part of the one flock of Jesus, while the season of grace is here, you must turn from ignoring the voice of Jesus if you have been guilty of that, and that is by not following his words to you through the Bible, which calls to you the way to follow him to eternal life through his teachings. That is the voice of his Jesus is going to judge if you listened to and obeyed, and followed him that way.

If you prove to listen to the voice of strangers, who may come among the fold as wolves in sheep clothing, and follow their false words which go against Christ's words, then you will prove to not belong to his fold, as his sheep do not *ever* listen to the voice of a stranger.

Thus, proving by your listening to the voice of stranger that you are not one of Jesus sheep, then you will be subject to being snatched away from the fold by the wolf in sheep clothing, falling to destruction.

The point behind this false doctrine is to get you to believe that no sheep standing in the middle of a flock of Christ can be snatched away from the fold of Christ's sheep.

But that is a demon lie because it conceals that not all the sheep milling around in the flock of Christ's sheep belong to Jesus. Some are wolves in sheep clothing; while some are sheep thinking they are part of that flock, but by responding to the voices of the wolves, prove they are not. Those are the ones not protected from being snatched away.

It is essential you realize that just by standing among other sheep part of Jesus flock, does not make one a sheep of Jesus, and, thereby, such a person can have a false idea they are safe from being snatched away, when only the true sheep are the ones Christ will protect, and he will let the others be snatched away, which he will identify by their responding to the voices of strangers.

Like a sheep you must follow Jesus example: you must follow Jesus through imitation of his righteous behavior by the good works he did, the self-control he practiced in every situation, the total obedience to God he continually showed, always doing only what pleased God and putting the works of God ahead of all, and

Chapter 7: Demon Doctrines Coming To A Church Near You

by the way he denied himself and bore his cross in sacrifice of love for God and his brothers as shown in the Bible. It is these examples and the commands of Jesus calling out to you he gave to the apostles for all future believers to obey, which you will be measured to see if you followed them.

This is not a test to see if you adhere to an inner voice of Jesus separate of the Bible; that is a deception if you have that idea that is what Jesus means by hearing his voice and following him, through some dynamic inner guidance apart and separate of his words in the Bible; instead this is a test by the criteria Jesus gave in the Scripture which is if you obey his word and follow his examples of godliness, two separate things---1) he has commands for you to follow, and 2) examples of a mindset to love of God and love of others you are required to imitate also.

Don't be delusional you are part of his flock, if you fail the test of the belief and obedience to his word, shown by any wicked fruits you may be guilty of producing, such as hatred to a brother, living an immoral life, and all the other sins specified in the New Testament which block a person from heaven, as it only takes one unrepented sin for you to lose out on salvation.

If you have believed nothing can snatch you away and as a result felt comfortable to sin and not have to worry about your salvation as a result of practicing sin, you need to lose that false sense of security while yet there is grace before the day of the Lord, and really examine whether you are a sheep of the Lord or not.

If you discover you have been following a stranger's voice, then you need to repent from that, confess to Jesus, ask for forgiveness, and turn from listening to the voices of strangers. Then, from now on firmly and with total resolve to be counted as one no one will snatch away from Christ, respond only to Christ's voice and follow only him in entirety. Nothing else will mark you to Christ as his than your responding in full to his voice, his instructions, and whether or not you will stray to the voice of another.

Jesus frees you from slavery to sin, but we are now slaves to righteousness (Romans 6:18).

If you belong to Jesus you hear his words and your will is to do them. "My sheep know my voice, my sheep listen to my voice" listen means to obey, to pay attention to and respond to it, which is to obey.

Hearing Jesus voice is also hearing God's voice; when you obey one, you obey the other. You will never see death (spiritual death/hell) if you hear and obey all of Jesus' words.

> Then said Jesus to those Jews which believed on him, If ye continue in my word, then are ye my disciples indeed; And ye shall know the truth, and the truth shall make you free.
> —*John 8:31-32, KJV*

7-7 Demon Doctrine: Fool You With Paulism

Sometimes Paul's teachings veered into a style I call 'Paulism'. The enemy uses 'Paulism' to lead people astray and so you need to be aware of it. In fact, more than one demon doctrine out there today, is a result of this 'Paulism'.

Peter gave the ultimate overview of the problem of this aspect of Paul's writing style I term 'Paulism'. Though I have come to personally give it this name as I studied Paul's writings, this problem is not something I invented, but it is scriptural and summarized by the apostle Peter in his second letter.

Now, mind you, Peter did not go into the details I will here, nor did he perhaps give it such thought as I have to see this pattern, but it was known then, this issue with his style of expression, and its potential problem that it could result in the unintended side effect to cause some people to be destroyed.

Apparently there had been enough casualties on a consistent basis back then that Peter had felt moved to leave this warning to believers to not fall into the same errors.

To show the issue is expressed similarly across different Bible translations, here is both the NIV and the NKJV of the same passage so you can see this issue is uniformly upheld:

> Bear in mind that our Lord's patience means salvation, just as our dear brother Paul also wrote you with the wisdom that God gave him. He writes the same way in all

Chapter 7: Demon Doctrines Coming To A Church Near You

his letters, speaking in them of these matters. His letters contain some things that are hard to understand, which ignorant and unstable people distort, as they do the other Scriptures, to their own destruction. Therefore, dear friends, since you already know this, be on your guard so that you may not be carried away by the error of lawless men and fall from your secure position.
—*2 Peter 3:15-17, NIV*

...and consider that the longsuffering of our Lord is salvation--as also our beloved brother Paul, according to the wisdom given to him, has written to you, as also in all his epistles, speaking in them of these things, in which are some things hard to understand, which untaught and unstable people twist to their own destruction, as they do also the rest of the Scriptures. You therefore, beloved, since you know this beforehand, beware lest you also fall from your own steadfastness, being led away with the error of the wicked;
—*2 Peter 3:15-17, NKJV*

It is put there as edification what can happen from Paul's writings if one is not careful when coming across those 'hard to understand' parts of Paul that I label 'Paulism' and twists some of the things Paul wrote.

What can happen is one can misinterpret some of the things Paul wrote to mean a license to be lawless. This Peter warned was the error, and one that lawless people were making, to their destruction.

As you can see, it is not a new problem of this day and age, instead it is a problem that began the moment Paul's writings went public, and casualties were happening not long after and continued to. People were twisting his letters, as they still do now, to interpret lawlessness is okay, and everything is permissible.

Of course you have to realize the warfare back-story to this, that this start of spiritual shipwrecking was the hallmark of Satan showing up to mess with God's will, to see who would fall for the enemy darts to let Satan move their heart to follow sin and stand on partial biblical falsehoods.

How do I know this? Because the Bible shows Satan is always prowling around, trying to trip people up with evil to consume them destructively.

> Be alert and of sober mind. Your enemy the devil prowls around like a roaring lion looking for someone to devour.
> —*1 Peter 5:8, NIV*

Devour is a consuming that destroys. Not just take a bite, or nibble on you, but to eat you ravenously, recklessly, until all gone.

One such Scripture example is in Acts when not long after the start of the early Church, when everyone was in one accord of heart and soul (Acts 4:32-35), we then see that idyllic scenario brought down in the next chapter by prowling Satan inspiring a believer named Ananias to lie to the Holy Spirit, him and his wife, resulting in their each falling over dead by the power of God when each was caught in that lie (Acts 5:1-10), no doubt their souls pounced on immediately by Satan to take down to his lair for devouring.

As this example shows, Satan was at the core of moving the husband and wife to be lawless, all for the goal to devour them if they made the mistake to follow his influence, which sadly they had, having been numbered up to that moment with those who believed and laying their possessions at the apostles' feet to be 'distributed to each as any had need' (Acts 4:35 ESV), this example also showing two Christians falling from grace when accepting the enemy's bait to sin.

First let me define 'Paulism' which is what I have dubbed those parts of Paul's writings that some did twist back then and some still are twisting today in error due to their hard to understand characteristics. It is error according to Peter and you have to believe the apostle whom Jesus dubbed as the 'rock' he would set the Church on (Matthew 16:18), is right to state it as error. Thus, this determination is not coming from someone today from a legalist teaching standpoint or a non-legalist standpoint, but it is coming from an original apostle.

Chapter 7: Demon Doctrines Coming To A Church Near You

Paulism Trademark

The trademark of the Paulism was its hard to understand nature.

Let's see why Paulism would be hard to understand: in a Paulism entry it would seem he was saying one thing yet he was not, and as well, it also sometimes would appear opposite of what he said elsewhere. It would sometimes be hard to make out if he was saying yes or no to something, actually promoting it or just using it to illustrate an aspect but not for the end it appeared. Paulism was part of Paul's style of expression, whether writing or talking, and purely a free-flowing style that was him.

This is where the weak would get in trouble, latching onto the parts that seemed to say what they liked or wanted to hear to their own destruction. Sometimes these contradictions did not lead to lawless ideas, where other times that was precisely the possibility. In those Paulisms, they came across as lawlessness, but down the road of the discourse proved righteousness. Ah, Paulism!

Wherever this style of Paul's popped up, it had the trait where you know he said something specific that could only be taken one way when read as itself, but then he said something else later on, same subject, negating that first idea from what it sounded like, with the last one what he ultimately meant. Listen to that: ultimately meant.

You could say Paulism bears a similarity to that well known "Who's on First?" Abbott & Costello patter routine, where it sounded like one thing, and you are sure that is it when you hear it, but, no, it turns out something entirely not, and he stated that to that end, making it even seem more head-shaking, double-taker, the 'hard to understand' that Peter said. Yet...the first ideas were points themselves which had their own separate merits and were not wrong to be said, but needed Paul to give that clarification to any thinking otherwise.

Maybe you have a family member who does that, who is quite a talker, and can manipulate concepts and facts like a magician can manipulate cups and balls, and you, having heard everything that relative has had to say, recognize all of these fact and concept manipulations, but all staying true in a convoluted sort of way, as that Aunt or Uncle makes his or her point to the first-time listener. And you know this is your relative's style of expressing him or herself.

Sometimes you know that verbose relative said something quite the contrary the talk before you had listened to on the same theme, but you know the core spot where that relative is coming from, that he or she is taking the listener to where that relative of yours is really coming from if the audience sits it out and hears your relative through, a place you know like the back of your hand because you have heard your relative say it half a dozen different ways over the years. So you can say in our Christian family we have such a relative and his name is Uncle Paul.

It is important to be on to Uncle Paul's style which has that distinct feature I dub 'Paulism' until you are so practiced in the Word that no one can throw you off or defeat you, by wielding some Paulism at you and stumping you and causing you to fall.

Here's a quick example of Paulism in action:

The lawless have run with this one:

Are we to sin because we are not under law but under grace?
—Romans 6:15, ESV

In this Paulism, that 'we are not under law but under grace', with the question 'are we to sin', only comes across as no accountability with grace which gives license to sin.

How can everything be allowed, though, if as a true believer, you gave up your freedom to do as you want?

It's not that you chose to give up that freedom when you want to be without freedom---it is that you conceded to permanently resign it when you committed yourself to Christ in the status of a slave. If then you are a slave, you are under the law of your master, and that was Paul's ultimate point in this Paulism which makes full circle in its end in the next three verses that as slaves to righteousness we are bound to not sin:

Do you not know that if you present yourselves to anyone

Chapter 7: Demon Doctrines Coming To A Church Near You

as obedient slaves, you are slaves of the one whom you obey, either of sin, which leads to death, or of obedience, which leads to righteousness? But thanks be to God, that you who were once slaves of sin have become obedient from the heart to the standard of teaching to which you were committed, and, having been set free from sin, have become slaves of righteousness.
—*Romans 6:16-18, ESV*

But those lawless people, forget out it. They turned deaf after Verse 15, and they've set up shop that gives 'thumbs up' to lawless behavior, fingers in their ears to anything after that, with loudly singing 'la la la' like stubborn little kids to drown anyone out who tries to communicate that to them, biting the inspiration of a demon to stay rebellious to the truth.

If you are a slave, you can only do what you are allowed to do by your master. Per Paul, all people are slaves of one kind or another, whether a slave to sin, or a slave to righteousness. As Christians, we are bound to our master, and our master is not named "License to Sin" but our master is named "Righteousness" and by that we are chained in slavery to. Ultimately, with regard to lawlessness and righteousness, that we are slaves to righteousness is what Paul ultimately meant in this Paulism.

Sometimes the place where Paul is really coming from when he speaks in Paulism isn't apparent until much later such as this other 5-star love of the lawless to quote:

All things are lawful for me, but not all things are helpful; all things are lawful for me, but not all things edify.
—*1 Corinthians 10:23, NKJV*

In this Paulism, again, Paul seems to stand that lawlessness through grace is in effect.

But you see the Paulism's true end four chapters later where you see the ultimate place Paul is coming from and his message is about:

Do not be deceived: "Bad company ruins good morals."

> Wake up from your drunken stupor, as is right, and do not go on sinning. For some have no knowledge of God. I say this to your shame.
> —*1 Corinthians 15:33-34, ESV*

Double-take! Excuse me, Uncle Paul, didn't you just say, "All things are lawful for me...?" Just kidding, Uncle Paul, I know you really were saying in 1 Corinthians 10:23 that those that are not helpful and do not edify, actually can drag down and are harmful.

Kidding aside, this trail of casualties led to Peter feeling the need to give a warning and instructions about this aspect of some of Paul's writings, not from disapproval of Paul, but from the standpoint of one who did approve of Paul and respected the wisdom given him, yet knowing from firsthand experience the negative effects on those who twisted his letters to a license to lawlessness, a spiritually fatal error.

In other words, the enemy takes advantage of Paulism to deceive people not mature in their knowledge of the ways of Jesus and God, just as the enemy takes advantage of anything or anyone for the same cause.

Always keep in mind that as Matthew 16 shows, Apostle Peter was used by Satan in Verses 21-23, after Peter had just gotten high praise in Verses 15-18 of his staunch standing in the faith to have been promoted as a rock in Christian faith, which is so the enemy's style to target what is good to God.

> "But what about you?" he asked. "Who do you say I am?" Simon Peter answered, "You are the Christ, the Son of the living God." Jesus replied, "Blessed are you, Simon son of Jonah, for this was not revealed to you by man, but by my Father in heaven. And I tell you that you are Peter, and on this rock I will build my church, and the gates of Hades will not overcome it."
> —*Matthew 16:15-18, NIV*

Seems like that was a gauntlet-thrown-down challenge from Jesus to the Devil because Satan appeared right after to challenge Jesus on that one in Verse 22:

Chapter 7: Demon Doctrines Coming To A Church Near You

> From that time on Jesus began to explain to his disciples that he must go to Jerusalem and suffer many things at the hands of the elders, chief priests and teachers of the law, and that he must be killed and on the third day be raised to life. Peter took him aside and began to rebuke him. "Never, Lord!" he said. "This shall never happen to you!" Jesus turned and said to Peter, "Get behind me, Satan! You are a stumbling block to me; you do not have in mind the things of God, but the things of men."
> —*Matthew 16:21-23, NIV*

Really, the reason why is because this is an active war and you are always, whether you realize it or not, under attack by the enemy to try to destroy you.

So taking a moment to discuss Paulism is relevant to your knowledge of defeating enemy schemes, and this Paulism is definitely used by the enemy to deceive about the importance of following God's commandments.

Here's one good generic example on Paulism, generic in that it doesn't deal with lawlessness but just is an example of the outright contradictory aspect of Paulisms. This example is on Galatians 3 and Romans 9:

> Brethren, I speak in the manner of men: Though it is only a man's covenant, yet if it is confirmed, no one annuls or adds to it. Now to Abraham and his Seed were the promises made. He does not say, "And to seeds," as of many, but as of one, "And to your Seed," who is Christ. And this I say, that the law, which was four hundred and thirty years later, cannot annul the covenant that was confirmed before by God in Christ, that it should make the promise of no effect. For if the inheritance is of the law, it is no longer of promise; but God gave it to Abraham by promise. What purpose then does the law serve? It was added because of transgressions, till the Seed should come to whom the promise was made; and it was appointed through angels by the hand of a mediator.

—Galatians 3:15-19, NKJV

But it is not that the word of God has taken no effect. For they are not all Israel who are of Israel, nor are they all children because they are the seed of Abraham; but, "In Isaac your seed shall be called." That is, those who are the children of the flesh, these are not the children of God; but the children of the promise are counted as the seed.

—Romans 9:6-8, NKJV

Paul goes on to make his argument in Galatians 3 that the singular 'seed' was Christ 430 years later.

If you had been one of the party of Paul who did the rounds with Uncle Paul in the different countries he hit on his tour for the Way, this talk to the Galatians would have had you shaking your head and doing a double take, as you remembered distinctly good ol' Uncle Paul had referred to the 'seed' in the plural form previously on the Roman stage when you had been standing back in the wings while he had given that discourse, a discourse which later found its way into the Bible at Romans 9:7-8.

... nor are they all children because they are the seed of Abraham...but the children of the promise are counted as the seed.

—Romans 9:6-8, NKJV

However, you keep your mouth shut at the wings of the Galatians church stage, knowing Uncle Paul's way of talking like the back of your hand, understanding this is his style to stress a meaning he might have used in a totally opposite way before, the current meaning relevant to his point, this one his 'what is currently pertinent' style alone and not mixed with his double-taker 'point u-turn' style which was the one which lawless people could make errors on, both techniques part of his Paulism repertoire.

At times Paul, aware some of his angles could be misconstrued, would come back with, depending on your Bible translation, 'by no means' or 'certainly not' did he mean that, to attempt to clarify he was not making the point it sounded like, such as these two:

> But if our unrighteousness demonstrates the righteousness of God, what shall we say? Is God unjust who inflicts wrath? (I speak as a man.) Certainly not! For then how will God judge the world?
> —*Romans 3:5-6, NKJV*

> For we hold that one is justified by faith apart from works of the law... Do we then overthrow the law by this faith? By no means! On the contrary, we uphold the law.
> —*Romans 3:28-31, ESV*

But he was not always around to correct every possibility where everyone could go with some of his points.

Revelatory Nugget of the Paulism Disclaimer

So his impressive writings are making it all over the ancient world because they are good, but disclaimers had to come in from an apostle because there were casualties in the Christian walk arising out of Paulism, enough so that it made it into a warning that stands in the Bible to this day.

What is important about that? Because all things in the Bible are good for edifying, and it is by no coincidence, then, that Peter's disclaimer made its way and stands fixed towards the end of the Bible, as it is further instructions on how to deal with Paulisms, that they exist and they require care handling. It is there to read as instructions so the same does not happen to anyone at all through time, reading Paul's amazing discourses.

The care involves not taking someone else's word on Paul, never hang on just a statement of his because of how wonderful it sounds, without having read the before and after of all of Paul's chapters in one sitting as he wrote so much you can forget he said something else pages and pages before.

That would have been impossible years ago, but today very

possible by listening to Paul's writings in audio Bible, such as offered for free at the time of this writing at www.Bible.is, where you can hear all of Paul in under 7 hours, while you do various things, but one of those times sitting and reading along with the audio.

Then your mind will be led to those Paulism places and they will jump out such as the one in Acts, and one in Galatians given above, and so on. And then you will see Paul's fundamental lawful message. Then you follow that session with the other Apostles afterwards.

In this way, you can avoid getting carried away with the error of lawless people reading Paulism can do to such ignorant and unstable to use Peter's language to describe such people. Why were they ignorant? Because they were ignorant of all of Paul, and his whole council he would give, in context to the rest of the apostles and Jesus.

As Peter inferred in 2 Peter 3:15, the way Paul's teachings led were not to a wayward end, if you were able to follow his sometimes ornate and convoluted ways, and see the entire panorama that Paul taught which always led back to the full ways of Jesus, of self control, the judgment of Christ, righteousness, and keeping from the immoral behaviors which Paul flat-out stated kept one from the kingdom of heaven, and fulfilling the 10 commandments through the two commandments of Jesus.

Peter is the ultimate authority on where Paul was coming from. Peter knew. He was there and he stated the issue with the truth of where Paul is coming from: lawful not lawless.

Through time, Peter, the apostle, stands telling us: "To interpret Paul means lawless is an error, one that will take you to destruction." It stands as a Scripture in 2 Peter, stands as a teaching in the New Testament, with no coincidence after all of Paul's writings.

Your defense is to know about it, be on guard about it, and take care not to fall to it, rejecting any teachings that arise from it promoting lawless behavior, and that means sin. You can count that License to Sin same as those funny licenses you can get at some novelty stores like the License to Grow Old. That License to Sin is nothing more than a novelty fraud created by Satan. If you got suckered into taking one, now is the time to take it out of your wallet and shred it.

There is nothing wrong with those Paulism areas of Paul's writings; it is what people do with them that can be wrong. It is important you are wise to this, so you cannot be misled by any, which you can only do if you are hip to the pitfall of not handling any Paulism with careful attention, knowing some have been snared by the enemy when they did not.

> God's truth stands firm like a foundation stone with this inscription: "The Lord knows those who are his," and "Those who claim they belong to the Lord must turn away from all wickedness."
> —*2 Timothy 2:19, NLT*

7-8 Demon Doctrines: How You Enter Heaven

Jesus was very specific about who will enter the kingdom of heaven. In several Scriptures he specifically stated who. Sometimes it was through a question that revealed the exact answer, and other times he specifically spelled it out.

Here is where demonic schemes are ripe: where false doctrines abound that focus on a word of the Lord, giving a partial truth, and not incorporating all his words.

Fundamental Foundation

In the New Testament, Hebrews chapter 3 and 4 give examples how disobedience equals disbelief and disbelief equals disobedience:

> And with whom was he provoked for forty years? Was it not with those who sinned, whose bodies fell in the wilderness? And to whom did he swear that they would not enter his rest, but to those who were disobedient? So we see that they were unable to enter because of unbelief.
> —*Hebrews 3:17-19, ESV*

> And again in this passage he said, "They shall not enter my rest." Since therefore it remains for some to enter it, and those who formerly received the good news failed to enter because of disobedience, again he appoints a certain day, "Today," saying through David so long afterward, in the words already quoted, "Today, if you hear his voice, do not harden your hearts.
> —*Hebrews 4:5-7, ESV*

By visiting Hebrews 4:5 words "They shall not enter my rest" coupled with Hebrews 4:6 "those who formerly received the good news failed to enter because of disobedience," it is clear obedience is needed in order to enter heaven, and by Hebrews 4:1 "Therefore, since the promise of entering his rest still stands, let us be careful that none of you be found to have fallen short of it" that although that is an Old Testament example, that this is an example in the New Testament as a warning given in a letter to Jewish Christians, that the belief-equals-obedience measure to enter heaven is still applicable to Christian believers.

> Let us, therefore, make every effort to enter that rest, so that no one will fall by following their example of disobedience. For the word of God is living and active. Sharper than any double-edged sword, it penetrates even to dividing soul and spirit, joints and marrow; it judges the thoughts and attitudes of the heart. Nothing in all creation is hidden from God's sight. Everything is uncovered and laid bare before the eyes of him to whom we must give account. Therefore, since we have a great high priest who has gone through the heavens, Jesus the Son of God, let us hold firmly to the faith we profess.
> —*Hebrews 4:11-14, NIV*

Notice in Hebrews 4:11 the words, so that no one will fall by following their example of disobedience and coupled with Hebrews 3:12 "Take care, brothers, lest there be in any of you an evil, unbelieving heart, leading you to fall away from the living God," that an unbelieving heart is the same as disobedience. So to have a believing heart, to hold firm "to the faith to profess" as Hebrews 4:14, is to be obedient to God; there is no separation between the two words of unbelief and disobedience, and belief and obedience.

On the reverse example how belief equals obedience to God are these Scriptures from 1-John, John and Revelation:

> And by this we know that we have come to know him, if we keep his commandments. Whoever says "I know him" but does not keep his commandments is a liar, and the truth is not in him,
> —*1 John 2:3-4 ESV*

The words 'knowing' in Verse 3 and 'know' in Verse 4 same as believing, and that stated belief only true if backed up by obedience, keeping his commandments.

> And all who believe in God's Son have eternal life. Those who don't obey the Son will never experience eternal life, but the wrath of God remains upon them.
> —*John 3:36, NLT*

Verse 36 shows how this 'believe' is equal with obeying. By order of sentence structure where "Those who don't obey" is counted different as someone who believes, establishing whoever believes as to eternal-life belief, obeys Jesus.

The New Living Testament (NLT) version of John 3:36 is more accurate to the original Greek which specifies those who don't obey the Son, as opposed to the King James Version which says those who don't believe, which can cloud an important issue that obedience is part of having eternal life.

The original Greek states: (I am putting the English translation of the Greek here) "the [one] believing on the Son has life eternal; the [one] moreover not obeying the Son not will see life but the wrath of God abides on him." The original Greek word for the 'not obeying' given as *apeithōn* which means not obeying from the word, *apeitheó* which means 'to disobey', as you can see no cousin to the King James word choice of 'believeth not' which is how demon doctrines come to be: the particular editors mulling over interpretations accepted the demonic influence to change it entirely to reinforce belief alone, acting as a reinforcement to the theory belief alone, without obedience involved, all needed to have eternal life.

Pretty important difference that specifically the one not obeying Jesus is the one who will not see life. This is why it is good to compare translations to the original Greek to find if there is any kind of discrepancy that could lead to a salvation error, something easy to do on the Internet with free online Bible tools that provide Interlinear searches.

Not all Bible discrepancies are crucial doctrinal errors, but this particular one is because it reinforces a demon doctrine that omits the need to obey Jesus.

> Then the dragon was enraged at the woman and went off to make war against the rest of her offspring--those who obey God's commandments and hold to the testimony of Jesus.
> —*Revelation 12:17, NIV*

The language above in Revelation 12:17 is especially important to note in describing those considered God's heaven-bound faithful servants: "those who obey God's commandments and hold to the testimony of Jesus."

That 'those' is presented as a singular description of one group is the item to take note of. See that it is not described as two separate groups, or it would have been stated as thus ""those who obey God's commandments and those who hold to the testimony of Jesus" making them two distinct groups.

However, that is not the case, although some leaders in independent Bible commentaries shove that distinction in there anyways, a hallmark of another kind of demon doctrine, which is when words are added to Scripture that are not there, perverting or changing significantly the meaning to deceive, the deception the motive of the demon influencing that term addition.

In that case those commentators following the demon influence to conform the actual Scriptures to a more popular belief people like better, in a comfort zone they can live with that doesn't conflict with their current lifestyles, so as not to risk convicting them of sin which could have inconvenient consequences for them in any repentance process.

Adding a 'those' that is not there allows a tremendous deception that Christians are those defined just by those who hold to the testimony of Jesus, not those who obey God's commandments, the evil of that leading astray Christians to believe obedience to God's commandments do not apply to them.

The original Greek in Revelation 12:17 does not even have a 'those' it just has it as shown in this next table:

meta	tōn	loipōn
with	the	rest

| tou | spermatos | autēs |
| of the | children | of her |

| tōn | tērountōn | tas |
| the | keeping | the |

| entolas | tou | Theou |
| commandments | of the | of God |

| kai | echontōn | tēn |
| and | holding | the |

| martyrian | Iēsou |
| testimony | of Jesus |

So in Verse 17, in the original Greek it is stated as "with the rest of the children of her the keeping the commandments of the God and holding the testimony of Jesus" showing the same and one group of children. Thus, these children being the ones who keep the commandments of God AND hold the testimony of Jesus.

To state they are two different groups, Jews who are the ones some Christians feel are the only bound to the commandments of

God, and Christians, who are the ones who hold the testimony of Jesus, is to add words that define another set of children, and ignoring there is only ONE set of children defined in Revelation.

All the same, not so radical information because this is said similar elsewhere, and this second Scripture of Revelation 14:12 which says the same as the above Revelation 12:17 serves as the nail that seals the coffin on that demon doctrine, emphatically clarifying Christians, referred to as saints, as the ones defined to believe in Jesus AND keeping God's commandments.

> This calls for patient endurance on the part of the saints who obey God's commandments and remain faithful to Jesus.
> —*Revelation 14: 12, NIV*

See how there is no 'those' that can be moved around or ignored or added in order to remove the 'who obey God's commandments' from the Christian, 'saints' being the key word that defines those Christians as those who reached the eternally saved state, and just keep obedience to God's commandments to Jews.

Do not confuse that obeying God's commandments we are called to follow as Christians has anything to do with any of the external Jewish rituals of foods, seasons, circumcision, etc. Also, the way we fulfill obeying those commandments are through the new way, which is that freedom we have in Christ, the way instructed by Christ which leaves us not held to the letter of the law when we are obedient to Jesus, but as an auto by-product from following him.

Thus, why belief as those Scriptures show, by itself, separate and without obedience, is insufficient to meet the belief that leaves one not condemned.

I repeat and let this bore into you and sear you: INSUFFICIENT. That kind of belief is impossible to leave one not condemned because demons also believe and testify in this belief, as Luke 4:41 below states. Note it is demons plural, meaning this kind of testimony was not an isolated incident, but common, the difference of their testimony being always without and separate of

Chapter 7: Demon Doctrines Coming To A Church Near You

obedience to Christ's teachings:

> And devils also came out of many, crying out, and saying, Thou art Christ the Son of God. And he rebuking them suffered them not to speak : for they knew that he was Christ.
> —Luke 4:41, KJV

> And whenever the unclean spirits saw him, they fell down before him and cried out, "You are the Son of God." And he strictly ordered them not to make him known.
> —Mark 3:11-12, ESV

If the demons gave testimony in front of many, they recognized Jesus as the Son of God, and recognized he was the Messiah, the Christ, and were not imputed righteousness from that belief, then it stands to reason such belief, separate of obedience, is insufficient to be saved, and that belief alone does not bring about righteousness.

You can't have exceptions: either just believing saves or it does not. There is no conflict with this conclusion because further Scriptures go on to detail the kind of belief Jesus means, which is the kind of belief Hebrews 3 and 4 show God means, which is that kind of belief from the heart that is equivalent with obedience.

> At evening, when the sun had set, they brought to Him all who were sick and those who were demon-possessed. And the whole city was gathered together at the door. Then He healed many who were sick with various diseases, and cast out many demons; and He did not allow the demons to speak, because they knew Him.
> —Mark 1:32-33, NKJV

It is this kind of 'knowing' Him that Jesus does not accept as belief to salvation, as he inferred in Luke 6:46 which is knowing Him, recognizing him, yet being one that does not follow what he says; in that case he doesn't even want you to call him Lord, because he is not Lord to those who do not do what he says.

> But why do you call Me 'Lord, Lord,' and do not do the things which I say?
>
> —*Luke 6:46, NKJV*

So a demon calling Jesus by his title, never results in that demon's salvation because demons never can obey his teachings from their evil hearts.

Further support the belief Jesus means involves obeying him, is supplied by these Scriptures:

> If you love Me, keep My commandments. And I will pray the Father, and He will give you another Helper, that He may abide with you forever-- the Spirit of truth, whom the world cannot receive, because it neither sees Him nor knows Him; but you know Him, for He dwells with you and will be in you.
>
> —*John 14:15-17, NKJV*

> But why do you call Me 'Lord, Lord,' and do not do the things which I say? Whoever comes to Me, and hears My sayings and does them, I will show you whom he is like: He is like a man building a house, who dug deep and laid the foundation on the rock. And when the flood arose, the stream beat vehemently against that house, and could not shake it, for it was founded on the rock. But he who heard and did nothing is like a man who built a house on the earth without a foundation, against which the stream beat vehemently; and immediately it fell. And the ruin of that house was great.
>
> —*Luke 6:46-49, NKJV*

Here in the final Verse 49 of Luke 6 the Lord makes clear that the one who hears his words and does nothing will fall under the steady violent enemy attacks, with great ruin, inferring eternal destruction, which is to say the house that person set up was in a known danger spot (where a stream beat vehemently), yet the person ignored that problem and set up house without any

Chapter 7: Demon Doctrines Coming To A Church Near You

attention to the instructions he heard how to build that house to survive those forces.

Thus to just recognize Jesus as Lord, and not obey his instructions, is to set yourself up to ruination, a fall from grace, with a result of a great ruin to your salvation plan.

The same need to obey Jesus is reiterated several times over later by several of the apostles in these Scriptures:

> And being made perfect, he became the source of eternal salvation to all who obey him
> —*Hebrews 5:9, ESV*

> For the time has come for judgment to begin at the house of God; and if it begins with us first, what will be the end of those who do not obey the gospel of God?
> —*1 Peter 4:17, NKJV*

To drive further home this important scriptural truth, here are over ten Scriptures you must obey Jesus teachings in order to be saved:

> ...but for those who are self-seeking and do not obey the truth, but obey unrighteousness, there will be wrath and fury.
> —*Romans 2:8, ESV*

Not a slap on the hand, folks, but wrath and fury.

> If you love me, you will obey what I command. And I will ask the Father, and he will give you another Counselor to be with you forever-- the Spirit of truth. The world cannot accept him, because it neither sees him nor knows him. But you know him, for he lives with you and will be in you.
> —*John 14:15-17, NIV*

> Jesus answered him, "If anyone loves me, he will keep my word, and my Father will love him, and we will come to

him and make our home with him. Whoever does not love me does not keep my words. And the word that you hear is not mine but the Father's who sent me.
—John 14:23-24, ESV

If you keep my commandments, you will abide in my love, just as I have kept my Father's commandments and abide in his love.
—John 15:10, ESV

Keep a close watch on yourself and on the teaching. Persist in this, for by so doing you will save both yourself and your hearers.
—1 Timothy 4:16, ESV

...and whatever we ask we receive from him, because we keep his commandments and do what pleases him.
—1 John 3:22, ESV

For this is the love of God, that we keep his commandments. And his commandments are not burdensome.
—1 John 5:3 ESV

And this is love: that we walk in obedience to his commands. As you have heard from the beginning, his command is that you walk in love.
—2 John 1:6, NIV

Why would this doctrine of demons be around, about belief that requires nothing more than a straight belief? Same reason as others: so you have a false sense of salvation and commit offenses that disqualify you from heaven. There are many doctrines of demons that have made their way as firm dogmas in some churches today.

The way to combat them is by scriptural familiarity, your own familiarity, so you do not blindly trust the one who blinds (god of this world), even at times through the most revered devoted Christian, such as Peter was a temporary demon pawn in Matthew

16:23 (ESV)

> But he turned and said to Peter, "Get behind me, Satan! You are a hindrance to me. For you are not setting your mind on the things of God, but on the things of man."

A couple of such dogmas, Imputed Righteousness or the equally similar Justification by Faith, are based on this Romans 10 Scripture:

> For with the heart man believeth unto righteousness; and with the mouth confession is made unto salvation.
> —*Romans 10:10, KJV*

Note that the Greek word for 'unto' is 'eis' which means to or into (indicating the point reached or entered, of place, time, fig. purpose, result).

You believe into a state of righteousness, a state of obedience. If your belief in the core of your heart is 100% in something, your actions show that belief 100%; otherwise, your belief is not total.

For example, you can't totally believe in a leader of a system, and not follow through with whatever you are expected to do the leader says is necessary to prove your loyalty as that would show a heart not 100% committed.

In other words, true total belief, moves you to complete loyalty to that belief, and such loyalty is proved by the actions you take and not by the words you say, no matter how sincere you say them, as it is possible for you to fool yourself.

Only by the final actions you take, do you discover if you really feel such a way. This can sometimes lead you to find you really didn't feel as passionate or committed to something as you thought you were, because you just couldn't go through with a certain action which would prove your total conviction to whatever that is. Maybe it is a romantic interest, maybe it proves to be a job offer, but through your ultimate inaction, you discover, you were not that into it.

As you can see, then, your actions are the real measuring stick to your belief. That is why believing something without action, or as often scripturally referred to as 'works', to back it up, is not an indicator of genuine belief.

Notice in Romans 10:10 Scripture above that the confession with the mouth is not separate from that total belief; so lip service, or just speaking Jesus is savior and Son of God, as the demons did by dozens, is not enough. The belief to a point God counts as righteous, shown by your actions or works, is a necessary half to that salvation.

You believe unto a right standing with the Lord, because you are entirely convicted in that belief, and show that by the actions you take. This is the state of righteousness you believe in that leaves you free of condemnation, coupled with that confession. Without that genuine whole-hearted faith, the kind revealed by your actions, you are not genuinely converted.

Wrongfulness of Imputed Righteousness

The people who push imputed righteousness that requires nothing further from the believer than just believing to be justified by that faith, often do on a first half of a 'Paulism', referring to this Scripture Paul wrote, "what does the Scripture say? "Abraham believed God, and it was credited to him as righteousness." (Romans 4:3 NIV) to prove nothing more than believing, taking God at his word, was what God perceived as the belief, crediting to Abraham righteousness.

Here in Romans 16:26 Paul reveals the crucial second half of that Paulism, that definition of faith that requires obedience. This faith, this belief Paul writes about goes hand-in-hand with obedience.

> Now to Him who is able to establish you according to my gospel and the preaching of Jesus Christ, according to the revelation of the mystery kept secret since the world began but now has been made manifest, and by the prophetic Scriptures has been made known to all nations, according to the commandment of the everlasting God, for obedience to the faith
> —*Romans 16:25-26, NKJV*

Chapter 7: Demon Doctrines Coming To A Church Near You

When you understand that unbelief equals disobedience and belief equals obedience, then Verse 25 in Galatians gives the revelatory implications why 'we are no longer under the supervision of the law' because now that we are in a state of total belief which equals obedience, being obedient by that belief, we no longer have to be supervised to do what is right, because by obedience gotten by total faith, we follow the law from our heart by obeying Christ's commands without needing the supervision of the law.

> But the Scripture declares that the whole world is a prisoner of sin, so that what was promised, being given through faith in Jesus Christ, might be given to those who believe. Before this faith came, we were held prisoners by the law, locked up until faith should be revealed. So the law was put in charge to lead us to Christ that we might be justified by faith. Now that faith has come, we are no longer under the supervision of the law.
> —*Galatians 3:22-25, NIV*

It is important to see that the foundation that Paul lays on the Way of Jesus upholds active obedience to the teachings of Jesus as part of that faith, which includes fundamental steps as he related to Felix here.

> Now as he (Paul) reasoned about righteousness, self-control, and the judgment to come, Felix was afraid and answered, "Go away for now; when I have a convenient time I will call for you."
> —*Acts 24:25, NKJV*

As you can see Paul specifically included 'self-control' as a part of that way with righteousness. Self-control is a 'work' an act that takes personal effort, and self-control is necessary to stay righteous through obedience, and resist temptations of the flesh.

Thus, Paul is not promoting a 'believe' only in the name of Jesus to be saved, but the same fundamental teachings of Jesus which require obedience to his words, actions to ensure that obedience, an obedience which can only be achieved by a true faith.

In Romans 6:16-18 he makes clear that though we are not under the law, and under grace, we are slaves to obey Christ, slaves to righteous behavior.

> Do you not know that to whom you present yourselves slaves to obey, you are that one's slaves whom you obey, whether of sin leading to death, or of obedience leading to righteousness? But God be thanked that though you were slaves of sin, yet you obeyed from the heart that form of doctrine to which you were delivered. And having been set free from sin, you became slaves of righteousness.
> —*Romans 6:16-18, NIV*

If the righteousness were imputed, which means vicariously given, there would be no need to be slaves, as slavery is a condition that makes you forced to obey.

What is the definition of a slave? A slave is a person who is the legal property of another and forced to obey them. Let that sink in: forced to obey. Forced means required, mandated, obligatory. That slave status, takes away an outside 'alien' righteousness just given to us that leaves us without any obligation and always in that state.

In these final 3 Scriptures by Paul, you can see although earlier he speaks about a 'freedom in Christ' that freedom involves slavery, a forced obedience to the owner, with the result of that slavery leading to eternal life.

> But now that you have been set free from sin and have become slaves to God, the benefit you reap leads to holiness, and the result is eternal life.
> —*Romans 6:22, NIV*

> For he who was a slave when he was called by the Lord is the Lord's freedman; similarly, he who was a free man when he was called is Christ's slave.

Chapter 7: Demon Doctrines Coming To A Church Near You

—1 Corinthians 7:22, NIV

> Slaves, obey your earthly masters with respect and fear, and with sincerity of heart, just as you would obey Christ. Obey them not only to win their favor when their eye is on you, but like slaves of Christ, doing the will of God from your heart.
> *—Ephesians 6:5-11, NIV*

True belief is obedience to God's will.

I write so much about this imputed righteousness because the enemy has and is deceiving a lot of believers to their destruction through this partial doctrine, and thus, it deserves a special visit to crush for certain that enemy deceit. Truly that sort of belief that God considers unbelief could definitely lead to the wicked state of souls I saw in my 1972 vision.

Those people were surprised they were in judgment; they didn't know they were in wrong, having committed all kinds of acts God abhors to the point their souls were tremendously corrupted and they had taken on the nature of demons.

That could happen to someone who believes in justification by faith that involves no works, that leaves them free to live as they please and commit any sin they want, erroneously believing they are justified in the end by believing Jesus through a belief of recognition, a recognition that does not involve loyalty to all he said.

In addition, imputed righteousness theory ignores Verses 20 through 26 of James 2 below, which expounds further what that belief/faith actually is, which is synonymous with obedience, and obedience meaning putting into practice what is said, using Abraham as an example as Paul did, but in Genesis 22 involving the sacrifice of Abraham's son, where Abraham's actions from that belief were what God decreed righteous.

> You foolish man, do you want evidence that faith without deeds is useless? Was not our ancestor Abraham considered righteous for what he did when he offered his son Isaac on the altar? You see that his faith and his

actions were working together, and his faith was made complete by what he did. And the Scripture was fulfilled that says, "Abraham believed God, and it was credited to him as righteousness," and he was called God's friend. You see that a person is justified by what he does and not by faith alone. In the same way, was not even Rahab the prostitute considered righteous for what she did when she gave lodging to the spies and sent them off in a different direction? As the body without the spirit is dead, so faith without deeds is dead.
—*James 2:20-26, NIV*

I can almost see James parrying with a sword with Paul as he says to Paul Verse 20, "You foolish man, do you want evidence that faith without deed is useless," as Paul and he clash swords together, James challenging Paul's 'no works' example of Abraham through Romans 4:3.

Does this mean that Paul was wrong in Romans 4:3? Absolutely not, Romans 4:3 is a strict example when just belief alone justified a man. However, it is important to look at the further example in Genesis 22, when it was only by works that Abraham's belief was justified. And more importantly to note that it was a belief that was as a test by God. This is important because the genuineness of our faith God is testing to see if true. Thus, really, as James 2 explains, the example of Abraham's faith shown by works is the true definition of Christian faith.

Thus, to use only Abraham's faith example Paul gave in Romans as the end of all to what defines belief God counts as righteousness, discounts what Paul says further on in several places that believers are slaves to righteousness, and does not include the whole word Paul taught which gives a rounded complete picture of that belief, and instead paints a picture of a partial set of facts.

You have to consider that when God really wanted to test the genuineness of Abraham's faith that he put him through a test that was graded on Abraham's actions.

Some time later God tested Abraham. He said to him,

Chapter 7: Demon Doctrines Coming To A Church Near You

> "Abraham!" "Here I am," he replied. Then God said, "Take your son, your only son, Isaac, whom you love, and go to the region of Moriah. Sacrifice him there as a burnt offering on one of the mountains I will tell you about."
> —*Genesis 22:1-2, NIV*

Obviously if the first show of faith Paul gave in Romans 4:3 by believing God on his inheritance had been 'good enough' God would not have sought to put him later on to a test that would reveal his true level of faith.

> In this you greatly rejoice, though now for a little while, if need be, you have been grieved by various trials, that the genuineness of your faith, being much more precious than gold that perishes, though it is tested by fire, may be found to praise, honor, and glory at the revelation of Jesus Christ...
> —*1 Peter 1:6-7, NKJV*

> My brethren, count it all joy when you fall into various trials, knowing that the testing of your faith produces patience.
> —*James 1:2-3, NKJV*

God knew Abraham could have tied up his son, pretended to lift that knife, and never really meant to follow through, if he genuinely did not believe in God to have a real fear of him and be obedient. God, knowing the intent of every heart, was convinced Abraham had a real belief strictly on Abraham's actions. As you know that is the problem of lip service, someone can say everything that sounds right, even fooling themselves they mean it, but the only telling moment is if that person's acts back up what they state.

With imputed righteousness which is nearly the same as Justification by Faith, it sounds like you are complimenting God, instead you are calling him a liar if you uphold this theory.

God does not take kindly to this kind of rejection of his

standards as he so said,

> They have lied about the Lord, and said, "It is not He, neither will evil come upon us, nor shall we see sword or famine. And the prophets become wind, for the word is not in them. Thus it shall be done to them."
> —*Jeremiah 5:12-13, NKJV*

It is like you want to say God does not have standards, and God does not require anything in the salvation process, as God stated above in Jeremiah that after it was he who was punishing Jerusalem for wickedness, avenging himself, that the people were denying God punished at all, that no such judgments God would do, something which entirely made God increase his wrath on them. Remember, God has not changed who he is through all time, you are dealing with the same God today who does not take kindly to rejection of his ways, even if presented as a seeming compliment of his kindness and love.

So imputed righteousness in fact by inference denies the need to be obedient, that by belief at face value of the truth, a belief that convicts you indeed as the demons are truly convinced Jesus is Christ and the Son of God, that by that kind of belief you are made righteous.

If so, then all demons are made equally righteous, which they are not, so thus the theory already crumbles.

And what is the harm, other than men's egos brought down, if you have a change in mindset and belief to the point of total conviction that brings you to wholeheartedly obey with all your heart and strength all of Jesus words? The only ones who would have trouble with that, other than denominations so gripped by the enemy they cannot change from the revelations of that error, and enthusiastically dash the enemy's handiwork, and do an about face that brings the right faith that leaves one not condemned, would be demons that such deceived would turn from that falsehood and be saved genuinely by faith that brings total obedience.

In addition, it is flat out dismissing Jesus directly in all the times he said specifically to obey him. It is putting the teachings of

Chapter 7: Demon Doctrines Coming To A Church Near You

man over the teachings of God.

> And in vain they worship Me, Teaching as doctrines the commandments of men...
> —*Matthew 15:9, NKJV*

This is a huge doctrinal error, again a hallmark of the enemy. Why? Because it leads a person to have a false sense of salvation, exactly what the enemy wants. It makes a person believe all that other stuff that Jesus says, that nags their conscience a little because they don't pay attention to those other things Jesus says a believer must do or face wrath, does not apply to getting salvation, no matter how in conflict with justification by faith it does seem to be. Never will the popularity of a theory override what the Lord has said in the Bible, all that he said.

So just how has such a false doctrine become so widespread? Many are guilty of accepting at face value the mantra that just to believe Jesus is the savior means they are saved because they let others think for themselves, exactly the judgment error the enemy hopes you to make.

It is time to stop unquestioningly accepting Jesus more culturally popular words at face value, ignoring his implicit clarifications on his words, and traipsing through life living in unacceptable disobedience that leaves you too filthy to enter heaven. Now is the time to do a reverse and move in the right direction in full obedience.

In essence while you are justified by belief, it is a belief that obeys Jesus in full, where you fulfill all of the law by obeying Jesus commandments, rather than the letter of the law. This is a faith that is synonymous with obedience to the faith, and not a belief of recognition that has no obedience which is the type of belief demons have concerning Jesus, and the kind he rejects. Therefore, obedience to Jesus that equals belief in Jesus is essential to entering heaven.

> The Lord Jesus shall be revealed from heaven with his mighty angels, In flaming fire taking vengeance on them that ... obey not the gospel of our Lord Jesus Christ: Who

shall be punished with everlasting destruction from the presence of the Lord, and from the glory of his power.
—*2 Thessalonians 1:7-9, KJV*

As the demon doctrines given as examples in this chapter show, the purpose of demon doctrines is to fool you that sin is okay, hide from you that everyone, Christians including, will be judged for good or evil (2 Corinthians 5:10), and erase truth that leads to repentance so you die in your sins and end up in hell.

As you can see this is an all-out, hard-hitting warfare tactic made to get Christians to stray from the faith, a warning the Holy Spirit issued Apostle Timothy over two thousand years ago, so the people in latter times, which is us, would be duly warned and not be taken down by the enemy this way.

Thus consider yourself duly warned by the Holy Spirit. This means to stay on guard. It means to also be aware such deceiving spirits are out there now in droves speaking wrong doctrine to every believer's ear who will listen in order to lure them from the faith.

Understand some in high positions of faith will fall for these doctrines and for you to not be deceived that from their standing in the Church it makes those doctrines okay.

> For the time will come when men will not put up with sound doctrine. Instead, to suit their own desires, they will gather around them a great number of teachers to say what their itching ears want to hear. They will turn their ears away from the truth and turn aside to myths.
> —*1 Timothy 4:3-4, NIV*

***

Chapter 8

UNEXPECTED MARY SHRINE DEMON PHOTO

> What do I imply then? That food offered to idols is anything, or that an idol is anything? No, I imply that what pagans sacrifice they offer to demons and not to God. I do not want you to be participants with demons. You cannot drink the cup of the Lord and the cup of demons. You cannot partake of the table of the Lord and the table of demons.
> —*1 Corinthians 10:19-21, ESV*

In this chapter I share with you an experience I had in February 5, 2011 of a demon figure showing completely in two pictures I took of a statute of a Virgin Mary holding Baby Jesus, and partially showing in another, same figure, all in the same picture-snapping session. I had taken the photos not with the intent to capture a demon, but to send to a relative recovering in a nursing home from a hip injury, to lift her faith and believe in a healing as Saint Therese of the Child Jesus had received from that particular manifestation of Mary called Our Lady of the Smile.

You have to understand I was extremely devoted to the Virgin Mary, more than most, having run several online businesses making handmade rosaries, and held a leading website for years with thousands of visitors around the world who came to learn how to pray the rosary from my detailed instructions on my large website built just for that purpose.

My devotion to Mary had not started with those websites, however, it started as a little girl in Catholic School when I learned my birthday was on a super important day of Mary in the Church called the Assumption of the Blessed Virgin Mary, when she was said to supernaturally go to heaven both body and soul and be crowned Queen.

It was the Catechism of the Catholic Church that said this in paragraphs 966 and 974 which you can read at the Vatican website www.vatican.va or find by doing a search for the term "Catechism 966, 974" and also reading "Catechism 491" where it shows Pope Pius IX proclaimed in 1854 the dogma of the Immaculate Conception and why.

I hadn't questioned the validity of the Catholic Catechism as I had thought it was a condensed version of the Bible with a Catholic slant, because even though I went to Catholic elementary school, I can't remember even owning a catechism, much less reading it. Plus, the masses when I was a child were in Latin here in USA, and it was just a matter of sitting through the service hearing the priest talk in Latin having no idea what he was saying. At least in my case, there truly was actually very little studying and understanding the whys of any dogma, and even what they were. It was only later did I come to learn that was not so, about the Catechism being a condensed Bible, which explained why there were a lot of things there that were nowhere in the Bible.

Since pretty much left to my own imagination on this dogma, I had first thought the Assumption of Mary had been an event witnessed like an apparition, like the apostles had seen Jesus ascend into heaven. But when I found no Biblical references, nor did I come across any such events like the ones about Lourdes and other places Mary phenomenon was recorded, all the same I just had accepted that as true based on some kind of authority of knowledge I didn't know about yet.

So that I started to see a discrepancy of no Scriptures to back it up or existing stories existing on it like when Jesus went to heaven in front of the eyes of the apostles, and though it did seem weird, it still was not a faith stopper to me because it was upheld by parishes all around the world and did have apparitions to back up Jesus wanted his mother honored and worshipped as the Queen.

Plus, it seemed reasonable that where he might not listen to a person, his heart was always tender to the requests of his mother. In addition, the saying "To Jesus through Mary" didn't come

Chapter 8: Unexpected Mary Shrine Demon Photo

across as a clash with God's will if it was leading people to Jesus or so it was how I felt. This to me did not raise any red flags as it made sense about how a loving son would feel about his mother. As you can see I didn't come to know this about Mary through education, but I came to know it through the traditions of the Church.

Besides feeling a special connection to her because of my birthday on her Assumption day, it got stronger when I experienced in fifth grade a couple of very unusual experiences with the Virgin Mary of a supernatural nature.

In fact in chapter 1, I wrote about how I had run away in 5th grade, but what I didn't share at that time was on that day my classmate and I ran away together, both she and I had gone earlier into the church to pray over this in order to know what to do.

She and I had felt, like children do, not loved by our families and felt the answer was to run away. So we both knelt down together in front of the statutes inside of the church on the school grounds to pray to Joseph and Mary what to do.

Looking at the Virgin Mary statute's face as I knelt before it, I asked the statute as if speaking to Mary directly, if we should run away, explaining in simple ten-year-old talk how we felt unloved. To my surprise, the statute winked at me like an approval! I had not expected any reaction at all, and when that happened, it was a definite yes. No more than a couple of hours later, because of that, my classmate and I, followed through with our plan, and pretended like we were going to the bathroom, then just ran out of the school grounds to her house where she took some change and dollars out of a jar for us to start our new life with, a life with no plans beyond that.

What could go wrong if God's mother herself gives you a yes wink? It has to be right, right?

Well on that trip which lasted until late that night when after a day on our own going to who knows where because we really had no plan but just to go, after getting our life-on-the-run jar money, I nearly was hit by a train, not aware of it while my friend and I walked on the tracks near an overgrown wooded area close to the airport. I lived because my fast-acting classmate pushed me out of the way seconds before the train would have barreled over me.

It was that train driver who reported to police seeing us on the tracks, no doubt shaken he almost hit a little girl. And later in that night, after spending the afternoon next to a canal in the airport woods, in our makeshift new 'home' of woven branches until we ate all the bread and baloney we had bought at a store on the way of our aimless hike, we accepted a ride from a passing police car who took us to the airport station.

Yet being a child it had passed over my head that I had been nearly killed if not for my fast thinking friend, and still had felt that the reason I had been kept safe was due to the watching eye of Mary.

Well, even then it didn't take away my affinity towards Mary, but increased it, and what was to happen next a few months later was to really seal my devotion to her.

Although I had run away, a few months later my parents let me go on a weekend camping trip with the Girl Scout troop that I belonged to on June 6, 1968. It was there that another camp mate and I both saw an apparition of the Virgin Mary out in the Everglades woods at Turkey Point Wildlife Refuge while we were on a private hike together in the bright morning that led us to stumble across a pathway that took us to a clearing where a chickee hut shrine stood with a small Virgin Mary statute central to it, hanging on the only wall of the hut.

As we were making up a story to one another how the animals probably came out to worship before Mary, we got a real surprise of a life-size apparition of the Virgin Mary appearing out of the woods to our left. She floated a couple feet off the ground as she moved in a straight line not looking to us, just staying sideways as she floated. For the amount of time it takes for a person to walk that distance is how long it was we saw the apparition which had the quality of a hologram in that it was the Virgin Mary life-size, but she was see-through, I guess one could say like a ghost, but this was full blown daylight. She went on a straight beeline, passing in front of the chiki shrine, and into the opposite woods, going right through the trees and out of our sight. And that was the totality of it.

The apparition was dressed in the classic clothes seen on all Virgin Mary statutes, of white and blue and pretty much looked

Chapter 8: Unexpected Mary Shrine Demon Photo

like this picture I made of the event.

Turkey Point Wildlife Refuge, Florida Apparition June 7, 1968 - Vivian Gendernalik

Well it scared the heck out of us and we ran to find our troop leaders, expecting they would come back with us to look, but instead surprised they told us not to talk about it, surprised because all of us, troop leaders included were Catholics from the same parish, same school, and we had been taught Virgin Mary apparitions were special. But here we were being told to not talk about it.

Thus that was the end of it because the other girl and I had been too afraid to go back on our own there, and being this was an outing in the scout campgrounds far from where we lived, nothing would ever take us back there again where we might find ourselves brave enough to venture back.

As you can imagine, having a full-blown apparition of the Virgin Mary really impressed me favorably to the point I had wondered if it had been the possible start to another official Mary apparition in the world had we been able to go back there more than once, because many of the apparitions had started as just brief showings to the children the first few times, before it would turn to Mary actually speaking to the children.

So here I was born on the day of the Assumption of the Virgin Mary and had two supernatural experiences concerning Mary, both involving in some way a shrine and a statute of her, and as I had related before that after my 8th grade vision/visit with God about the end time, had been seriously contemplating becoming a nun, and that is where the nuns taught me how to make rosaries, which I would do after school to be donated to poor people.

That rosary making stuck with me through the years and between my supernatural experiences with Mary, when I was considering what kind of business I could do from home on the Internet, it seemed natural for me, if not ordained for me to run a rosary business. When Pope John Paul added an additional rosary mystery, the Mysteries of Light, I was interviewed October 17, 2002 by the Los Angeles Times for my opinion about it, because of my rosary business.

Thus, I was a very devoted person to the cause of the winning of the Immaculate Heart of Mary and spreading the devotion of praying the rosary daily, when I had gone to take that picture for my relative getting over a hip injury in February 2011.

At that time I had been still running my one authority website on teaching how to pray the Rosary, even though I had long sold my businesses to others before the death of my husband, when he could no longer help me ship out my orders of handcrafted rosaries, and my own health problems left me unable to single-handedly run the entire business myself.

So when my relative was having a difficult recovery from fracturing her hip region I wanted to petition that statute of which I had had my own miracle a few months before in which I had received a 5-figure settlement unheard of since I was unrepresented by an attorney, and attorneys from my research routinely got a fifth of that from the same hospital which had settled off the records to me on an injury to my late husband.

I was certain I would get a miracle for my relative, but I wanted her to know about it so that her spirits would be lifted. Thus, I ventured that night to do the petition to the parish where the statute was a few miles from my house.

It was approaching 9:30 at night though my camera's clock I always left set to spring Eastern Time an hour later. At that hour, I found no one in sight, but the shrine area was yet accessible, the gate not yet locked, which I was really happy about because I had the whole place to myself to do my petition and could take pictures, too, without feeling I was bothering someone in prayer.

Chapter 8: Unexpected Mary Shrine Demon Photo

I had taken my Minolta Dimage Z1, 3.2-mega-pixels digital camera to take the pictures of the beautiful statute both far and close up so my relative could see the statute, and have her faith strengthened.

When I took the pictures, I just took them, focusing on getting good shots. Then when I got home, I transferred the pictures to my computer hard drive to see what came out.

My plan was to print off with my photograph paper all the pictures that were in focus, and send them all to my relative, so she could look at them and get uplifted.

Altogether I had snapped about 14 pictures, starting with close ups of the statute, and from what I was seeing, the majority looked good. It's when I came to the pictures taken from the distance I had gotten the whim to take as I left the shrine grounds, with the thought for my relative to be able to see the whole of the shrine from a far view, as well as the side where there were a line of statutes of some saints, I was stunned what I saw.

In the wall directly behind the statute, on the right side of the picture, was a huge shadow of a figure with horns looking to the smaller shadow that belonged to the Our Lady of Smile statute.

First I had been surprised I had not noticed that while at the shrine as it was unmistakable in the picture. The reason had to be because the photo dwarfed the scene so I could see what was a shrine around eighteen feet tall at once in a small photo, and so those two shadow figures behind her dominated the picture.

I found the very next photo taken even further back, same thing, a giant demon-shaped shadow positioned next to the shadow of the Our Lady holding baby Jesus, so it looked like it was the force behind her shadow image, looking to her shadow. It was so clearly a demon figure there was no way I was sending those two pictures to my relative as it looked like a demon and I did not want to send her that in case she saw it too, which I didn't see how she could not.

So using the other pictures, the close-up ones, I sent my relatives those and not the two that came out with the giant shadow demon. Since this shrine was across the street from a row of residential houses, I wondered how the people there felt about looking at this giant demon shadow cast on the concave wall of that shrine unless it was something not visible and only freak snaps I had ended with.

I couldn't let it go, I had to go back another night and look.

Sure enough, big as can be, there was the same giant demon shadow, just as I had snapped, but now I was seeing it directly with my eyes. Now I could not help but see it, I guess those photos bringing to my eyes this shape existed.

Chapter 8: Unexpected Mary Shrine Demon Photo

Still, I felt there had to be some kind of logical reason why, even though I still thought it must not be a happy sight for some of the residents to look at, unless the angle of the view, as the shrine was sideways to any houses across the street, and the size of the shrine kept them from seeing that as I had not seen it the few times I had gone there at night as I had been focused on just the statute itself. If it had not been for those pictures and it had just stood out like a sore thumb, maybe I never would have seen what was now an undeniable shadow of a giant demon.

So with that intent, I examined every spotlight putting light on the statute and that back wall, matching up the different shadows, what made this shape, what made that shape. I could find what made the smaller Mary shadow to the left, but I could not find the cause of the large demon giant, what made up his horns, what cast the shadow of its head, nothing, just nothing added up to it. See here an enlarged image of the two rear shadow figures:

Since I can't be with you and point it out as I see it, I thought the next best thing I could do is outline the figures I am seeing for you to compare and see for yourself what I am seeing and if you can also see these images by comparing my outlining to the untouched photos above.

Mind you, in the paperback version of this book the images might not render that great, and may be better seen in an electronic reader with a larger screen resolution or a 10-inch plus tablet or pc screen, these better because you can see the pictures in color as well as higher dpi and larger image sizes. However, all the same, you may see it clearly enough as I was able to see in my proof copy of the paperback edition, even in the black and white lower quality printing.

With the best outline I can do in this next picture, which is still very rough considering I am not good at outlining with a mouse trackball, you can see what I am talking about. It even has a six-pack abs and buff male pectorals, lion cat-like nose, a full beard, and eyes that appear to have intentional evil amusement, its moustache looking like it rests above a cat-who-ate-the-canary smile.

It is a combination of a man-like face in a goat-shaped head, with horns of an ox, a forearm ending in a goat hoof, and a body like an upright humanoid goat, with human-like muscular chest. It is an absolutely amazing phenomenon to have captured in a photo of a Virgin Mary statute. The 'coincidence' of the shadows appearing just as they are, of a demon principality appearing to be the power behind that statute of Mary, is just too extraordinary.

> So they shall no more sacrifice their sacrifices to goat demons, after whom they whore. This shall be a statute forever for them throughout their generations.
> —*Leviticus 17:7, ESV*

What makes this Leviticus Scripture even weirder is that did I not point out to you that giant demon shadow appears to have a goat hoof it is resting its chin on? Is that not even weirder? And if you really look at it, the untouched picture and not the one I have mangled up with my outlining attempts, its face really looks like a goat.

Honestly, it looks like a goat which can stand upright and is wearing a long cloak, and can move its front leg like a person can move their arm. Could it not be that God is actually referring to a type of demon that is really like a goat, and not the form of an idol?

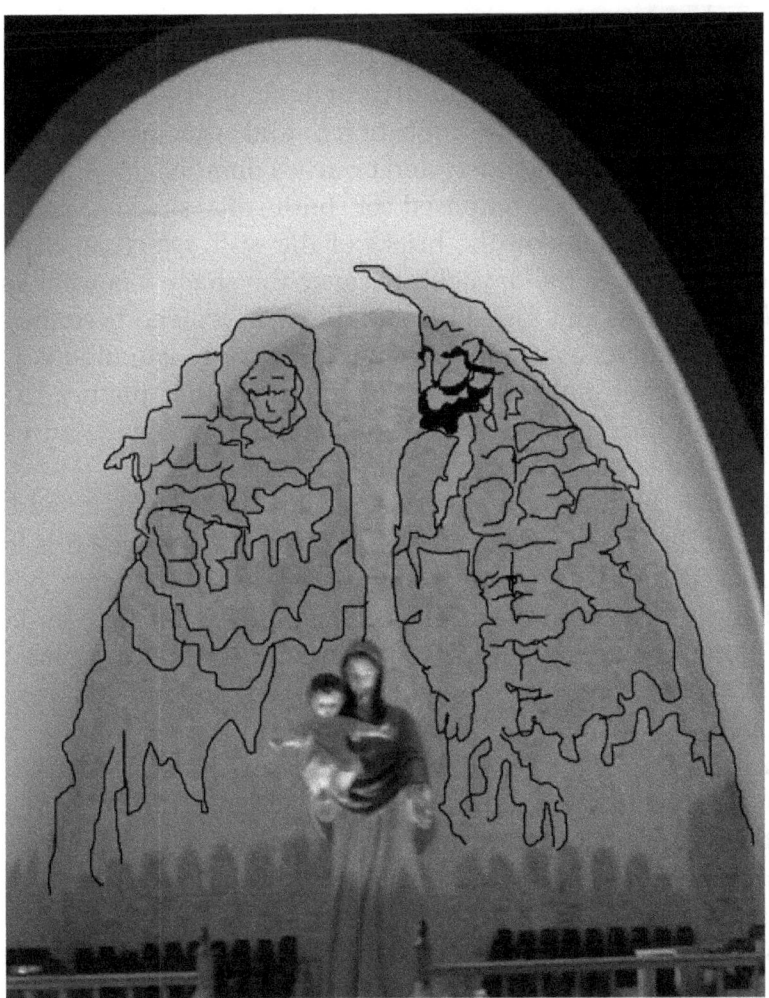

Friend, the coincidences here between the photos I got and the goat demons behind these idols is just too spot on! There is synchronicity, and then there is just weird. This is in the realm of supernatural weird.

And as strange that it coincides with a type of demon

mentioned in the Bible dealing with idolatry, see how it is looking to the direction of the shadow of Mary and the baby to the left, so much as if it is the force behind and serving on the statute's behalf. It really blows my mind because it almost looks like a cartoon because it looks like it was created specifically, a demon character right there, but it is an untouched phenomenon. I have seen other photos where people say they can see a holy image in an object and I have had to strain to make it out, but this one is so specific it is in your face. This is no little light orbs in a picture that you can blow off as spots of dust or reflections, and the photographer's imagination, this is absolutely and clearly a demon.

The imagery is composed of both the shadow and the coloration and stains on the bricks of the wall, which is why you would not see it in the daylight, because the shadow is what casts the demon horns and forms the shoulders, overall body shape and face shape, and its goat-hooved hand. It is simply astounding.

You can see now why I could not send that picture to my relative and how it could eventually lead me to a conviction I had long resisted.

I'd like to interrupt this description a moment to add an update to the above here on 3/23/14: I had not intended this but I was moved today to visit this statute again 3 years later, before finalizing my paperback proof and having it published, as I am near done correcting the mistakes in my proof copy and this affords me an opportunity to stick in any last minute updates like this one.

I hadn't been to this shrine in those 3 years and I thought it might be good to see if things were still the same, if the shrine was still there, and if the same shadows appeared. If so I planned to photograph different angles, including zooming up close, all with the same camera I had used back in 2011.

I found online that the shrine address was still showing it at the same location, which is around 7 miles from my house. As it turned out, having risen at 7 p.m. this evening from trying to get this book proof done in the midst of all of my physical ailments which as I have written earlier means often having to sleep as long as needed to be able to work on the book, which means going to bed 2 to 10 hours later each day, after having a quick 'breakfast' I

Chapter 8: Unexpected Mary Shrine Demon Photo

got there in the last ten minutes before the gates would be locked, just like I had back in 2011. And as before at that late hour, I was the only one there, which left me free to take all the photos I wanted.

To my surprise I found that the statue had received some cosmetic work, and some lighting changes. It was the new lighting that has totally changed what is cast on the back wall. No longer do you see the goat demon principality, because that apparently only showed in the different lighting previously there.

Now there is a new bright spotlight directly behind the statute that entirely lights up the back wall as shown in this next picture.

Shrine in 2014 with redone lighting vanquishing demon on wall
03.23.2014

It makes me wonder if someone did not come to the parish priest and said to him, "Excuse me, Father, but there is a large demon shadow appearing behind the Our Lady statute."

"What do you mean...let me take a look...oh, dear Lord!" He then picked up his cell phone and pressed autodial. "Maggie, this is Father. Please tell Frank the grounds man to put a spotlight behind Our Lady. That demon shadow's back again. Thanks, Maggie...oh, and listen, Maggie, and when he does, have him give her some new paint, she's getting a little faded 'round her veil." He turned back to the complainer. "There, that'll take care of it," he said with a nod, the complainer nodding also in agreement.

In the photos I snapped tonight of the redone statute and lighting, you can see the same stain on the wall near where the lower outer sleeve of the goat demon appeared in my 2011 photo, which I reshow here above so you can conveniently compare it to the new one just before. But now with the new spot light behind the statue, the 2011 shadows my camera captured are not seen.

Before in 2011, the spotlights were coming from the ground in front of the statute's platform, as you can see from the way the

Shrine in 2011 with lighting casting giant demon on the wall

lights hit the wall of the platform the statute stood on. Now in 2014 there is a single bright spotlight you can see behind the statute which now lights the back wall, and makes a bright spot of light behind the statute.

That new single spotlight in the back vanquishes the supernatural drama played out in the photos I took. Whether my pictures in 2011 were of paranormal origin which appeared only to my eyes and my camera's capture, or if they caught a paranormal appearance on that shrine's back wall from the kind of previous lighting used, now gone from the change of lighting, perhaps intentionally changed by the parish because that paranormal effect

Chapter 8: Unexpected Mary Shrine Demon Photo

had caused a disturbing shadow to appear exactly like one of those goat demons God gave a statute against sacrificing to in Leviticus 17:7, I don't have the answers to that.

However, ponder on this: Of all the things the play of shadows could have been, like a funny object like a duck, or a happy face, or even inspirational like an angel, or how about a butterfly, it was none of those benign things you could just shrug off. That it was a goat demon to which there exists a statute by God to no more sacrifice to them, and not just posed in a random position, but one that seemed intentionally to show that demon as the real force behind that statute, with a sinister cat-ate-the-canary expression towards that Mary shadow it was turned to, speaks a million words, ones that should convict.

Because of the late night hour that I captured those pictures, and the late hour that the 2011 shadows would appear, I may have been the only person to capture this paranormal phenomenon on two separate pictures that I still have on my hard drive, pictures which I almost lost in Sept 2013 during enemy warfare I write about in chapter 10 when my main computer died. Maybe these rare paranormal pictures could be one of those things the demon commander I write about in chapter 10 is ballistic against becoming public because it might topple a lot of their strongholds around the world built on this deceit. Time will only tell, as I do not have the perspective right now with the book not yet published as I type this.

That said, back to my description when I was examining the spotlights back in 2011: As I examined them I could not find why if the spotlights were making two shadows of the Virgin, why they were different in size and drastic in shape?

Even if it could be said, one spotlight from one angle gave one figure, and another the other of the same statute, I could not find anything that pointed to the larger one to account for those horns on the demon, nor the shape, or its goat-hooved hand that has been classically attributed as an appendage of the devil. I put my fingers on the spotlights and on the statute to see how they cast on the wall. For those horns going straight out to the sides like horns on a bull, I couldn't match them to anything.

That is when I started to wonder if it was really okay the way I venerated Mary as most good Catholics do. I had never had a big-giant-demon-behind-Mary photo which I had taken myself, a Mary devotee. Sure, I had seen blasphemous literature on Mary by Christians who created anti-Mary propaganda full of hate, which only painted any Mary adoration as something demonic, to me an ignorant view from people who really didn't know what Catholics did when they knelt before a statute which was just to use it as an object of focus to pray easier to the real Mary or the real Jesus. In fact I had felt they went out of the way to make such defaming pictures up as part of their anti-Mary campaigns.

You can believe more than once in my business of selling rosaries, I and the other owners of rosary sites would have to deal with a 'Christian' attacking us with hostile emails full of hate.

But these pictures I had taken out of devotion, so seeing a huge shadow shaped like a demon in those pictures was not a trick of somebody else to convince me praying to Mary is idolatry. I had taken these pictures. They were real pictures, and not tricks. So the impact of seeing that was sobering, and it caused me to stop and think.

I felt the pictures convicting me of the need to finally pay attention to the gargantuan discrepancies between what the Scriptures say and what the Catholic Church claimed about Mary, and the sources for which they drew those claims.

The only information I ever found as a Catholic to uphold Mary's special role as Queen of Heaven, and an intermediary for Jesus was Church-approved apparitions, and Church beliefs created by logical reasoning and not Scriptural facts. This certainly was food for thought because what was my source to depend on? Apparitions and opinions of men.

Same time I had seen Mary as a Girl Scout in 1968, multitudes were having joint visions of Mary appearing in Zeitoun, Egypt. So supernatural apparitions, and the reasoning of men adding different info to the Bible, were what I was to believe.

As the veil was getting lifted from my eyes, I could see there was no other source to attribute that supernatural phenomenon but other than the table of demons as Paul had called it in 1 Corinthians 10:21.

So I started to search what any one Catholic had to say about

Chapter 8: Unexpected Mary Shrine Demon Photo

it, and it led me on April 1st, 2011, a few weeks later to come across the testimony of Mary Ann Collins, the author of *Another Side of Catholicism: Insights from a Former Catholic Nun*.

I was open to what she said because she was not the typical hostile anti-Mary person, but she wrote coming from a place of a former Catholic nun, sharing her own soul searching if Mary adoration was a form of worship like worshipping God, arising from the clashes she had encountered with that form of adoration and what she knew to be true in the Bible.

From her I learned about this Scripture in the New Testament where Jesus corrected those trying to honor his mother:

> And it came to pass, as he spake these things, a certain woman of the company lifted up her voice, and said unto him, Blessed is the womb that bare thee, and the paps which thou hast sucked. But he said, Yea rather, blessed are they that hear the word of God, and keep it.
> —*Luke 11:27-28, KJV*

Even if the demon shadow was just an eerie fluke which someone more diligent than I could find that source to explain the large horned demon, these photos to me were a wake up call for me to not ignore what Jesus was saying here. He is the Son of God, he should know whether Mary was held above all women, all humans, and held a special blessing. And he did know, and he gave that answer which was no. Then he proceeded to say who were the really blessed, and it was the ones who obeyed God, and not the ones who gave birth to the Son of God.

In addition I always had the firm belief before that event that when I prayed before any statute of Mary it was just like praying before a photo, as a symbolic representation. I had been sure that was what I had been doing, and not idolatry as someone might say.

So if Verse 28 in Luke shows Jesus did react in such a way, it didn't make sense to me how it could be the will of Jesus his mother is worshipped as some Marian apparitions were teaching.

That made me determined to scour the whole Bible and find out what more the Bible had to say. So two days later I bought the complete audio Bible of the Word of Promise, with seventy-nine CDs, and I started to listen.

Then I came across the passages in the Old Testament that God considered it sin to go through the motions even bowing before an idol, even by those considered his people, and that it wasn't a heart issue, that it was the act itself which he considered disloyalty to him and sin (Numbers 25). It didn't matter the people might have been going through the motions for cultural reasons; it was flat out sin to the Lord that demanded the full sentence of death.

Anyone who would've even suggested such a thing to me that my praying to Mary was idolatry, I would've strongly disagreed with, not seeing it that way at all, feeling I was just honoring what Jesus wanted for his mother to share glory with her because he just wanted to out of his soft heart for her, as a loving son has for his mother. Yet I wasn't finding anywhere where Jesus had special plans for his mother.

Not only that I had thought giving adoration to Mary was Jesus will, but I could see from what I was finding in the Bible, it certainly was not his will to elevate his mother with glory and adore her.

On top of that I found there were certainly no verses backing up that Mary was born of an Immaculate Conception.

But I *was* finding Scriptures countering this such as here.

...for all have sinned and fall short of the glory of God
—*Rom 3:23, ESV*

If the Bible says all have sinned, then that 'all' had to include Mary as well, and so it was not possible she was born from an immaculate conception as that would call the Bible untrue. The Scriptures declaration that all have sinned and fall short of God's glory came over eighteen hundred years before Pope Pius IX proclaimed the dogma concerning Mary's immaculate conception. That would make the pope's proclamation in 1854 an addendum to the Bible, an *addition*, which the Bible relates is false doctrine and making that particular pope a false apostle.

Chapter 8: Unexpected Mary Shrine Demon Photo

> Now the Spirit expressly says that in latter times some will depart from the faith, giving heed to deceiving spirits and doctrines of demons, speaking lies in hypocrisy, having their own conscience seared with a hot iron, forbidding to marry, and commanding to abstain from foods which God created to be received with thanksgiving by those who believe and know the truth.
> — *1 Timothy 4:1-3, NKJV*

For a long period I had thought that whatever the Catholic Church authorities decided on earth, was agreed in heaven, like Matthew 16 said, making their proclamations God approved as a result, not that anyone had taught me that, but because that was the only Scripture that made sense to me why things that the popes said that were not in the Bible, were accepted by God in heaven.

> I will give you the keys of the Kingdom of heaven; what you prohibit on earth will be prohibited in heaven, and what you permit on earth will be permitted in heaven.
> —*Matthew 16:19, GNT*

I found that listening to the audio Bible let me pick up on things I never could before as clear as watching it happen live, that reading alone could never do for me.

After having heard an actor speak all of God's words since Genesis on his strong anger with idols, I heard for what seemed the first time for me, God's anger with the people in the cities of Judah and the streets of Jerusalem offering cakes to an idol that was considered by them the Queen of Heaven.

> The children gather wood, and the fathers kindle the fire, and the women knead the dough, to make cakes to the queen of heaven, and to offer libations to strange gods, and to provoke me to anger.
> —*Jeremiah 7:18, RHE*

That it provoked God to anger the people worked to make cakes to the queen of heaven, made clear there was no queen in heaven and it was idolatry.

In addition, nowhere in the future Scriptures was this prophesized a real queen of heaven would reign one day totally God approved and God recognized, but on the other hand the deity of Jesus was prophesized in the Old Testament.

> I will proclaim the decree of the LORD: He said to me, You are my Son; today I have become your Father.
> —*Psalm 2:7, NIV*

> The Lord says to my lord: Sit at my right hand until I make your enemies a footstool for your feet.
> —*Psalm 110:1, NIV*

In the Old Testament Mary was indeed referred to, but as a virgin who gives birth to the Messiah, and not as some queen.

> Therefore the Lord himself shall give you a sign. Behold a virgin shall conceive, and bear a son and his name shall be called Emmanuel.
> —*Isaiah 7:14, RHE*

> Behold a virgin shall be with child, and bring forth a son, and they shall call his name Emmanuel, which being interpreted is, God with us.
> —*Matthew 1:23, RHE*

In addition, God specified utterly clear he was a jealous God; he clearly did not take to sharing his glory or reign with any idol.

> Do not worship any other god, for the LORD, whose name is Jealous, is a jealous God.
> —*Exodus 34:14, RHE*

Statutes of the Virgin Mary are by sheer definition graven images, graven meaning no more than something that is carved or sculpted. Because those statutes are something graven, they meet

Chapter 8: Unexpected Mary Shrine Demon Photo

the definition what graven is. You take away all the religiosity and any statute of Mary is by definition a graven/sculpted/carved image of an artist's idea of Mary. You kneel, bow or pray before it, you are counted by God as going against his command not to do that action.

So this Scripture here hits that with a double whammy.

> I the Lord, this is my name: I will not give my glory to another, nor my praise to graven things.
> —Isaiah 42:8, RHE

Mary was just a young virgin girl married to Joseph from the lineage of King David. Never was any sort of particular wisdom attributed to her, nor any sort of special or unusual characteristics such as had been attributed to Ruth in the Old Testament who was exalted for showing admirable loyalty to her mother-in-law (Ruth 1:16). However, Mary had found favor with God to be the one to bear Jesus.

> And he came to her and said, "Greetings, O favored one, the Lord is with you!" But she was greatly troubled at the saying, and tried to discern what sort of greeting this might be. And the angel said to her, "Do not be afraid, Mary, for you have found favor with God. And behold, you will conceive in your womb and bear a son, and you shall call his name Jesus."
> —Luke 1:28-31, ESV

But beyond that announcement by Gabriel that she had found favor to be the one to conceive Jesus, all the marvels Gabriel described following that were about the merits of Jesus, how he would be the Son of God, how he would reign, and how he would be holy. Mary even acknowledged her servant status with her final words in reply to Gabriel.

> He will be great and will be called the Son of the Most High. And the Lord God will give to him the throne of his

father David, and he will reign over the house of Jacob forever, and of his kingdom there will be no end. ... And the angel answered her, The Holy Spirit will come upon you, and the power of the Most High will overshadow you; therefore the child to be born will be called holy—the Son of God. ... And Mary said, "Behold, I am the servant of the Lord; let it be to me according to your word." And the angel departed from her.
—Luke 1:32-38, ESV

In the Bible Mary had not been the only one to find favor with God, Moses also God had said had found favor with him.

Moses said to the LORD, "See, you say to me, 'Bring up this people,' but you have not let me know whom you will send with me. Yet you have said, 'I know you by name, and you have also found favor in my sight.'"
—Exodus 33:12, ESV

Did that make Moses then a mediator for God after his death? Did this favor then get Moses a special ascension into heaven? Not even. In fact not at all, he died as a normal person does, and in a way that was a punishment so he would be blocked from seeing the Promised Land, because he had failed one time to follow God's command to only tell a rock to give water, but instead had struck the rock twice to get water flowing for the people (Numbers 20:12). And no matter how much Moses had begged God to please change his mind on that punishment, God had refused, so that favor did not mean he had a limitless blessing that had made him more than a man.

Then I pleaded with the Lord at that time, saying: 'O Lord God, You have begun to show Your servant Your greatness and Your mighty hand, for what god is there in heaven or on earth who can do anything like Your works and Your mighty deeds? I pray, let me cross over and see the good land beyond the Jordan, those pleasant mountains, and Lebanon.' But the Lord was angry with

Chapter 8: Unexpected Mary Shrine Demon Photo

me on your account, and would not listen to me. So the Lord said to me: 'Enough of that! Speak no more to Me of this matter.'
—Deuteronomy 3:23-26, NKJV

So if that favor had not elevated Moses in any special way more than a man to be seated and crowned next to God as a co-mediator and intercessor on prayer, why would the favor Mary had received to bear Jesus in her womb, result in a favor more than just the way that Gabriel described it, which was given the role to conceive and give birth to Jesus, and co-parent along with Joseph.

Because if Mary's womb had remained special beyond that Jesus would not have denied that as he did when in Luke 11:27 a woman out of the crowd shouted to him:

Blessed is the womb that bore you (NIV)

To which he disagreed in Luke 11:28 when he said:

Blessed rather are those who hear the word of God and obey it (NIV)

The word 'rather' which means 'more properly, or correctly speaking', that more correctly speaking, more truly, is that blessed are those who hear the word of God AND obey it, not hearing it alone, but ALSO obeying it.

That word choice of 'rather' then indicating Mary did not remain after she gave birth to Jesus, blessed among all women, did not retain that special blessing or obtain holiness, as the surrounding ground that the burning bush God spoke to Moses from did become holy as well as the incense censers which the 250 men in Korah's rebellion offered, had turned holy from the offering to God.

> And when the Lord saw that he went forward to see, he called to him out of the midst of the bush and said: "Moses, Moses." And he answered: "Here I am." And he said:, "Come not nigh hither, put off the shoes from thy

feet; for the place, whereon thou standest, is holy ground."

—Exodus 3:4-5, RHE

And a fire coming out from the Lord, destroyed the two hundred and fifty men that offered the incense. And the Lord spoke to Moses, saying: "Command Eleazar the son of Aaron the priest to take up the censers that lie in the burning, and to scatter the fire of one side and the other: because they are sanctified."

—Numbers 16:35-37, RHE

Notice that their offerings turned holy, and not the men holding them, who were burnt alive. Like Aaron's sons, Nadab and Abiu, who were burnt alive in the same manner from the wrath of God shooting out as a fire that consumed them before the Israelites in that they were not totally burned away, but their carcasses remained, so had the 250 left behind burnt carcasses.

And Nadab and Abiu, the sons of Aaron, taking their censers, put fire therein, and incense on it, offering before the Lord strange fire: which was not commanded them. And fire coming out from the Lord destroyed them: and they died before the Lord... And Moses called Misael and Elisaphan, the sons of Oziel, the uncle of Aaron, and said to them: "Go and take away your brethren from before the sanctuary, and carry them without the camp." And they went forthwith and took them as they lay, vested with linen tunicks, and cast them forth, as had been commanded them.

—Leviticus 10: 1-5, RHE

Yet it was only the offered censers which became holy as being given as offerings to God, and not any portion whatsoever of the physical bodies of those men.

Jesus was the offering being given to God in a process that would take 33 years to complete.

Chapter 8: Unexpected Mary Shrine Demon Photo

> ...Christ, our Passover lamb, has been sacrificed.
> —*1 Corinthians 5:7b, NIV*

Only the offering Mary carried was the holy object, and not her physical body, nor was her personage in any way elevated from that process to holy by God. As you can see from what happened with Aaron's sons and the 250 men, only the objects in offering to God or declared holy by God had been turned holy. In addition, Jesus denied Mary retaining a special blessing as a result of having born him in Luke 11:28.

Scripture shows as well in 2 Samuel that physical contact itself with something containing God does not turn someone holy, does not protect the person, does not transfer any thing good to them or special power to them, even if what they are doing is good and noble, like carrying a baby to term as Mary had.

> And when they came to the floor of Nachon, Oza put forth his hand to the ark of God, and took hold of it: because the oxen kicked and made it lean aside. And the indignation of the Lord was enkindled against Oza, and he struck him for his rashness: and he died there before the ark of God.
> —*2 Samuel 6:6-7, RHE*

We see instead that poor Oza, or Uzzah as other Bible translations call him, died beside the ark from the anger kindled from God at the error he would receive special recognition by that act from God, at least enough to be safe and be in God's favor, in order to keep the ark from falling. But, no, Oza was given nothing special from that contact, and instead, stayed in God's eyes a normal man with not even a shred of praise or glory that only belongs to God.

If such physical contact transferred holiness then that man's touch would have been accepted by God, but it was immediately rejected. Thus Mary's prolonged contact with Jesus, the fetus, did nothing to transfer his deity to her.

Yet, all the same, all this does not have to be said, because what Jesus said about anyone who hears God's word and obeys it being more blessed in Luke 11: 28, is enough. That would be a paperboy who fully follows God's word is more blessed than Mary, a pizza delivery guy who fully follows God's word is more blessed than Mary, and a dishwasher in a dead-end job who wholeheartedly obeys God's word is more blessed than Mary, per the Son of God, who was her real son by physical birth.

If you still have to seek the opinion of someone else to confirm to you if what Jesus said is true or not, you have to take a moment in order to realize just what you are doing: You are putting the opinion of a human if Jesus is saying what is true or not, over Jesus. Thus if the person tells you no, and you accept that as true, you are then counting Jesus as a liar.

It would show you are suffering from brain-washing of obedience to the wrong source: the authority of human institution over the authority of God. If you can't believe the word of God, you have a faith problem.

While you are a human being is the good time to discover you are having a faith problem because this is the only time the problem can be corrected and your prognosis for full recovery excellent. Rather than letting the enemy overwhelm you with excessive despair (2 Corinthians 2:7) to be dragged down that way, it is instead a time in rejoicing in God's mercy extended to you yet, and get your faith level back up to full strength to "all the counsel of God" (Acts 20:27 RHE).

The Catholic Bible, which is the Douay-Rheims Bible, abbreviated as RHE, says it:

> And the base things of the world and the things that are contemptible, hath God chosen: and things that are not, that he might bring to nought things that are: That no flesh should glory in his sight. ... That, as it is written: He that glorieth may glory in the Lord.
> —*1 Corinthians 1:28-31, RHE*

As God's word does not return void, and stands, I couldn't turn from the fact, she too, would be counted in that crowd of no man, no person.

Chapter 8: Unexpected Mary Shrine Demon Photo

Coming across all these Biblical truths, and reading what Paul wrote about offering sacrifices is only offering to a demon, and seeing, even if purely coincidental the spitting image of a demonic principality ruler as the power behind that particular statue, at that point I didn't need to see anymore in order to stop rebelling and let the Lord convict me through all those Scriptures I had come across which said the same thing that those photos did, that bowing a knee to any statute, praying to it, leaving donations to it, written prayers to it, was doing so not to God, but to demons.

I got it finally that exactly what God said is *exactly* how it is: we are not to bow or kneel to any likeness to anything that is in heaven, that God will not share his glory with any man, that Jesus denies his mother more blessed than people who obey God, that Jesus does not recognize his mother more important than a committed true follower, that God has wrath against setting up a queen in heaven he did not ordain, that the real Mary would be more pleased we are strictly obeying Jesus and God, and would not be grieved, if she were the true Mary, his *true* earth mother, as she would only be in full commitment to the will of God...unlike a demon who would react with rage twofold, that you are no longer falling for their deceit, that you are slipping out of their clutches as you close your ears to their lies and hear what God is saying, only acknowledging that as true.

Thus it really became unimportant whether that shadow form was really what it seemed or a tremendous coincidence when the conviction hit me, knowing demons are real, having had the encounters that I have had with demonic principalities. What mattered was it is literally a symbolic portrayal of what you are doing according to Scriptures, when you pray before any likeness of anything that is in heaven, including departed relatives or famous religious persons. You are doing so to a demon force behind that carved image or likeness and that is sin, guilty of breaking the 2nd Commandment of God.

> Thou shalt not make to thyself a graven thing, nor the likeness of any thing that is in heaven above, or in the earth beneath, nor of those things that are in the waters under the earth. Thou shalt not adore them, nor serve

them: I am the Lord thy God, mighty, jealous, visiting the iniquity of the fathers upon the children, unto the third and fourth generation of them that hate me: And shewing mercy unto thousands to them that love me, and keep my commandments.
—*Exodus 20:4-6, RHE*

Twice I had gotten 'miracle' results from coming to that shrine and praying to the statute, offering money in the donation box, putting my written petition. Having to face when it was made known to me the wrong I did, not by some person, but by the passages in the Bible, I could see I was going through classic offering to demons by what God had said himself of whoring after demons.

You can be guilty of unintentionally doing idolatry and still have to pay the price; it is very much like breaking a local traffic law you didn't realize you did, yet all the same held accountable to that wrong and being legally held to make good on the resulting ticket, with no wiggle room, that traffic law being final.

If anyone of the common people sins unintentionally in doing any one of the things that by the LORD's commandments ought not to be done, and realizes his guilt, or the sin which he has committed is made known to him, he shall bring for his offering a goat, a female without blemish, for his sin which he has committed.
—*Leviticus 4:27-28, ESV*

Even then, because of the big 'miracles' I had gotten from that, it was hard to resist the lure to come to that shrine to get help on my troubles. I was sure I would indeed get whatever new help I needed, but this time I knew it would be by the hand of a demon and not God. When I resisted, hostile troubles increased to me as if a striking out by the enemy for not coming back to them, resisting this deceit.

I had to be wiser than the people in the cities of Judah giving cakes to the Queen of Heaven that when their 'blessings' dried up when they had stopped upholding that demon source, they rejected God's word, and ran back to the arms of their Queen, only wanting the 'blessings' back, first of all rejecting God's forgiveness of their prior sin, and selling their souls for the earthly blessings they got, turning their back to God to their destruction.

> Then all the men that knew that their wives <u>sacrificed to **other gods**</u>: and all the women of whom there stood by a great multitude, and all the people of them that dwelt in the land of Egypt in Phatures, answered Jeremias, saying: "As for the word which thou hast spoken to us in the name of the Lord, we will not hearken to thee: But <u>we will certainly</u> do every word that shall proceed out of our own mouth, to <u>sacrifice to the **queen of heaven**</u>, and to pour out drink offerings to her, as we and our fathers have done, our kings, and our princes in the cities of Juda, and in the streets of Jerusalem: and we were filled with bread, and it was well with us, and we saw no evil. **But since we left off to offer sacrifice to the queen of heaven**, and to pour out frank offerings to her, **we have wanted all things**, and have been consumed by the sword, and by famine."
>
> —*Jeremiah 44:15-18 RHE*

> And Jeremias said to all the people and to all the women: "Hear ye the word of the Lord, all Juda, you that dwell in the land of Egypt: Thus saith the Lord of hosts the God of Israel, saying: 'You and your wives have spoken with your mouth, and fulfilled with your hands, saying: Let us perform our vows which we have made, to offer sacrifice to the queen of heaven, and to pour out drink offerings to her: you have fulfilled your vows, and have performed them indeed. Therefore hear ye the word of the Lord, all Juda, you that dwell in the land of Egypt: Behold I have sworn by my great name, saith the Lord: that my name shall no more be named in the mouth of any man of Juda, in the land of Egypt, saying: The Lord God liveth. Behold I will watch over them for evil, and not for good: and all the men of Juda that are in the land of Egypt, shall be

consumed, by the sword, and by famine, till there be an end of them.'
>—*Jeremiah 44:24-27, RHE*

There is nothing in the Bible to back up Mary worship or Mary intermediary but there is plenty in the Bible to back up such acts incur God's wrath. This kind of addition to the salvation plan of Jesus is what is called a false doctrine in the Scriptures and an error.

> But there were also false prophets among the people, even as there shall be among you lying teachers who shall bring in sects of perdition and deny the Lord who bought them: bringing upon themselves swift destruction. And many shall follow their riotousness, through whom the way of truth shall be evil spoken of.
>—*2 Peter 2:1-2, RHE*

Does this not sound like the way Christianity is being spoken evil of because of the recent years child abuse scandals in the Catholic Church?

> While they promise them liberty, they themselves are slaves of corruption; for by whom a person is overcome, by him also he is brought into bondage. For if, after they have escaped the pollutions of the world through the knowledge of the Lord and Savior Jesus Christ, they are again entangled in them and overcome, the latter end is worse for them than the beginning. For it would have been better for them not to have known the way of righteousness, than having known it, to turn from the holy commandment delivered to them.
>—*2 Peter 2:19-21, ESV*

See to it that no one takes you captive by philosophy and empty deceit, according to human tradition, according to the elemental spirits of the world, and not according to Christ.

—Colossians 2:8, ESV

Do you know when you practice doctrinal error you give a legal right to demons to you?

Essentially a demonic legal right is when you sin this gives demons the right to harass you or cause you trouble and stay with you. Even though it sounds weird, it is actually Scriptural.

> Afterwards, Jesus findeth him in the temple and saith to him: Behold thou art made whole: sin no more, lest some worse thing happen to thee.
> *—John 5:14, RHE*

The 'worse' that Jesus is inferring is sickness or possession from a demon as a result of that sin, and as you see, getting delivered from that demonic affliction and then you go back to it, a worse demonic problem can happen to you as this Scripture shows here that if one demon is sent out of you and it can come back, it may bring along worse demons than itself to set up house in you.

> Then he goeth, and taketh with him seven other spirits more wicked than himself, and they enter in and dwell there: and the last state of that man is made worse than the first. So shall it be also to this wicked generation.
> *—Matthew 12:45, RHE*

It begins when the enemy tempts you to think something wrong, like Mary shares the glory with Christ for redeeming mankind because she 'renounced her mother's rights' as Pope Benedict XV (1914-1922) wrote, and that she is trusted with the prayers and praises of God's children because she knows humans, having been one as Catechism of the Catholic Church says in Paragraph 2675.

These are two wrong things to think, wrong because they breach God's commandments which is to have no other gods before God, which is what you are making Mary as if you share Christ's glory with her, as no man shares in God's glory, and elevating her to Jesus' role as Scripture says God gave Jesus the authority and power to pass the judgment because having been son of a human, he is aptly equipped to both have the total understanding of the human condition, and pass just judgment. Jesus experience as a Son of man is enough and he does not need the services of another human's experience to be trusted with the prayers and praises of God's children, which really is a blasphemous stance.

> For as the Father hath life in himself, so he hath given to the Son also to have life in himself. And he hath given him power to do judgment, because he is the Son of man.
> —*John 5:26-27, RHE*

> Neither is there salvation in any other. For there is no other name under heaven given to men, whereby we must be saved.
> —*Acts 4:12, RHE*

> Therefore I said to you that you shall die in your sins. For if you believe not that I am he, you shall die in your sin.
> —*John 8:24, RHE*

> Jesus said to him, I am the way, and the truth, and the life. <u>No one</u> comes to the Father <u>except through **me**</u>.
> —*John 14:6, ESV*

When you accept this idea and make it a habit to go through Mary to get to God, a door opens for the enemy to bother you or stay with you even when you cast them out, which is what demonic legal rights are. Consequently, behind this wrong habit can lay a demonic influence that is hard to resist.

Due to such demonic legal rights, there is no wonder all the controversy with the morale behavior of many priests in recent years. Can you not see the pattern, that with error that leads to destruction, doorways are open to demons to lead you there? It can happen to anybody in any branch of the body of Christ and, thus, is not a Catholic-only problem.

When I had been utterly convicted and saw my error, I had to spring-clean my house, get it right with the Lord, and do as God commanded, clear out all the idols. It was hard because it was like burying a loved one, but as the Old Testament showed, as long as someone held onto an idol object, God's curses stayed, his wrath stayed. In addition, I had to terminate my website teaching the rosary as I was incurring responsibility for leading people to that same error of using Mary as the go-between to Jesus.

I know many people will find it hard to no longer pray a devotion that defined their lives. To help in that transition, I received Holy Spirit inspiration on the only rosary one could pray in full line with the Scriptures, and urge such a person to substitute the Hail Mary for this scripturally acceptable prayer instead:

Hail Jesus

HAIL JESUS, full of glory
You are the Lord
Blessed are you above all creation
Blessed are you Slain Lamb God resurrected, Jesus
Holy Jesus, Son of God
Pray for us sinners,
Now and at the hour of our death,
Amen

As you can see, it is a line per line following the Hail Mary, but with the proper turn that gives Jesus his full glory and petitions him directly for the prayer.

I call this the True Rosary, because it is the only way to say those familiar rosary prayers giving true focus to Jesus, no go-between.

> Jesus saith to him: I am the way, and the truth, and the life. No man cometh to the Father, but by me.
> —*John 14:6, RHE*

In the True Rosary, you pray the normal Apostles' Creed, Our

Father, and Glory Be where they normally are said, but in place of the Hail Mary, pray the Hail Jesus instead. And you can either fully drop the Hail, Holy Queen prayer at the end, which deifies Mary, resisting the beloved traditions of men over the things of God, which is Scriptural error, or pray the Hail, Holy King, a version I made which gives all the glory to Jesus, yet contains all the words you are familiar with, to give a match per word match of the rosary to the True Rosary.

Hail, Holy King

HAIL, HOLY KING, our Seat of Mercy, our life, our sweetness and our hope! To thee do we cry, poor banished children of Eve; to thee do we send up our sighs, mourning and weeping in this vale of tears. Turn then, most gracious advocate, thine eyes of mercy toward us, and after this our exile, manifest to us, blessed firstfruits from the tomb, Jesus. O clement, O loving, O sweet Jesus Christ!
V. Pray for us, O Holy Son of God.
R. That we may be made worthy of God's promises in Christ.
Let us pray. O GOD, whose only begotten Son, by His life, death, and resurrection, has purchased for us the rewards of eternal life, grant, we beseech Thee, that meditating upon these mysteries of the Most Holy Rosary of the Blessed Jesus Christ, we may imitate what they contain and obtain what they promise, through the same Christ Our Lord. Amen.

I challenge you to pray the rosary with the Hail Jesus and the Hail, Holy King and watch if your life is not transformed by lifting the proper praise and prayer to the proper source. I also challenge you to use your beads just as they were originally intended: as a string abacus just to count, and not as an object to revere, a form of idolatry.
I challenge you as well that when you go to Church to not bow, or give petitions to, or light candles to any statute or image. I challenge you when prayers to Mary might be lifted to not pray along, but pray inwardly instead to Jesus. I say this realizing you may be so heavily ingrained into attending a particular church,

you may find it too difficult to part with such a church which may put unscriptural focus on Mary, and for that is why I put those challenges concerning when you go to church should you yet insist on remaining part of that parish.

Yet not all Catholics do bend a knee or uplift Mary in adoration, or petition, or acknowledge the Saints as intermediaries. However, do be wise such continued affiliation can be a snare to anyone if they are not careful to stand against and not partake in any unscriptural worship or prayer. That is one of the strongest tools the enemy uses: likeability, the likeability of a person, the likeability of a place or organization.

> They shall not dwell in your land, lest they make you sin against Me. For if you serve their gods, it will surely be a snare to you.
> —*Exodus 23:33, NKJV*

> ...Thy eye shall not spare them, neither shalt thou serve their gods, lest they be thy ruin.
> —*Deuteronomy 7:16, RHE*

In addition, I challenge you to lift your prayer to the Lord directly, no object before you, so your prayer is in Spirit as the Father seeks. I also urge you to do your own housecleaning and get rid of all statutes you have knelt before, or bowed to or just prayed to no matter what you rationalize, making sure to repent to Jesus.

If you find you cannot stop lifting Mary over Jesus, then you need to come to Jesus for aid against this resistance, this rebellion, and repent and confess this sin to the Lord, asking him to wash it with his precious blood, sanctifying you. You have to know the real Mary would be delighted the true glory is shining on her son, both in praise and petition.

> While he was still speaking to the people, behold, his mother and his brothers stood outside, asking to speak to him. But he replied to the man who told him, "**Who is my mother**, and who are my brothers**?**" And stretching out his hand toward his disciples, he said, "Here are my

mother and my brothers! For **whoever does the will of my Father in heaven is my** brother and sister and **mother**."

—Matthew 12:46-50, ESV

***

Chapter 9

WHEN PEOPLE TURN INTO DEMON PAWNS

> The man who had the evil spirit in him attacked them with such violence that he overpowered them all. They ran away from his house, wounded and with their clothes torn off.
>
> —*Acts 19:16, GNT*

This chapter is to equip you with the understanding demons can take control of people and make them do things to try to block God's will for your life, cause you tremendous grief, and if possible, hurt you severely. As you see the consequences are extreme already, which is the hallmark of demon handiwork.

When you gain the knowledge this really happens you will have the right perspective to deal with warfare attacks on you from the enemy using this method straight out of an end-world movie where people are turning into demons to take down people, and keep them from making it to heaven.

Not all these attacks involve physical violence, but they do involve an unreasonable reaction in some measure against you as if it involves a vendetta to stop you. What is even trickier about this is good Christians can turn into demon pawns momentarily if they choose to obey Satan's influence at that time.

As Satan is the Father of Lies, he can masterfully cloak something to appear righteous in a way, an assault which can only be defeated by keeping scriptural knowledge forefront to know if that impulse is with God's will or against it.

Because the warfare is so devious, these wicked strategies can pass over anyone's head, which is why anyone at times may unwittingly find themselves delivering Satan's work, as Peter did per my favorite Scripture I like to use on such an example because we all know Peter was not evil, yet here he was serving as the enemy's mouthpiece to his own ignorance.

> Then Peter took Him aside and began to rebuke Him, saying, "Far be it from You, Lord; this shall not happen to You!" But He turned and said to Peter, "Get behind Me, Satan! You are an offense to Me, for you are not mindful of the things of God, but the things of men."
> —*Matthew 16:22-23, NKJV*

I say this so you do not fall into the sin of judgment against anyone who turns into a demon pawn, whether temporarily or ongoing, as we battle against unseen principalities with honed skills of influence that can seem from within us, but which are enemy sent. Anyone is at risk to be used by the enemy if they fail to resist the enemy's influence.

People being used by the devil, and people doing the devil's work, actually happens. First of all you have to understand that the demonic principalities really are real, and they really are warring against us. I pray that at this time of this book, you have come to be convinced the world of the demonic is true, because otherwise you are operating at a huge, huge dangerous disadvantage.

Fortunately for you, I pray, I happened to have a tremendously eye-opening experience that demons can use people and they can make them into their pawns, ordinary people, on the fly, which indicates the demonic is monitoring you as you go about your every move.

While I have had many experiences with demon pawns since this one I am about to tell you, this one is the one where God revealed to me the process so I could see with my own eyes the demonic behind it, and know for certain it wasn't my opinion but an actual event, as somebody else would go through that confrontation with the pawn on my behalf, two people whom before this event, I didn't even know, which were the person fighting against the scheme and the person who was the demon pawn.

From this I got my rock-solid lesson about the demon pawn

process which has served me through my life in recognizing such situations and acting accordingly, knowing from firsthand experience there are times these confounding hostile attitudes from people to you are really due to demons and not your paranoia someone is out to get you because they don't like your looks.

You may live long enough to encounter such a situation or situations where a person is treating you in a way that is hell bent; you can only describe it as hell bent. And there is no foundation and there is no reason why they are acting so erratic.

I actually gave an example in the first chapter of this book from the nurse who went ballistic, out of character for her profession and age, using profanity and everything from keeping me from being born. While her behavior meets the criteria of a human demon pawn, I was a baby and I did not see the process.

But this example I am giving, was when I was an adult and I actually received the experience in this case to have my spiritual eyes open for the first time to witness the demonic principality behind it. I mean I didn't feel my spiritual eyes open, however, I know my spiritual eyes were opened because I could see this supernatural occurrence as if it was part of the same reality, one with that human turned demon pawn, an event I had never seen before.

The phenomenon I saw with my eyes was just a few minutes, but the events that followed with that person gave the revelation what I had seen, though I had not understood the phenomenon until over 2 decades later through formal Biblical study and revelations through those studies.

So let me start.

September 12th, 1982

On this warm, sunny day in Miami, Florida, I rode off in my rusted, faded-green 1972 Chevy Impala hardtop sedan to buy a male Shetland Sheepdog. I wanted this puppy to be a companion to my female Sheltie, China.

There was one small problem, though. I only had fifty dollars and the two places advertising puppies sold theirs from $150 to $175! I worked part-time then as a processing clerk in Miami

Children's Hospital and didn't make that much money, a little over $6 an hour, working less than 20 hours a week. I had a plan, however.

I bought along one of my contracts from Dog World Magazine created just to purchase a dog on time payments, which I had made available as an option for the people who had bought puppies I had offered for sale couple years back from my late Doberman pet. I hoped that I could make a deal with one of the two sellers to let me purchase a puppy with fifty dollars down and monthly payments of $50.

As I drove with all windows rolled down because there was no air conditioner in my car, I prayed one of them would say yes. It was my only way to get a much-needed companion for poor China, who was suffering trauma from my separation from my ex, moving me into my mother's house and away from her other two dog pals.

I went to the breeders in South Dade first, a husband and wife. They lived in the Perrine/Homestead area in a middle class neighborhood, in a ranch-style house. The wife greeted me at the door. I stepped into the house which led almost immediately to the kitchen. From there I could see the living room to the left.

The husband, a little bit gruff, came in, leading the puppies. They were huge! They almost looked like collie puppies. China's father was a champion and she was the proper height. Whichever puppy I got from here would dwarf her. These were clearly puppy mill producers—people who were only concerned with putting out a lot of puppies without caring about the quality, if they conformed to the breed. All the same, beggars can't be choosy.

I presented my offer to the couple. The man became upset and refused. His behavior seemed to embarrass the woman. I asked if I could use their phone. It was a long drive to the other breeders and I wanted to be sure they were there. I used the phone in their kitchen while they listened.

I thanked them and then went to my car as the husband followed me out, standing on the porch watching me, as a courtesy I thought.

Then a peculiar thing happened that I thought only happened in movies.

As I started my car and looked over at the man his eyes

Chapter 9: When People Turn Into Demon Pawns

glowed a malicious yellow.

An actual sick yellow light emanated and filled his eyes, so all I saw was this evil light.

I didn't know what to make of that.

It was broad daylight outside and I was outdoors in the hot sun, in the Homestead area, it can't get sunnier than that.

It must have been around 1 o'clock in the afternoon, clear sky, I am in my car, and there are no trees around and the man standing outside his ranch-style house, so to see a light shine, you turn a flashlight on in the bright afternoon, a lot of times you can't even see the light because the brightness of the day drowns it out.

It has to get a little to evening to even see the light in the bright sun. Bright sunlight cancels out light of flashlight bulbs the size of his eyes.

In addition, he was not that far from me, his property in a regular residential area in Florida, where it was a modest size block, where the yard might have about 25 feet from the front door to the street where my car was parked.

My car was sideways in the street to the house that when I started the car I just turned my head to the right to look at the guy when I was met with a scene right out of a *Transformers* movie where these strong beams of lights are in the man's eyes, strong enough beams of yellow light that I could see them like bright lights in his eyes. In fact there was no pupil, no white of his eyes; there were no eyes even that I could see.

It was all yellow light filling his eyes that were in place of his eyes, and not in the size of his eyes, but went out in beams like a special effects move.

I didn't know then that yellow is considered the color of evil. I didn't know anything like that as I witnessed a malicious yellow light beaming from his eyes.

If I had a little flashlight in the broad daylight it would not have the power to shine like that as the Florida sun kills the light being able to show.

Only in night can you see the beams of light coming out but not in the broad daylight. So this had to be some kind of light that not only filled his whole eyes, but it also, emanated out like a character in a special effects movie so all I saw was evil.

The light was evil. I could see it was evil, yellow by and of itself is not evil, but that light, and that yellow color to it, I knew somehow was evil. So I didn't know what that meant. I was like in my mind thinking wow... I never saw that and I had no idea what that meant.

Soon, however, I would learn what that evil light was about as the man turned before my eyes into the first demon pawn I laid my eyes on, the veil ripped from my eyes to see the manifestation of the demon that took him over through the appearance of the evil malicious light filling his eyes, which would lead him to go through a deep evil deed and attempt to in extreme measures to try to thwart me to get a dog. It was an amazing thing.

When it was over, it was the first time I had seen that and what I saw was followed by an evil demonic plot and scheme that this fellow tried to do.

I could see when I was in that house there was something about that guy that made the wife act like she felt humiliated by him, like there was some kind of verbal abuse and he was a guy that was abusive.

So I can see now that this fellow had made a legal right the demons could take over from his anger, his rage, and who knows what else there was there. I am not sure, but I dimly recollect him holding a can of a beer of some kind and there could have been an alcohol addiction also giving a legal right, but I witnessed a man at that instant taken over by a demon.

My eyes were opened to see this so I could then have the understanding why this man was going to behave in an evil scheme against me.

> My dear children, you belong to God and have defeated them; because God's Spirit, who is in you, is greater than the devil, who is in the world.
> —*1 John 4:4, NCV*

> We have not received this world's spirit; instead, we have received the Spirit sent by God, so that we may know all that God has given us.
> —*1 Corinthians 2:12, GNT*

Chapter 9: When People Turn Into Demon Pawns

In fact this scheme was such an outrage to the person whose home I went to next that the person ended up going out of the way to try to get that man in jail.

After a 20-plus mile drive from there, I got to the next breeders, a woman named Linda in the NW area of Miami. Here was another husband and wife, but this couple was pleasant and warm. The tiny puppy they brought out for me to see in their small apartment conformed perfectly to the breed. I was delighted.

They told me he was the runt of the litter. I found him beautiful and charming. Here I went again, presenting my offer. But, to my joy, they happily agreed to my terms. I left ecstatic with the beautiful little puppy I named Chinling, which is the tallest mountain in China, what I'd hope he would become for China, her tallest mountain.

The picture here of him as a puppy I took that very day of the event, same afternoon I saw that man's eyes light up with evil yellow light.

Chinling (5½ weeks old) 1st day home with China (1 year and 8 months old).

Then a strange thing happened. To my surprise, the lady I

purchased little Chinling from called me at my house that night, having gotten my phone number off the contract I had given her.

She called to confess to me how the guy I had gone to see before I had come to her house had called her as I was on the way from his house to hers.

He had identified himself as Mr. Burke from the American Kennel Club. He said he was warning her about a woman traveling about town with a scam to steal purebred puppies. She carried a time payment contract with her and would pretend to make a contract and disappear with the animals. He said she had stolen many puppies that way.

Well the woman told me she worked as a police dispatcher and she traced his address in the classified on puppies to the breeder's house using a Bresslers book.

When she'd called his house it was the same man's voice that had just telephoned her. She'd talked with her husband and they decided to judge for themselves what kind of person I was. She said the moment she saw me she knew the man had been lying.

She later called him after I left and told him she worked for the police department and she would file charges against him for fraud and lying.

A few weeks later she wrote me a letter telling me she had called the American Kennel Club to see what could be done about this mean man misrepresenting himself as a representative of the AKC.

But after she wrote a four page letter to the AKC her husband advised her they didn't really have any proof other than his voice being identified over the phone and that he might try to sue them for liable. But she had wished for concrete evidence, because she had wanted to see this guy hung for being such a creep.

Why did this man, a literal complete stranger to me, want to deny me from getting a puppy?

Some people are just creeps, like the lady I had bought Chinling from had said. But when I think back at how important a part Chinling played in my life, I know there was another reason, one that has to do with the warfare we are in.

So why would a demon influence a person so far just to keep someone from getting a puppy? Many times Chinling was the only reason I wanted to live, because I was going through very difficult times. When he was alive he gave me critical joy and companionship.

Because of that I have come to believe the demonic behind the evil glow out of that guy's eyes wanted to prevent me from having such a lifesaving companion.

Me and my darling Chinling

This man had let Satan fill his heart to invent a vicious lie to stop me from getting my wonderful Chinling who over the years would bring both China and me so much delight.

> But Peter said, "Ananias, why has Satan filled your heart to lie to the Holy Spirit and to keep back for yourself part of the proceeds of the land?"
>
> —*Acts 5:3, ESV*

Now these sorts of things happen a lot. For the most part we cannot see when these demons take over the people, such as Judas at the Last Supper, when Satan entered him that possession did not result in visible physical signs to show Satan within him---yet, this was known by Jesus, as this was understood to have happened by the very Scripture that describes this as what happened to Judas.

Maybe Jesus alone saw Satan enter Judas at that time, perhaps even seeing Judas' eyes fill at the possession with a malicious evil light as Satan was successfully in control.

We do not know, and I am speculating on this because the very moment that Satan entered Judas is specified and perhaps it was so noted because the Lord had seen the visible manifestation of Satan's possession of Judas same as I had seen the visible manifestation of that man's possession by a demonic force.

> Jesus answered, "It is he to whom I will give this morsel of bread when I have dipped it." So when he had dipped the morsel, he gave it to Judas, the son of Simon Iscariot. Then after he had taken the morsel, Satan entered into him. Jesus said to him, "What you are going to do, do quickly."
>
> —*John 14:26-27, ESV*

When the people who have these legal entryways into them are taken over by the demons to do their evil schemes against you, whatever it is, they will go out of the way to try to fulfill their scheme against you, fueled by demonic fury to attempt to thwart God's will for you.

The thing to know about this is there are 3 types of human demon pawns:

Chapter 9: When People Turn Into Demon Pawns

1) A Peter case where you don't necessarily have a legal entry by the demon but you are enticed/influenced by their bait and you jump on it and you temporarily do work for the devil, and not even being evil at the time, you don't even realize that what you said or did is a plot of the devil and fell for it. If you resist that you would not do it, you will not have a temporary entry way like Peter.

2) Then there are those who have an open legal entry and they are used at will to carry out schemes of the enemy and they don't change forms from human, they are still human beings, but somewhere along the road they have some unrepented sin, and a legal entry and a big one too, where they can be taken complete control over by the enemy and used to follow through something that if they were able to step back and think, they would question, What am I doing, why am I acting like this, why am I going crazy about this person, why am I so upset about it, why am I doing this to them? But they are too much in the grip of the demonic power they cannot fight it. They think it is all them and they do not know they are a pawn of the enemy.

3) The third type of demon pawn you may run into is the willing pawns of the enemy. They are actually in satanic matters and they willingly of their own choice, work out devious plans of their master and you can find these kinds of people, the willing demon pawns in every single place people can be. A lot of them are in power positions by this time of history; the enemy has been seeding their own kind. More than you would realize, there a lot of them are in very top positions and they control a lot of things.

So how do you know when you are facing any of these three types of demon pawns?

Whenever you run into a situation that seems purely evil, purely demonic, defies understanding, is just sheer evil, that is a hallmark that the person is a demon pawn and has come under the control of the enemy to do confounding things to steal, kill and destroy, that is the fundamental enemy agenda.

Whether the person is temporarily influenced, or used routinely without their knowledge by the enemy, or a direct

Satanist who is consciously working things for the dark kingdom of their master, sometimes you can tell, but a lot of the times you are left scratching your head if that is what happened to you with that mean person.

For any of those it is good to lift a prayer to the Lord to help set them free from the devil's snare, even the willing satanic workers because they also are victims. These people think they are getting special concessions when they get to the afterlife, but they are going to be met with an evil booby trap instead.

> Maybe they will come to their senses. Maybe they will escape the devil's trap. He has taken them prisoner to do what he wanted.
> —2 Timothy 2:26, NIRV

In the second type of demon pawn who is unaware they are under control by the enemy, sometimes in instances like mine, you can actually see the case when the enemy actually enters the person and you have the visible signs to your eyes and you can see it, then you have no doubt.

When you can see something like that be aware that that party is going to attempt some kind of enemy scheme to cause you harm.

If asked about the why behind that person's hostility to you, the person being controlled will have no reason to give you which makes sense for such schemes or reactions, just lame explanations that do not make sense for such behavior.

If you see such a thing just be alert that that party is meeting a scheme of a demon to you if you are their target, and know this is a spiritual warfare against you where regular human reasoning and interactions will fail.

That I even came to know about the details on this one was unusual itself which is what leads me to think it was for my edification for thirty-three years later, when it would serve a purpose through this book I would write concerning overcoming enemy schemes to make it to heaven.

It was unusual I came to know the details because both people did not know me at both ends, but the Holy Spirit moved this woman to telephone me personally afterwards to actually reveal

Chapter 9: When People Turn Into Demon Pawns

the whole thing to me and that is how I came to know this.

So if you happen to see such a manifestation of evil on someone's face that is clearly of supernatural origin, how do you handle it?

Before I answer that, I must tell you years later I saw a different manifestation of such a possession on another person's face, this one my late husband, which did not involve seeing a malicious light, but this time involved my seeing momentarily his face morph into a monster's face visible to me for about 3 seconds as the monster face glared back at me in rage-filled hate.

I believe my husband had been folding his clothes in the bedroom, it was mid afternoon, and I had come in to hand him something, I don't remember what.

He seemed grumpy and I said something to him like, "How about a smile?" and he turned and gave me a hideous smile, full of hate, showing his teeth, excessive viciousness I had never seen and he had never done anything like that, very uncalled for, and when that viciousness came on his face, his facial expression became a monster's face for about three seconds.

I am talking real monster, not symbolic, but as seen on the back cover of this book in the facial features becoming a demon monster's face.

Having all the experience with supernatural and demonic trouble I have had, I mentally registered his face turned into a monster's face, I saw the monster in his face, I took note of it, didn't know what to make of it, but I certainly was not going to let that monster realize I clearly saw it.

I did not like that it had happen, because to put it mildly that is not a good sign when a monster demon shows itself on the face of someone you know.

Still the only way to handle something like that when you confront it in a family member, or anyone you are alone with, is with a poker face, as you don't fan the flame so to say, because the demonic does not respond to anything with peace. Joy, peace and good come from the Spirit of the Lord, but anger, discord and evil only come from the enemy.

As you can see by the fashion by which my husband showed he had turned into a pawn of a demon, that demonic possession can manifest itself appears to be as varied as the demons behind each of the schemes.

Of course I had hoped that was to be the start and end of it, but no. Soon I would come to know the demonic scheme, and find myself saved only by the grace of God.

In this second case, I was to soon learn why I saw that monster face because he plotted to kill me shortly after, by putting shards of glass into my breakfast cereal of oats which I by habit would prepare the night before and put in the refrigerator, as these were oats I would get at a natural food market's in Plantation, Florida, out of their open bin where a customer could scoop out the portion he/she wanted.

When it happened I had thought somehow broken glass had found its way innocently into their mix, and called the store the minute I found the shards in my cereal I had served myself to eat.

In fact when I had glimpsed the thick sharp pieces of clear glass same size as the oats in my cereal bowl, only by the Holy Spirit's prompting, first thing that came out of my mouth is, "The devil is trying to kill me. Yay! I must be going to do something for God!"

I was kind of thrilled and pleased as punch with that realization part, because usually if the demonic tries to off you it can be because you are or are going to be trouble to their kingdom. Of course, I was thrilled with that part, not the getting nearly killed part but I was delighted I might end up actually doing something worth it for God, enough the devil wanted to do me in.

If the devil might find it trouble enough then that would mean that work might really have value to God by God's standard and that possibility made me glad, as up to that point I didn't see that I was accomplishing anything that would make the devil find me a threat. I was just making rosaries, not much of a deal there, or else all rosary makers would be on demon hit lists which they were not. At the time I was in my rosary business and far from any of these developments now in my life.

Well, after the store manager did a thorough search of that oat bin with me on the phone as I totally took the pieces of glass out and put them in a Zip-Lock bag, very concerned themselves, and could find no evidence, my husband, who had been sitting across

Chapter 9: When People Turn Into Demon Pawns

from me at the breakfast table, whom I had seen that monster appear on his face the day before, said, "You probably are going to think I tried to kill you."

To which I said, "No I don't." And I didn't think so, even though I had seen that monster on his face to which I had said nothing to him about when I had seen it.

Well, God takes care of his own servants, whether they are in good standing with him at the time or not if there are purposes yet for them, as later on that day as I went into his office moved to get something I can't remember now, not very important and not routine, something caught my eye at the bottom of the 2-gallon waste basket next to his desk.

What did I see? Broken shards of glass, exact match as in my cereal.

There was absolutely no mistaking that glass. It amazed me that it would even be there sitting for me to see if my eyes came that way. I believe that was the Holy Spirit who led me to come into the room then while the trash was not taken out and have me go where my eyes would fall on the inside of the little can, which I did not ordinarily go doing as he had his office and I had mine, and I certainly didn't care what he threw into his trash can.

He was the one who emptied all trash cans, so apparently he had felt no need to rush and dispose the evidence.

I guess a lot of people would have called the police on their spouse, but I had seen that monster appear on his face, and I knew it was a demon and I had seen that demon hate, not knowing what to make of it, but aware it showed itself to me. I am sure that demon did not plan on revealing itself to me, but God had opened my spiritual eyes to see that.

I didn't have any impulse to call the police even though I knew as I looked at the glass that is what people would have considered the 'right' thing to do.

All these things raced through my mind, the consequences of calling the police, that that was what such evidence called for. I was sad, not mad, that he could be influenced such a way to attempt what would have been a very painful death. I guess the demonic reasoning was it was glass and it would not show digested.

All I did was take out a couple of pieces and leave the rest so it would be as he expected and not raise his suspicions that I knew if maybe he could not handle that I knew and be moved worse by the demonic. Those pieces I saved with the others I had put in that bag. And if he tried it again, then I would have to think about going to the police.

To me it was two wrongs don't make a right. I didn't want to see our relationship over. If he went to jail both our lives would be destroyed. He would be publicly shamed and there would be no going back.

It was like if the devil did not succeed in killing me physically, he would see if he could set off a reaction in me that would lead to the destruction of my life another way. So what I did is I kept mum to my husband that I had seen the glass in his trash can, and he never, ever knew all the years we remained married until his death.

He passed on never with the knowledge my eyes had seen that glass in his office trash can. He never knew I had kept some pieces of it hidden in a drawer all those years.

I knew that monster was behind it, and now I knew what the plan of that monster had been.

What I did do was step up the prayers for my husband, as I already had to say protection prayers around him because since right at the time we got married, I learned why his first wife waited for him to fall asleep for many years before she passed on, because he had developed a condition which he described as hypnopompic hallucinations where as he fell asleep (which would be more accurately called hypnagogic as they occurred as he fell asleep or shortly after), or soon after, he would see around his bed visions, some dreamlike such as animals.

One of those times as a reaction he had struck out to hit one, and by accident slugged his sleeping first wife. From that point on she had waited for him to be asleep for some time before coming to the bed herself.

After learning about his condition, I, myself, believed he was having them for a reason other than what he thought, which he thought was due to eating prepared meats like sausage. However, I believed the true source was demonic because of the nature of this

Chapter 9: When People Turn Into Demon Pawns

one 'hallucination' which would repeat itself, and the others would not.

The first time he had described it to me, I had thought, Oh my gosh, demons, but had said nothing of that to him. This one alone would come back, consistently reoccurring same way every time. This is what he described it as: he would see every time small hooded beings in robes, faces not visible covered in blackness. They stood around his bed, side by side, watching him, though he could not see their faces, he knew they were looking at him, just looking.

I can tell you the moment he told me about this routine 'hypnopompic' experience, which he brushed off with the 'scientific' medical reason he attributed them to, I knew, coming from my experiences of the demonic, I was highly concerned what he was seeing were demons who had a legal right to him and were attached to him.

I didn't want to tell him that, because I didn't want to frighten him, and I didn't want him to feel doomed demons were waiting to take him to hell, and I never told him that, but just dealt with this warfare on him privately in my prayers for him which I lifted to God.

My hunch seemed confirmed that as I prayed for him secretly, then stretches of time would happen without him having any of those 'hypnopompic' hallucinations as he called them, those hooded demon-like dark figures would not appear in his room, nor would he get any kind of those 'hypnopompic' experiences.

I refrained from telling him that so he would not get scared or alarmed that it appeared he was awaited upon by a demonic group. I never told him that the times he had periods of no such experience correlated with my prayers and quiet warfare. I did not want to fill him with a spirit of fear and open him to further things. I especially did not want him to have even the slightest idea that I got a spiritual impression they seemed to be demons waiting for his soul and having some kind of ownership to him.

As I have seen supernatural manifestation jointly with other people, the hypnopompic and hypnagogic hallucination theories just do not explain away the supernatural, and are not the sole reasons people see things any time surrounding sleep, or wake time, though the secular world wants to box them that way. There are a lot of gray areas these terms just can't account for, especially when two or more people witness the same thing without any kind of planted suggestion, or any substance involved which can trigger any such hallucinations, nor in poor lightning, but in broad daylight. The point I am trying to drive is the supernatural is real and the enemy wants you to think otherwise so you stay a good little victim coming along with them to hell.

For instance while living with my ex whom I write about in chapter 4, one such experience is where I woke to find hovering over me about three feet above me, a life-size image of my husband sitting cross-legged in a meditative posture, not upright, but face down to cover my whole body protectively. His form was not solid like a physical body, but hologram is the best explanation. I woke my husband right up, who was next to me, the image disappearing then, telling him what I just saw.

He smiled at that, getting up and walking around the bed to my side of the bed, to which he pulled out something from under the mattress where I lay. It was a hand-drawn pentagram on leather he had made earlier that day just for the purpose to protect me.

What he was trying to protect me from were the troubling spirits I complained to him I was getting bothered by in that room when he left to work. His smile had been because he was pleased to get proof his occult magic was working, interpreting that image of himself over me as a result of his pentagram and protective incantations.

What he had done had been unknown to me, and I certainly did not feel a little flat piece of soft leather he had tucked underneath my side of the mattress. This is just one example that hypnopompic hallucination explanation can't account for, as it was a supernatural reality of a spiritual manifestation.

What that actual form of his really was is unknown to me, but that it was invoked through an occult pentagram and sorcery, scripturally the Bible says it is due to a demon, making my husband's incantations being given to a demon ready to respond to such requests. And why? To get ownership to him in the end, through all the sins they got him to do involving the occult. For a while sin appears good, then one day one has to pay.

From my own experiences then, I know that every ghostly figure or apparition you see is not solely medical reasons as the devil wants you to buy so you brush off the supernatural, which is brushing off the whole demonic principality Jesus warned about, so you dismiss the spiritual truths against them in the Bible, put there to protect you from the wiles of the devil so believers can resist and make it to heaven.

Bishop Earthquake Kelly writes about in his book *BOUND to LOSE DESTINED to WIN* demons that frequented around him as he grew up who revealed when he got to hell that he was now their property, an ownership they got for his falling for their lies. In my husband's case, because I didn't want those demons to win, I did what I could to pray for his protection although I did not have the knowledge I have now to do that warfare. Yet I never saw that demonic monster on his face again, and never got served another glass pie à la mode again.

I believed his 'hallucinations' were due to his great interest in ghosts which had led him to travel the country when he had retired just to visit places where ghosts were said to frequent not because he was into the occult, but because he had pursued tales of the dead for writing purposes, publishing many macabre horror poems, as well as working on writing fiction for children involving witchcraft, which I was helping him with.

As a sidebar I can tell you, it doesn't matter why or how you dabble with the occult, whether as a practitioner or as story teller, the trouble all is the same you get. In this case, by chasing after ghosts, and putting energy into writing macabre poetry, working on a witchcraft series, my late husband did not know he was breaking God's command to not contact the dead, have nothing to do with witchcraft, nor deal with the occult in any way.

By his fervent interest and pursuits of that, he left this big gaping legal right to him, which could allow down the road, a hate monster demon to take him over to get him to serve me chopped glass in my breakfast cereal.

> There shall not be found among you anyone ... who practices witchcraft, or a soothsayer, or one who

interprets omens, or a sorcerer, or one who conjures spells, or a medium, or a spiritist, or one who calls up the dead. For all who do these things are an abomination to the Lord, and because of these abominations the Lord your God drives them out from before you.
—*Deuteronomy 18:10-12, NKJV*

That was the only time something like that happened because I stepped the prayers up, now on the alert of the situation, having seen its origin. That possession was so different than the loving man I would see, one who did a lot of things before and after to help me to live and played a pivotal role in my life.

But not many people get the opportunity to see the demonic force behind the evil schemes that birth themselves in either strangers or people you know. So they only believe the offending party is acting fully on their own and can take it to heart personally against that person. But sometimes these same people are the victims of the demonic which through an earlier sin have left open a portal to the demonic to use them at will.

It explains in a lot of cases why somebody who never did anything hostile in any shape or form suddenly goes over the edge and acts totally out of character and commits an irretrievable demonic evil.

When and if you do spot such a manifestation of a person turning into a demon pawn, do not approach them. Do not go back to them if it is someone you can walk away from as in a business transaction or service.

If it is a loved one, be on guard you are the intended target of a hostile enemy attempt. If you sleep in the same house, I would barricade your door at night, I would watch your back, and most importantly I would never let the enemy know you are on to them, as this could lead to an outright attack with you alone and no help around.

In addition, you need to get active in spiritual warfare by taking this in prayer, daily to God in Jesus name, to get rid of the enemy, keep you safe, and deliver your loved one. Spiritual warfare is real, and in such a case you could count your friend or family member as under the control by the demonic realm, and act

Chapter 9: When People Turn Into Demon Pawns

accordingly, never confronting the party with this information as that person is under an active possession and not in their right mind, never letting the enemy know you are on to their control of that person.

What you need to do is you need to pray, prayer is the step to do. First you need to confess any sins and ask Jesus to wash them clean with his blood and sanctify you, and close all legal entryways. You need to cover yourself in the blood of Jesus.

> And they have defeated him because of the blood of the Lamb...
> —*Revelation 12:11, NLT*

> ...the blood of Jesus Christ His Son cleanses us from all sin
> —*1 John 1:7, NKJV*

You need to put on the armor of the Lord.

> Put on the whole armor of God, that you may be able to stand against the wiles of the devil...take up the whole armor of God, that you may be able to withstand in the evil day, and having done all, to stand. Stand therefore, having girded your waist with truth, having put on the breastplate of righteousness, and having shod your feet with the preparation of the gospel of peace; above all, taking the shield of faith with which you will be able to quench all the fiery darts of the wicked one. And take the helmet of salvation, and the sword of the Spirit, which is the word of God; praying always with all prayer and supplication in the Spirit, being watchful to this end with all perseverance and supplication for all the saints-
> —*Ephesians 6:11-18, NKJV*

Then you need to rebuke the enemy in the Name of Jesus, order them to leave your loved one, leave your house, and never return by the power and authority of the Name of Jesus, by his might, his shed blood, not any merit of yours, but his mighty holy power. You command the devil in the name of Jesus to leave and not return. And then you thank God for banishing the enemy from your lives, bestowing on you the gifts Jesus purchased for you at the cross. As you see, it is not by your might, not by your works, but by the Spirit of God that you get rid of the demons.

> But if it is by the Spirit of God that I cast out demons, then the kingdom of God has come upon you.
> —*Matthew 12:28, ESV*

You continue rebuking the enemy like this each day until you receive total victory and the enemy departs.

> After Jesus had gone indoors, his disciples asked him privately, "Why couldn't we drive it out?" He replied, "This kind can come out only by prayer."
> —*Mark 9:28-29, NIV*

That is a crucial part of the warfare: the persistence to continue in your prayer for as many weeks or months or even years it takes to get your victory. This is actually normal, as banishing some demonic strongholds takes continuous coming against that demonic force with the very same commands and the very same lifting in thanks to God for that victory, BEFORE you see that victory, as that is where your faith comes to play.

> Beloved, think it not strange concerning the fiery trial which is to try you, as though some strange thing happened unto you:
> —*1 Peter 4:12, KJV*

The faith you hold is that it is in the Lord's timing when he will answer your prayer. If you give up before that timing, you will not get the deliverance you need. Not because of the Lord, but because of your failure to stand in faith.

In brief I can give you an illustration about that with a little lump that appeared on my long-haired standard Dachshund right after he got his 3-year Rabies vaccine 5 months ago. It was one-

Chapter 9: When People Turn Into Demon Pawns

inch in diameter and in his right 'arm pit', if that is what you call that area of a dog.

I could grasp it, it was like a little football, that did not hurt him, and could have been a fatty tumor or otherwise. Being on disability and food stamps, I had $0 to get him any veterinarian examination, still paying off an old veterinarian bill on another dog, from two years ago, having no access to any credit out there for vets bills. So Veterinarian Jesus was the only one I had to turn to.

In addition, when my husband was alive and we could afford all the right care for our dogs, including insurance coverage on each, when a precious dog of mine did get diagnosed with cancer, all the treatments did was cause him more suffering and fear, not able to save him from the cancer he had, nor improve his life's quality, although we paid thousands of dollars trying. From that I had learned I could do all the right things by the world, and still not save my dog, which helped me to not feel deprived at least this time that I could not afford vet care, because I knew already it is all God's call in the end.

Thus, knowing this takes continual prayer, I began the process, but being in the front-line of this warfare, my energy to attack it is not optimal. Thus, I was just lifting it in prayer once a day, briefly. I would talk right to the lump, commanding it in Jesus' name to leave my dog, leave the house, and not come back, but not calling it a tumor, but the source of the curse of that lump.

There was no change at all for the 1st couple of months, but I knew that was how it might work. And even worse, my energy to put into it, got sparser as I juggled working on this book, and dealing with increasing enemy hits to me. A couple of weeks ago, however, I noticed it had reduced ¾ in size, and I could feel, like a spiritual sense, that it was on its way out. I know it is a matter of time before it is all gone.

Did I stop my prayers then when I saw the shrinkage? No, I know to continue praying against it and commanding it and thanking God in Jesus name each time, until it has fully disappeared.

Same principle goes for rebuking any demonic principality controlling someone. When you understand what is 'normal' in effort to overcome demonic problems like these, you will not get prematurely discouraged, and you will systematically keep coming against the enemy until victory is achieved, confident you have victory already through Christ.

> But thanks be to God! He gives us the victory through our Lord Jesus Christ. Therefore, my dear brothers, stand firm. Let nothing move you.
> —*1 Corinthians 15:56-58 NIV*

> I can do all things through Christ who strengthens me.
> —*Philippians 4:13, NKJV*

Then you need to also assess if you have any unrepented sin as you need to close that right up, because sometimes that can give the enemy the right to harass you through one of their pawns. I have a lot of reasons then because I was living in the normal sins of the world, finding acceptable and entertaining any reading material or movie or television show on any occult subject, although I viewed myself as a Christian.

That was one way that I was open to this sort of thing, but you do not have to be in any kind of sin, because when Satan took over Judas Jesus was not in any sin. Satan wanted to first of all finish off his human booty he'd long ago gotten ownership to, which was Judas, and then get more chances to tempt Jesus to work against his father, God.

The point is you need to immediately take spiritual warfare by bringing in the big guns and the big guns are lifting this up to God in the throne room, before you make another move. You can pray with your mind from the core of your heart (your spirit) as you leave the area.

> For if I pray in a tongue, my spirit prays, but my mind is unfruitful. So what shall I do? I will pray with my spirit, but I will also pray with my mind; I will sing with my spirit, but I will also sing with my mind.
> —*1 Corinthians 14:14-15, NIV*

Chapter 9: When People Turn Into Demon Pawns

While you are leaving, without trying to draw attention to yourself, keep a watch on that person as you don't know what they might try to do, you don't know what the devil has for them to do. It could be a scheme that involves defaming you. Or it could be a physical harm to you. You have to watch that person while they are in your line of sight, and then when they are out of your sight, and you are gone, you still have to be aware, if you get any kind of problem, that that party may be behind it.

So you have to be very careful how you handle that situation because you may not have a revelation of it as I got on mine. You need to also guard yourself against sinning by holding anger or unforgiveness to the pawn so Satan doesn't snare you that way.

I want to take a moment to use this incident in my life to touch on how we are called to forgive and just what that means by God's measure.

When I saw that glass in my cereal and then in his garbage can, I had added the shards from his can to the pieces of glass I had gotten out of my cereal to the same plastic Ziploc bag, both matches. I wrote in permanent black marker on that clear bag that he had tried to kill me with that and the date, stating pieces had come from his office garbage can.

I had also told this to my mother when it had happened, so someone at least would be aware if something did happen to me later on, this had taken place. And then I had hid that bag in a dresser drawer where he would never find it, though I did know it was there. I looked at it every few years considering what happened, and it became almost a souvenir of almost being killed by somebody close to you.

After my husband had died, one day, though, as I was going through my spiritual house-cleaning of standing right with the Lord, I felt an inner prompting that it was essential I throw away that bag, even though I held no ill will to my late husband over it, and had never mentioned to him I had found the matching shards in his office trash can, in fact never spoke of the matter again, and had continued on as usual as if it never took place.

Yet even though I thought that was enough, I understood that just by the act of holding on to that bag, I was still holding something against him, and had not really forgiven him in full. I can tell you since I really need to have God's full forgiveness myself, and any other mercy points God has out there, because I am convinced my standards are corrupt compared to the holy Lord, I knew I had to be obedient to that prompting, no matter what I thought otherwise, and throw it out.

I knew when I had thrown it out, only then I had been marked as having forgiven him. I say this so you see an example from my life, where according to the world I was justified to hold onto something that was justifiable to hold onto, even with neutrality as I had felt, just as a souvenir of an unbelievable event, and so it would be understandable to continue holding that object, and that memory about such an incident.

Yet, God's measure is not the world's measure and in order to get the forgiveness we all need from God, we have to purge from ourselves offenses by others against us or be held accountable to the sin of unforgiveness. It is not just saying or thinking you forgive, you have to let go of everything.

Yes there are definitely times where it is normal to feel trespassed, offended and harmed by another, yet we have to entirely forgive in order to get God's forgiveness.

If you have access to a computer, I would suggest you watch the free version of Ian McCormack story 'A Glimpse of Eternity' which is available to watch through various video places like youtube.com or at his site aglimpseofeternity.org as his God encounter of this issue in that film holds a great example of how God holds us all to forgive others no matter how deep the offense. I had not seen his story at the time of my conviction, I was to see it later, that along with Daniel Ekechukwu, a Nigerian Pastor taken to hell on account of one unforgiveness most people would find acceptable, both whom were the inspiration behind my writing my song 'My Unforgiving Heart Is Right'.

My Unforgiving Heart Is Right
Lyrics and Music by Vivian Gendernalik

I've faced ruthless scorn from cold hearts
I've faced evil hate bent to rip me apart
And anyone knowing the harm done would testify

Chapter 9: When People Turn Into Demon Pawns

My unforgiving heart is justified

I've faced cruelty that'd make you cry
From callous people not caring if I die
Abuse in all its various ugly forms
An unforgiving heart is the norm

God I know you will treat me
With the same mercy as I have on others
You forgive me if I forgive from my heart
You refuse to cancel my debt if I believe
My unforgiving heart is right

I want my outrage unremitting
And not budge from staying unforgiving
But Jesus made clear my unforgiving heart is right
If hell is my goal for eternal life

God I know you will treat me
With the same mercy as I have on others
You forgive me if I forgive from my heart
You refuse to cancel my debt if I believe
My unforgiving heart is right

My unforgiving heart is right
If hell is my goal for eternal life

© 2013 Vivian Gendernalik -- All Rights Reserved.

  Back to the subject of demon pawns: Not all encounters with demon pawns are life-threatening or even very long, time wise. However, they can pop up in situations where whatever they do acts like an insurmountable block to you, and there is no reason behind it. Again, the goal the enemy tries to do is stack on you straw after straw after straw of this little grief, that little grief, at all times with the goal to see if any will break your will, and lead to your destruction, whether to get you to commit suicide or go on a rampage that lands you in jail. The person doesn't have to be visibly hostile; they are just dead set against you to a passionate level that defies reasoning for that time they are dealing with you.

April 2012

Another demon pawn incidence typical of such pawn encounters you can run into, I had was with a business I hired a couple years ago. The party whom I will call a secretary for the sake of telling this story, having just gotten my file sent to the office he was in from their satellite office I had signed up in, right off behaved bizarrely upset about me to me on my scheduled introductory call, snapping and short-tempered.

Four days later, not to my surprise as I had recognized the behavior as a possible hallmark of a potential pawn situation, that same secretary had managed to convince the owner to have me dumped as a client on some idea the secretary said was my motive for being a client, which my own statements given on my new client sheet proved otherwise, if the owner had taken a moment to read what I had written as my need for hiring him. This was without the secretary having even met me in person as I signed up with the business long-distance through another party, or having asked me if his 'idea' was right or not.

Instead the employee presented this to the owner as 'fact' and stood in his office while he telephoned me to let me know based on the secretary's statement of my motive and not my intake sheet, that he could not handle me.

Once the owner had stated the reason why, because of some false belief the secretary had presented to him, and I, surprised, informed him this was not so, and even told him about my statement on the intake sheet. The owner, seeing my sheet, then had apologized that there had been a mistake and that indeed he could help me.

However, at that time of my life, I well understood how the enemy uses people they have legal rights to through some loophole of unrepented sin, to recognize from the secretary's exaggerated short-tempered behavior to me, a stranger, what was going on and I performed all the steps given here, lifting it to the throne room of God, because when you have to do business with a place where

Chapter 9: When People Turn Into Demon Pawns

someone can be 'switched on' by the enemy to target you, particularly if you are a 'militant' Christian soldier who takes fighting the enemy seriously, you will be on the receiving end of many such schemes out of the blue, uncharacteristic for that business, except when you, the enemy's hated target, come to that place.

Why? The motive will always be to rob, kill, steal, or destroy or all the same time whatever your need is from that business or relationship. The enemy plays dirty so go in with your spiritual coveralls at all time, expecting that dirt and you will be ready to take the slings of dirt, expect them, deal with them in Christ, and to the fury of the enemy, get your business done all the same, because in Jesus you have victory.

As I stated in the steps, I made sure not to confront the party in any way because rationalization does not work when the enemy is driving them to fill a dirty plan against you. Instead, I lifted that person up to the throne room of God for help to that party to close that legal right, but again in private and in care for that party, as we are called not to judge or we risk being judged.

I could tell by this person's outlandish reactions to me he didn't even know me, just briefly on the phone, I knew that he had some kind of legal right that the enemy could enter into him to try to use him to block help I needed and to act with irrational, the key flag for a demon pawn, responses to me, saying strange things I never did, always getting bent out of shape in just the two weeks I was a client, long distance, never having gone to their office at any time, and then plotting to get me out of there.

See the weird part? Plotted, yes, against a stranger he never met, getting irrationally enraged, without justification, in other words, getting hell bent against me, literally. That was exactly one year I had gotten the conviction from the Bible concerning that giant shadow of a demon behind the Our Lady of the Smile statute. So it was known in the spiritual realm my eyes were being opened about this deception and investigating all the other ways the Scriptures say the enemy is deceiving us.

For certain the demonic realm was red-hot enraged. So why it may have seemed random, the enemy had stepped up warfare against me as I was, unknown to me, going to be writing in 6 months Christian music on standing against the enemy and resisting sins, and a year later, writing this book about overcoming enemy schemes to make it to heaven, subjects I am sure are not high on the devil's Like list.

I knew that the help I was going to get from that business was crucial to my surviving at the time, and unknown to me, crucial to do God's work because if I had not gotten that help, I wouldn't have written the songs for the kingdom and I would not have written this book because I would not have been in the space and place to do it.

So you see now a pattern...hot-button encounters that can rob, steal and destroy on all kinds of levels, levels that can derail you from heaven if you let the enemy move you that way, which is to react in a way that makes you commit a sin that disqualifies you from heaven.

In the case of that business, I knew from his uncalled-for rage at me, the way he contrived a lie to have me dropped and stood in the room to listen to the owner's call to drop me as if to see the plot through, he was the enemy pawn; however, knowing what I was dealing with, I just dealt with this situation, not calling the person on his behavior, because I knew already from experience this is not a person thing, it is a demon thing.

Because of that I was able to deal with it in the right way, which was to lift it to the Lord, ask him to overcome this enemy attack, and point out what was going on for his assistance, while I was dealing with this call, which lets you know I was praying within as it happened to the Lord so you know God does hear you even if you do not have the opportunity to open your mouth, and he will render aid to you.

And I did get a turnabout in what seemed a doomed situation, as the Lord intervened from the demonic work, and had the owner's eyes opened immediately that these issues were not so. Thus, what was set to be a destruction to me, was turned, and I got the full help I needed, for all the time I needed it, conscious however, that this key employee in that business had a legal entryway for the enemy to use. So I would make a concerted effort the times I needed to have communication with that service, to go through anyone else first, and if I still only had that person left as the one with the answers, I would remain aware at any moment it could turn explosive on his end, could result in false information from that person, and had to keep that in mind with all my dealings with that person.

At the same time, I also lifted that person up to God in prayer because he had legal rights that let this happen to him. Why? Because if I am to really follow Jesus, I have to treat this person the way he said to or stand condemned if I don't because I am behaving according to the world instead, and not according to what pleases God as Jesus explained in Luke 6.

> But I tell you who hear me: Love your enemies, do good to those who hate you, bless those who curse you, pray for those who mistreat you.
> —*Luke 6:27-28, NIV*

These are not refrigerator magnet sayings. They are actually verbatim instructions Jesus gave us to follow of which we are called to do as his followers.

The Lord says we must pray for those who hate us, curse us and abuse us. Either you follow what Jesus says and be counted obedient, or you dismiss his words and follow the evil Satan has fed your heart through entertainment propaganda. How you actually handle these demon pawn confrontations is how you actually prove yourself a hearer of the word who obeys the instructions given. Not only is it important to know how people can become pawns of the demonic to interfere with God's will, but it is important to know that how you handle it is revealing to Jesus if you are really his follower or you prove dross to be tossed away.

> Someone asked him, "Lord, are only a few people going to be saved?" He said to them, "Make every effort to enter through the narrow door, because many, I tell you, will try to enter and will not be able to. Once the owner of the house gets up and closes the door, you will stand outside knocking and pleading, 'Sir, open the door for us.' "But he will answer, 'I don't know you or where you come from.'

> Then you will say, 'We ate and drank with you, and you taught in our streets.' But he will reply, 'I don't know you or where you come from. Away from me, all you evildoers!'
> —*Luke 13:23-27, NIV*

This is a revelation light bulb moment then to understand it is super important how you handle your share of demon pawn situations, understanding now they are refining you with fire that with these fiery trials you are showing your true colors, your true heart.

> And I will put this third into the fire, and refine them as one refines silver, and test them as gold is tested. They will call upon my name, and I will answer them. I will say, 'They are my people'; and they will say, 'The Lord is my God.'
> —*Zechariah 13:9, ESV*

By knowing this is what is going on, you get the edge to understand the why of the scenario and get the opportunity to consciously put on your best behavior to show the Lord you stand true to his teachings. It is not by how faithful you are to go to Church, it is not about how much you share about Jesus, it is how you reveal yourself in the fiery trials the Lord will determine if you are obedient to him or not, which shows the genuineness of your faith, and are part of his flock or not.

> So that the tested genuineness of your faith—more precious than gold that perishes though it is tested by fire—may be found to result in praise and glory and honor at the revelation of Jesus Christ.
> —*1 Peter 1:7, ESV*

That is so against what Satan wants you to feel over demon pawn encounters. Through popular shows he gives his own example what to do in these confrontations, which all lead to sin, no surprise. However, since many people do not have knowledge of the ways of God, they do not realize these popular models on these anti-Christ behaviors are against the teachings of Christ and result in condemnation.

While it is normal to get angry with such behavior, and you will not get judged for getting angry, you can get angry, but you have to refrain from sinning as a result of that anger. And that is handled by the self-control followers of Christ as called to do.

Thus, it was my Christian duty to stay obedient to the Bible and pray for this man every time I had a confrontation with him as that is the only attitude God deems right. Such prayer means to lift that pawn of the enemy with genuine care to God. Why? In order that God may have mercy on such a person and save that person from the devil's snare trapping that woman or man or youth in slavery to wickedness.

> Be angry, and do not sin: do not let the sun go down on your wrath.
> —*Ephesians 4:2, NKJV*

Satan wants you to take that acceptable anger, and then sin. He wants you to cross the line of righteousness and give evil for evil and sin. He wants you to believe if you do not, you are not acting normal, and you are not respectable, and your feelings are fraudulent, those of a spineless worthless person. Whatever hot-button he can push in you to get you to follow his influence, he will, whether approval from others, or vanity or shame or otherwise, he doesn't care, as long as he deceives you right into hell.

He uses movies, television series, novels and the like to teach the deceit that going on the offensive to offenses you experience is not only rightful to do, but makes you more attractive and powerful behaving that way.

It is an enemy deceit made to get you to believe this so you have an unrepented sin of which you are unaware is a sin that keeps you from heaven all the same. Oh how devious the enemy to honey-coat evil so you bite into it without any objections, oblivious of the line you have just crossed that you need to step back from before it is too late.

> Woe unto them that call evil good, and good evil; that put darkness for light, and light for darkness; that put bitter for sweet, and sweet for bitter!
> —*Isaiah 5:20, KJV*

That is the scheme of a diabolical entity to make evil look like the right way to be, so you are never aware you have fallen into a demonic snare, and have this sin within you which you don't realize you need to confess while there is time to get forgiveness.

> ...in accordance with the work of Satan displayed in ... every sort of evil that deceives those who are perishing. They perish because they refused to love the truth and so be saved. For this reason God sends them a powerful delusion so that they will believe the lie and so that all will be condemned who ... have delighted in wickedness.
> —*2 Thessalonians 2:9-12, NIV*

January 2014

Again, let me give you an example from my own life, which is all I can really talk about with certainty that precisely gives such an example which took place at a department store this same month I am writing this, January 2014.

Of course I could say nothing to the person who experienced this demon pawn hostility directed on my behalf, which would have given that person the understanding of the why the inexplicable extreme behavior they had taken the brunt of from the pawn, when trying to help me. Oh, but I knew, being in the thick of this warfare and in the front lines doing this book and being ¾ of the way near to completing it to the enemy's great anger.

Essentially what happened is I had ordered online from the department store's website, a 20-inch girl's bike as the 24 beach cruiser I had gotten was too high for my short legs and my foot would get caught on the bar as I tried to get off.

Now I will keep this store nameless because it is not about

Chapter 9: When People Turn Into Demon Pawns

using this book to get back at the establishment, which it would become if I used the name, but instead it is about giving a good, everyday-example of a demon pawn example that is not life-threatening, not immediately at least, because it did hold all the hot-buttons in it which might lead a person to despair from the grief and just blow their top in violence, or commit suicide because it is a straw that breaks their resolve.

From the cash my father gave me for Christmas I had gotten a bike not to ride it but because I needed to have an emergency back up transportation if I found myself in the same fix I had this summer, where my car battery had died when I was entirely broke and faced the possibility of weeks with no transportation and no way to take myself any place, not having the money for a taxi or the health to deal with trying to catch and ride and walk to and fro any bus.

I could more sit on a small bike and pedal than walk the blocks to get where any free transportation existed, if push came to shove; yet I would probably pay the price for a bike ride anyways as a disabled senior citizen, (remember that I am not the same youngster as in the pictures shown in the prior chapters), still that would be the lesser of the hardships.

Plus, having tried the electric moped route as a backup vehicle, and getting stuck with a machine that needed maintenance I could not do or afford, a bicycle was the best option with the least long-term problems since it can just lay around in my garage not needing gas or electricity, and not take up much room. Thus, my intent had been to get a bike for my height small and light enough for me to handle.

But all I had found right after this last Christmas, which was Christmas 2013 as I write this, in this particular shopping chain which was the only of three different chains I could find a bike for the cash my father had given me, were bikes for people with longer, more flexible legs. Yet when I made a trip to one of the stores and found some bikes yet there after the Christmas shopping craze, I thought I would try the lowest, height wise, one there, a 24 inch girl's cruiser. However, after buying it in the store and taking it home, I learned it was just too high.

But it took a couple of weeks for this shopping chain to have back in stock their girl cruiser bike in the height I could manage, which is 20 inches. Soon as I saw it back in stock in their online store, as I had a window of time to return this bigger bike and get the cash back to use to get the smaller bike, I ordered it online, as it said a store in the nearby city to me had 4 in stock.

At the point of time, this department store chain has a system in place so you can order online and go to any store to pay cash for that order. So I did, taking back the bike to the store where I got it, to get refunded, where I then paid for my order on the smaller bike, using my refunded cash.

At this chain of stores, when you do an order like I did online to order the item and pick up at the store the same day, you have to wait for the local store to contact you when you can come to the store to pick up that bike in a few hours. Well that contact never came, which I realize can happen because sometimes their online stock does not reflect what is really in a store, so you can pay for something not there and your money is hung up in the process to get refunded.

That led me to go to that store and see if such an issue was why I got no contact.

Everybody was nice, but right off no one could find my order in their store computer, although I had my online email receipt with the order number and the matching store receipt where I had paid the cash, matching to my online order number. Well, the order number was the problem, and the reason was, in hindsight because no one had the answers then, that their system had cancelled the order after I had paid the cash in the other store, because the store supposedly having the stock, didn't have the inventory.

With my order number not being found by the store's computer, it made it non-existent as a result, as if the computer did not recognize the order number, even though store staff saw the receipts and could verify the receipts existed in my store online account. But without my order number getting acknowledged in the store computer so it would pull up the order and let them work with it, it was as good as no order and they could do nothing on their end until someone got the order to patch through from the online end to the store's end.

Chapter 9: When People Turn Into Demon Pawns

So no one could give me my cash back and no one could give me a bike.

So it was like I gave the store my father's $100 Christmas present to me and was supposed to be happy with that and walk away to the 'oh well' situation. Yeah, right, hmmm? See, a real worldly hot-button meant to blast emotions, thus a devil-inspired catch-22.

Thus it was a problem that needed a manager to try to sort in that store with their corporate online business. I truly appreciated all the effort the staff was going through to help fix this situation they had not run into before. All that was needed was for them to get an override or fix from the higher up corporate that deals with the online orders for store pickups same day. So the manager called on my behalf to fix the problem, and I thought it would not take long with a manager at the helm.

As I stood on the customer side of the counter, with my semi-annual doctor appointment an hour away, already having been 90 minutes in the store trying to get a bicycle or a cash refund, I saw by the turn that was happening in the conversation the manager was having with the corporate end on the phone, a demon pawn situation had just arisen, because the manager started to say with great offense, "Excuse me....! Excuse me.....! She paid with cash, there is no return to a credit card. Excuse me......! You are yelling at me.... You're yelling....Stop shouting!.... Excuse me......! Excuse me......! How can this be fraud, she paid with cash! Excuse me......!..... Why forty-eight hour wait, it's cash! Yes, she is here in front of me. Excuse me....! Excuse me.....! Hello?...... hello!?..... hellll-lo!...... .....hello!?......hello!?.....hello......! She hung up! She was screaming, screaming!!"

As I had witnessed the manager, she had been calm as much as she could be trying to get through to someone on the other end of the line who was screaming angrily to her partway in the conversation, a point that was apparent to me the enemy had entered that person to make something simple an impossible roadblock for me that involved days of back and forth as if I had used funny money to pay cash and an inordinate time of days before any process would be allowed to even let the order be cancelled, and even then, never the order appearing in the store's computer so no one in any store could help.

Apparently the person on the other side of the phone had to have some kind of legal entry way that the enemy could take over to set in place as much grief as possible to me, recognizable by the extreme unwarranted reactions that had no basis and continued with no basis for such behavior through all the different people in that corporate side, concerning my order, no matter which of the managers in the local store tried to resolve the problem.

A few days later, still locked in the refund grief, I had a word of knowledge from the Holy Spirit that this day I would get my money back, and would get a right-size bicycle online. But I had no spare cash, just my grocery money same amount a new bicycle would cost.

When I went online to their site, I did see they had the bicycle in stock online and this time to be delivered straight to a person's home, which would avoid the Same Day Store Pickup grief I was in, where there could turn out to be no bicycles in stock again after I pay for it, though the online site would say otherwise.

Still I called their customer service number yet again to see if my locked-up cash order was 'unlocked' now and I could get my money back in the store. I was told yes, yet I made sure to make clear I had to know for certain because I wanted to get the same item online to be sent to my house, but to do so would take my month's grocery money, which I could only do if I knew my cash refund could be had. Although she kept insisting because she could see the order on her end the store would also be able to see it, I had her ask a manager to be sure, and spent about half an hour getting verification.

Well, I am sure you can spot where this is going now, because of course after I did order on that assurance, I went to the store expecting it would be as the customer service rep and her manager had assured me, and found out otherwise, that no, my cash order was still locked in the same days long limbo of not appearing and so, no, they could not give me a refund to my cash payment I had done in advance of receiving any item.

Now the problem had escalated because I had depended on what the customer service lady and her manager had told me before I did spend my grocery money for the replacement bicycle,

Chapter 9: When People Turn Into Demon Pawns

so getting that cash refund was more important now.

When I explained this new complication to the store management, again the management got on the phone to the corporate and again they heard, "no, no, no" to my cash refund, even though twice the time had passed since the corporate told them my order would show up in their store computer. Did that deter me from believing the word of knowledge I had that morning that I would get my money back this day?

No, I could see that getting my money back involved my standing firm in faith, believing that if the Lord had impressed me with that information he would get me my refund, that it would happen. Still I was getting shrugs of helplessness from the management, though they were courteous and sympathetic, but their hands were tied.

So I kept telling them what led me to the problem of spending my grocery money, their own customer service, that I had called first to be sure there would be no hang up yet on getting my cash refund this day, to be sure my order finally was appearing in the computers of the local stores, before paying for the replacement bike that day with my debit card because the bikes sold out fast online, showing them that email receipt so they could verify it, which they did, just explaining this like I would explain to a friend, just telling the truth, even though it involved sharing my embarrassing lack of money situation, but the same things I was telling them from the get-go that day.

Though I said nothing new, this time I could see the Spirit of the Lord work in their heart and change the management's hearts to say yes against a firm, fixed 'no' still in place from the corporate end, and the management just gave me my money back, having no way they would be compensated for the money from the corporate who treated the transaction with a legitimate printed receipt as if it never happened, throwing it into a limbo they kept saying would end at x point, but that x point would come, and prove untrue.

You see that store was not the one to get my $100 cash, it was another store. But without it showing up in their store by my order number if they refunded the money, they would not get credit for the refund, and it would be like they just took $100 out of the register without any order attached to it and just gave it to someone. In other words, the electronic accounting stood the final rule in this store chain, even if it could not be corrected and physical receipts did nothing.

Yet on my end, because I am commanded to love others as myself, and treat them as such, I tried my maximum effort to see how the store could get their credit for giving me my refund, because I am ordered by Jesus to be my brother's keeper. If it had been my store, I surely would have wanted to get my just compensation for giving a refund to a customer, and could understand their issue. But since it remained an impossibility, and I had done all I could, I could in peace know no theft on my hands, and accept the refund the devil wanted to rob from me, or trip me up in my standing with God.

You see how the demon pawn situation made abnormal grief over something? That kind of grief is spiritual warfare. The enemy is trying to crack you, to get you to sin, prove you are not a child of God. Whether you do a sin that will get you to hell from it, or you despair and commit suicide over it, Satan does not care which, only that it results in your destruction.

Knowing this, through all that grief I went through, at no time did a bad word, or a scowl, or insults to the store employees come from me. I did my best to follow the commands of Jesus the whole way, kindness, patience, truthfulness, perseverance, letting others go before me as I waited for the help being given to me in the store, courteous to the employees, being of good cheer to the staff, although due to my disability it was physically difficult for me to be there, keep standing there so long.

If it would have reached a point in that I could see it would cross too bad territory, I knew I had to face walking from it, and forgiving, and no, I can't afford to lose $100, but I can less afford to lose my soul over a $100. Now of course, I would never use that online option again, so there you go, as it does not mean you have to repeat by choice an act that led to grief from a pawn at a particular place.

The value of this is when you recognize what is going on, you don't put futile effort into trying to overcome it the way of men, as it will not be won that way, as it is spiritual warfare. You turn to the proper way to combat such encounters, which is lifting that

Chapter 9: When People Turn Into Demon Pawns

prayer to Jesus, coming to God in Jesus name to win the battle for you, hearing his guidance to you in the spirit, following that guidance, and by that way overcome that enemy scheme.

If you find yourself also having to deal with a demon pawn in a place of business, and it is a place you can't get around having to deal with, you have to walk in wisdom, know that person is a pawn being used, and lift it to Jesus, and don't confront that person. Act in humility and turn the other cheek, oh yes, do turn the other cheek, and ask Jesus to take you through it.

You will not be able to win with that person ever because as long as they have that demon working through them there is no winning with a person like that, it is all lose, lose, lose. But if that business is the only place that can aid you, Jesus will keep his hand on you in spite of the demon pawns in there. Yes, sometimes you have to use a place that you know has got demon pawns in there, people who can become demon pawns, and they actually behave that way with you, but you still need that service.

Know that if the Lord wants you to use that service, he will help you to get through it. You have to know this more so in these times as it is getting harder because of the increasing number of people being raised without God who are now working in many jobs today, which means there are many more people living in sins which give legal entry to the demonic. So there are more people the enemy can use, and the warfare is getting more aggressive as signs of what is going on in the world today, show the day of the Lord gets closer and closer. Thus, on a stronger basis you are going to be dealing with running into demon pawns.

You are going to have to be dealing with important places to you that are heavily controlled by these pawns where Satan is. It's going to be perilous, more perilous than ever. If you realize that, if you understand what is going on, because remember this is all warfare, you will be able to get the protection and the things that you need from those particular places, while not jeopardizing your salvation.

Did you think you were not going to be having grief? Do you think you are going to be sitting in the front lines, watching television and flipping through channels, and having a lovely time? No. It is grief. Battle is grief, grief, grief. That is why Paul and the other disciples repeatedly made sure to say to a group of disciples in Act 14 to keep on in faith, that they had to go through a lot of difficulties to get into the kingdom of heaven.

> And when they had preached the gospel to that city, and had taught many, they returned again to Lystra, and to Iconium, and Antioch, Confirming the souls of the disciples, and exhorting them to continue in the faith, and that we must through much tribulation enter into the kingdom of God.
> —*Acts 14:21-22, KJV*

God will get you through it despite these tribulations facing every believer. You, however, must walk tight in the spirit in order to be able to handle this increasing grief. You must walk in the veils of the Father in order to be able to deal properly with the demon pawn scenario.

When you understand this, it makes it easier to deal with as far as you know what is going on. You know why you are getting this kind of grief from who could be a stranger to you, and so you keep it in the right perspective and don't fall into the enemy scheme to get you to break. You know why the demon pawn is targeting you, you know why the pawn is trying to do you in even though he or she doesn't know you because it is not the person, it is the demonic spirit in that person.

This isn't just like 15 humans here and there; we are in a thing of warfare of the angels of heaven who fell, which was 1/3rd of the angels. These are minimally millions and millions and millions. As you can see, there are a lot of demons to go around. They are all kinds of sizes and are into all places, and this is getting desperate times for them because their days are numbered now.

> For if God did not spare angels when they sinned, but sent them to hell, putting them into gloomy dungeons to be held for judgment;
> —*2 Peter 2:4, NIV*

It is getting closer to when that appointment scheduled for

them thousands and thousands of years ago, which they have not lost sight of in their demon appointment books, when the Lord is coming after them to torment them.

> When he arrived at the other side in the region of the Gadarenes, two demon-possessed men coming from the tombs met him. They were so violent that no one could pass that way. "What do you want with us, Son of God?" they shouted. "Have you come here to torture us before the appointed time?"
> —*Matthew 8:28-29, NIV*

What that says there is a time the demons know they are going to be taken to their appointed torture. When the two demons said that in Matthew 8 it is because there is a time and they know this for sure. And this time now is coming closer.

As this time comes closer, their desperation is climbing and their desire and hatred to harm people is also climbing, and they are going out of the way. You don't even have to be an active soldier; you just have to be a person for them to want to cause you great destruction.

It seems incredible all this stuff, eyes that light, Satan taking over people to cause other people harm and do people in, but the thing is it seems incredible, it seems outlandish but the thing to remember it is all Biblically true, and it is all true what is in the Bible.

What the Bible says about the demonic, about the warfare, about the examples there like Judas who was taken over by Satan, that was not a symbolic thing, it was a literal thing. It was because he had a legal entry, he was a thief, and would not repent of that.

These things I am explaining they seem mind-blowing but they are right out of the Bible, because everything in the Bible you have to embrace every part of it, the whole teachings. It is not just about salvation to heaven. All the many times Jesus addressed demons and he talked about demons and they cast out demons, and the warfare with the principalities of darkness are in the Bible because they are a reality. Jesus was not talking about these things symbolically. The experiences I am relating to you here are true, are real. They are just a continued manifestation what Jesus and the apostles experienced in the Bible, experienced then. It is still a reality of the world, and the earth, exactly as they said. I am not relating anything out of the ordinary; this is all Biblical. It is all exactly the way as Jesus said.

That is the most important thing you have to realize. Everything about the demons and the warfare is exactly what Jesus said. If you believe Jesus on one thing, you have to believe Jesus on everything. Jesus said those things because they were factual things of existence.

If at any time you think the war is not raging at every venue the demonic can strike out at people to snare them, you don't have the right perspective.

Now if some evil behaviors can be blamed on a demon, does that exonerate the possessed party from any sin that person may do as a result of demon influence? No, not at all, for they accepted Satan's lead and let it happen to them, and went with his enticement, embraced the evil idea, and went full throttle with it, instead of rebuking it and resisting it as a righteous person will. If they end up murdering, if they end up stealing, they have that on them, which resulted out of their unrepented sin state, if they are not delivered. Will the Lord forgive them if they repent genuinely in time? Absolutely.

The other flipside is if you find yourself under such an influence and wonder, Why am I so enraged over this? I don't even know this person. Why are they making me so mad? You can bet a demon is trying to stir you if there is no rational explanation; a demon is trying to influence you to do its work of destruction on that person. It goes without saying, resist, and don't aid the enemy. Now if you have some kind of open doorway in yourself, you have to repent in order to get that closed up.

Did my knowing what was going on in any of these demon pawn situations make it any easier to deal with? No. Grief is grief. This generally happens in pivotal key things that you really need, that is when the enemy tries to take you down.

It still is difficult even when you know and understand the phenomenon, but you will understand it is not personal, and you will understand the irrational nature of it. This will help you from

Chapter 9: When People Turn Into Demon Pawns

inner angst wondering why a stranger is treating you so evil. You will know that person has some kind of wide-open entry the devil has full rights to access due to sin that person has not repented of, and they can be freely used as a pawn by the enemy, on demand of the situation, to block you from essential help you need.

You will have understanding why it may be no one else but you who has and is getting this kind of hostile treatment even though you have never met any of those people/person before. This will keep you from anguishing, why this person or party is treating you this way though they just met you.

You will instead get light-bulb moments of revelation knowing why, that this is what the enemy is trying to do to you in the warfare, and you will then know to lift it to the Lord and present the situation on your end to him. It will be completely unfair and it is entirely unfair what the enemy is trying to do to you, but Jesus overcame that for you at the cross.

Know you have to step lightly around such a person because they have an open doorway where they can be used by the enemy and you will only get back irrational devious plotting and that person will not be able to explain why they are spouting lie, lie and lie about you. You will know why, though it will still be difficult as all struggles in war are. They will go to confounding levels of lies to achieve stopping you from getting you what you need, and it will not end. Now if you can circumvent that person or party if you spot them as a pawn, you need to because that person is a demonic pawn to you and you are only going to have grief.

It really is like a movie where the person looks normal and all of a sudden they become a weird creature. That is what happens to people who become pawns of the demonic, they don't necessarily turn into creatures, but their behavior becomes monstrous. They all of a sudden become monsters, but they are not becoming a monster themselves, they are showing the demonic within them using them.

> With shrieks, evil spirits came out of many...
> —*Acts 8:7, NIV*

The evil spirit shook the man violently and came out of

him with a shriek.
—*Mark 1:26, NIV*

A clue you can observe in such a human pawn in the grips of the enemy at the time to carry out an enemy act of destruction, is that that person can't seem to stop his or herself from carrying out a hate or destructive act against someone. They are all hate driven, all destruction driven, all evil driven during that 'spell' of enemy control, to where they can't give you any rational reason, but all anger, or rage or evil replies.

You see when they have an open legal right to them to demon access, and there is an entry way into them, when they are with this breach, they really are like robots/pawns on standby the demons can take over to do whatever plan they want. It really is a physical thing. It is not a symbolic illusion I am talking about, it is an actual process as shown in the Bible.

If you do not see the process, they look like they are being a mean person doing something really evil and wicked and they will be evilly set on hindering you in something crucial so you suffer grief.

We wanted very much to come, and I, Paul, tried again and again, but Satan prevented us.
—*1 Thessalonians 2:18, NLT*

As I have shown, there are ways you can recognize by their fruits a person is at that time a devil pawn: by how they are hell-bent against you for no reason, defying understanding. In this warfare there is no controlling when or if you will cross paths in the future with another demon pawn. This time, though, you should be ready to recognize such a person by their out-of-place hostile reaction to whatever it is you are before them to accomplish. It may not always be apparent to you the merit of what you are attempting to do, but if you encounter such a pawn it usually has stakes that can cause you to stumble now or further on in your future in a serious way, whether as a reaction to that pawn, or as a consequence of what that pawn worked to deprive you of.

You can take confidence it is not your imagination and you are

Chapter 9: When People Turn Into Demon Pawns

not paranoid, and deal with it accordingly, standing firm in the victory you have in Christ. The main thing is:

- Don't despair.
- Don't let a pawn push you over the edge so you sin.
- Don't let a pawn lead you to hell by taking the enemy bait to fight back with an eye for an eye, or return evil for evil.
- Handle the demon pawn with the spirit of godly righteousness and you will do well.
- Whatever you need which may directly involve the pawn's involvement in some way in that item, whatever God has for you concerning that issue, trust him to supply it to you despite a pawn putting all effort to block you from that, and confidently through the Spirit of Christ, keep on that need, lifting it to Jesus in your mind during any face off with a pawn, and know God will lead you to getting what you need through the fruit of the Spirit which is patience, peace, joy, love, and goodwill.

Keep foremost you are undergoing a test, to sift you as wheat, to see if you pass in your faith, and hold to the faith, and see if you still stand firm to the whole counsel of the Lord.

As Jesus, turn the other cheek, be gracious to your enemy, suffering cheerfully, having complete assurance God rules, and in any worldly 'no' from a pawn, knowing if it is God's will for you, that God is God and he will give you a yes, even though all is no, from every pawn mouth, even the highest in authority. That requires standing in faith and patiently insisting on what you need in faith, repeating your need in patience to others also able to help in that business or situation, repeating it often, being intractable in patience, and God will move all the hearts necessary to go around the no's and give you the things you need.

Encountering a demon pawn can be viewed as a situation to sift you as wheat, and see if you stay obedient to following the commands of Jesus. Thus, rather than griping when you run into one, that is the time to snap to the opportunity to prove to Jesus you are a real child of His, by reacting to the situation according to how he has instructed to deal with all these scenarios which fall under his two commandments to Love God with all your heart, soul and mind, and to Love your neighbor as yourself.

Satan wants you to show a different set of colors when he sifts you for God. He wants you to reveal you have a black streak in your heart that shows you belong to him. Knowing this, refuse to play into his setup. You run into a demon pawn checking you out at a store cash register, abnormally cold-hearted and hateful to you, who gives you the wrong change, you realize there or don't realize until you leave and come home, here's what you do, realizing this:

On God's permission, Satan just depressed the minute clock on the test, gloating already you will flunk, and he will get one more proof you're not a child of light, without the test even underway. The test is to see if you walk as Jesus, if you are obedient to him in full.

Know this and do not do what the world approves of: do not return evil for evil to a demon pawn. Do not exact the last toll of justice for this provable offense against you. Do not give judgment on the character of the pawn, or what drives that pawn to act like that.

Within reason, where you do not sell your soul for it, seek to see if you can get a refund, but if it turns to evil level to do so, release that money, release the offender, lift the issue to Jesus and ask him to keep you from sinning, refusing to take the enemy's hot-button issue bait. Afterwards, pray for the Lord to not hold the act accountable to the pawn, in order that you fulfill the command to forgive those who trespass against you. Then consider the test done, and pray to the Lord you did well, and just let it go.

Satan wants you to follow his example to handle the situation as he has influenced many writers to portray in stories which involve evil for evil, offense for offense, worldly justified anger to the maximum level for human vengeance over God's vengeance, judgment over mercy, because his examples oppose the commands of Jesus, and result in condemnation.

So next time you run into a demon pawn, know you have run

into a Sifting-Wheat test, and take care to perform correctly so you ace each test and your faith found proven. Just because you know it is a test is not going to make the difficulties you may be dragged through any easier, but you will have the right attitude to handle the demon pawn putting you through it.

> And the Lord said, "Simon, Simon! Indeed, Satan has asked for you, that he may sift you as wheat. But I have prayed for you, that your faith should not fail; and when you have returned to Me, strengthen your brethren."
> —*Luke 22:31-32, NKJV*

***

Chapter 10

BE AFRAID, BE VERY AFRAID

> Fall on us, and hide us from the face of him that sitteth on the throne, and from the wrath of the Lamb: For the great day of his wrath is come; and who shall be able to stand?
> —*Revelation 6:16-17, KJV*

Either you will be around on the day of the Lord which will hit the earth with bigger destruction than the flood that engulfed the world at the time of Noah, and be faced with the horror of God's wrath, or you will die before then and find yourself undergoing a personal day of the Lord trembling in terror as your mind panics wondering if you are ready to his measure or not.

> Wail, for the day of the LORD is near; as destruction from the Almighty it will come!
> —*Isaiah 13:6 ESV*

So no matter which, you are going to be experiencing a terrifying day of the Lord, same as if you are going to a court where your life hangs in the balance, and even if you are certain you are innocent, a fear still grips you until it is over in face of a severe, unyielding judge. You have to be comatose to not experience a true terror until you find how it goes for you, as there is unknown territory that can happen in the experience you have never gone through.

Sooner than you think, the day of the Lord that involves the world is on the horizon. As I wrote earlier in chapter 6 it is not a day you wish to rush to as it involves terrors to all on the planet when it comes because of the horrifying events of the stars falling, the sky rolling up like a scroll, and the knowledge to your very core all of physical existence is ending because God's terrifying judgment is here, a supernatural understanding everyone will have when it comes.

Yet, because you will have some kind of day of the Lord you will go through, the urgency to get yourself right with the Lord is extreme, and applies to you!

There is no difference in the terror you will feel coming to either of those days not ready to meet Jesus. What is worse, any of the two, your personal day, or the world's day, is coming at a time you will not expect, and so you will not have the luxury of advanced warning where you will know you have a certain window of time to get your house in order.

At whichever of the two is the time you are ordained to meet your God, at that instant your time to repent is over and gone any more chances to avail yourself of the cleansing through Jesus blood of any sins in you which you have yet to confess and repent of, whether known to you or unknown to you are within you by God's standards.

Nothing will feel more terrifying than that moment you know the door of grace shut in your face at a grossly unexpected moment ahead of the idea of time you believed you had remaining to be completely prepared to meet Jesus in eternity.

I can't jack up the urgency enough either way your day to meet the righteous judge is racing to you, cloaked like a thief, and will hit you without warning. Thus it is urgent you take advantage of this final period of grace to be prepared to face Jesus. There will not be a second chance to turn the clock of grace back and get an extension of time. Jesus does not want you to perish.

He came from his glorious throne just to be slaughtered like a lamb to keep you from this wrath if you avail yourself of the mercy he purchased for you on the cross, all yours if you repent, turn from sins completely, and follow his teachings to be fully prepared when he arrives for you.

It is important you do not brush this off before all time runs out for you to avoid a terror of a righteous holy God come to dole his wrath on all evil. If you only take it seriously, you can avoid the utter hopelessness which will fill the unprepared.

The devil knows this time is on the rise, so the panic in the demonic principality is also on the rise which brings me to an experience I had not too long ago you need to pay attention to so it will build up your faith the demonic threat to you is real, and you can take action to have your spiritual house entirely ready. Honestly if you understand what is going to happen to you sooner than later, nothing the world has to offer will hold any meaning or value to you, as you obtain the true perspective that it's always been all about God's itinerary since the creation of earth and not ours.

March 9, 2013 - Ruler Of Principality Upset

March 9th, 2013 I lay in bed on my stomach, head to the left. As I lay there it was like a communication channel was switched open. Of all the experiences I have had in my life this was new. It seemed the Holy Spirit opened this communication frequency long enough for me to listen to a conversation about 2 feet from my ear so I could know exactly how threatened the demonic kingdom felt about something I was part of, which unknown to me coincided with the date I would finish this book exactly one year later in 2014 on March 9th.

A male demonic voice spoke exceedingly angry, super angry to unseen listeners to his right, very close. I couldn't quite understand what he said, but I knew what he spoke about, as if it was revealed to me, much the way someone can interpret tongues.

It was as if Satan himself came personally to point me out, point out the threat, point out that I was close to making something happen that was a threat to them, something that would tip the war in a very threatening way to them, and he was highly upset the situation had gotten to where it was.

If it was not Satan himself, it was a high-ranking ruler in his kingdom from the authority in his voice.

Let me tell you what that voice sounded like. It was not human to begin with, yet it was distinctly manlike in that it spoke words like people, but it was demonic and of a big monster-like being, monstrous in that its voice had a peculiar resonance and depth like a giant would, but a monster giant that spoke with evil in his entire tone.

The phenomenon of the voice was precisely like the Lord of Darkness demon played by Tim Curry in the 1985 film titled *Legend*, as far as the strange depth resonating special effects given to Tim Curry's voice to make him sound like a large monster demon.

Except the voice I heard was far older, comparing Curry's demon like a young man to this voice being senior, not as in feeble senior, but in very much potent, but a very-mature, advanced- age male like a high general, seasoned mature being.

The demon's voice spoke of girth, like an elephant has girth. It spoke of tremendous size.

Its voice conveyed this was a being that if he held me I would be like a small poodle in his hand. He could hold me with one hand. I am not talking one arm, I am talking one hand. He could actually put his hand around my torso and hold me like a small dog, because he was that big, from what that voice spoke of, the size of the creature behind that huge voice.

Actually this demon had to be about 30 feet in height, or 30 to 50 feet wide from the resonating volume of its voice.

What I would have seen if I had turned, which I was getting the distinct information not to, who knows what? Maybe I would have seen something very shocking to look at, besides being in trouble that it would see me looking at it, something too shocking for me to look at and not freak out, which may have been the reason I was getting the distinct impression spiritually not to look, even peek, but stay laying there playing possum as I was, keeping my eyes shut.

So it probably no doubt had to be supernaturally within my room, since it was talking about two feet away from my head, and had to have been hunched over.

If I had been dumb enough to disregard the unspoken warning coming to me not to turn and look, I might have seen the front half of its body leaning through my ceiling and wall, it's giant demon head down to me to talk to the smaller, normal size, as far as human size, demons, and just talking right at me as it spoke about me, saying these orders, saying this information that it was really highly upset about.

I really want to take the moment to convey to you in full what hearing its voice was like so you have a more proper understanding of what this demon commander really was like.

Reflecting on my experience brings to mind this YouTube story I saw around three months after my experience titled *Shawn Weed's Hell Testimony (Full)* of a Marine vet who underwent an unexpected near-death experience (NDE) as a result of some clowning around with a couple of Marine buddies that backfired after one of them put a noose around his neck during the prank, and he ended up actually getting hung.

That led then to him finding himself out of his body, where he spent like 15 minutes watching his friends panicking trying to get the noose off of his dead body and succeeding.

That was when he got the idea to try to go back into his body once the noose was off of his neck.

But when his spirit head met his physical head as he lay back into his now prone body, he found himself in another reality, which was a totally black place, a black which he described as a substance you could feel.

As he tried to figure out where he was, and find a way out, then finding none, and then starting to panic, from there a tremendous demon came for him and snatched him in one hand, and took off running with him faster than a cheetah can run, to what he understood was the lake of fire described in the Bible in order to throw him in to it.

This demon he described in great detail as he got a super close-up look at him while it painfully held him in just one of its huge hands.

He had described it as thirteen feet tall and very broad, with its hand as wide as the top of the Marine's own shoulder, going from the edge of his neck to the end of his shoulder, what is the width a shoulder-pad would be, not the width of the demon's flat palm, but the width of the side of its hand being as wide as a shoulder pad would be on that Marine vet's shoulder.

So 13 feet tall, but super bulky, and built like the incredible Hulk-type massive abnormal muscles, though he did not describe it as the Hulk, but from how he detailed its bulky abnormally huge muscles it fits the description of the Hulk.

The girth that he described I would say minimally had to be

the type of girth of the demon I heard had to have, but honestly it seemed to me from its voice it easily could have been twice that size, to even 26 to 30 feet without even a stretch of the imagination.

However, the chest it had to have to give such a giant's voice, most certainly was larger than any elephant on this earth, because this voice I heard had a tremendous resonance of a monster giant. There is no comparison to such a voice I have heard in my life, not even an elephant's trumpeting that I have heard live at zoos.

However, if a T-Rex could talk, that might have been what it sounded like as far as this big chest resonance and power of the voice, like the *Legend* demon performed by Tim Curry, but if it was right in the room with me and not through stereo speakers which really can't capture the true volume and girth conveyed in that giant's voice.

If you want to hear an amazing detailed description of a demon, and what it feels to be like in its grip, that is a good video to watch, but you have to get to around the 25 minute mark for that part of the story to kick in, as the first part involves the antics with his Marine buddies that led him to have an NDE.

There was a happy ending to it in that he ended up being rescued by Archangel Michael who conveyed to him it was not his time to die, and still he had a name in heaven if he lived for God. This information was new to the Marine, ultra shocked by this news, as he had been clueless this was needed to enter heaven, not having learned anything like that from his occasional church attending.

Like most of us do, he had thought because of the deception of the enemy, that being a nice guy who treated people decently would keep him from hell. But he testifies he learned otherwise, that as the Bible says is how it is, that we are to live for God.

So the kind of size he was talking about, really it was at least the smallest size this demon commander talking two feet above my head as I lay there in bed had to be, though, as I said, he really came across, really twice the size of that, like a T-Rex's height and mass, as given for one of the most complete specimen's found on a Tyrannosaurus rex which is 13 feet tall at the hips (4 m) and 40 feet long (12.3 m), as provided in a research article published in

2011, titled A Computational Analysis of Limb and Body Dimensions in Tyrannosaurus rex with Implications for Locomotion, Ontogeny, and Growth **Citation:** Hutchinson JR, Bates KT, Molnar J, Allen V, Makovicky PJ (2011) A Computational Analysis of Limb and Body Dimensions in Tyrannosaurus rex with Implications for Locomotion, and Growth. PLoS ONE 6(10): e26037. doi:10.1371/journal.pone.0026037.

Getting back to the demon commander raging next to my ear: first of all he raged like he was super upset I had gotten to the point where I was. It was a fury panic, if you can imagine a monster voice going on like that.

As I said, he spoke in a language not of this world. I made no sense of any of the words, none similar to any language we know on earth.

Yet, as I said, the Spirit gave me a knowing of the conversation, like instant understanding as this demon general raged. I use the words 'general' and 'commander' interchangeably because I knew, the same way as I was given understanding of the contents of what he was saying, that he was a top power, though I cannot say if he really was Satan or who, but definitely top, as I had my head turned away from him, my eyes covered with a sleep mask I usually wear, so seeing was not something I could do even if I had been dumb enough to disregard this supernatural understanding not to do so while this took place, besides my own common sense to keep them closed.

In addition to the knowing not to look, I had the understanding his presence was there because the problem was big enough that he had to come in person himself, to deal with it personally.

He was going off the walls hyper upset, just two feet from my ears. It was a combination of hyper-upset and panic.

Then I understood he was giving commands to wreck destruction on me. At the same time, it was like they could not touch me, as if I was in some kind of protection, which had to be the Holy Spirit who was giving me this whole protected experience where I understood to just play possum like I was sleeping.

Through the same kind of indirect knowing, I got the

information this commander was barking orders to a group of hit demons, not just one. Somehow this knowing conveyed to me these demons listening in total respect to this ballistic commander were not monsters in size themselves, but like people size and smaller, and several were there. The big giant commander was over my head as I lay in bed, my face turned away, and his henchmen were further out to the room, to the foot of the bed.

The information this demon was giving to those listening was something those listening didn't even know. I heard about 8 seconds, then the channel was switched off, almost as if the Holy Spirit did not want me to know the details so I would not be overcome and faint from that. It seemed that I had been tuned in to the pertinent part to get the essential summary of my predicament.

Then later when I got up I got hit with several overwhelming troubles from before breakfast to after dinner, ones clearly meant to do me in or drive me over the edge.

The important part of my sharing these problems that hit me, and continue to hit me, is so you can see how the enemy does warfare and get some understanding about some negative things which might be happening to you as well, and put those troubles into the right perspective, and know how to overcome them and endure against them.

This is not too dissimilar to my first experience with a demon pawn as I wrote about in chapter 9 where my spiritual eyes were opened to see the actual process of evil possessing someone with malicious intent against me, and then a third-party filling me in on the details to what that meant.

Here in this March 9th experience, my spiritual ears were opened to hear firsthand the demonic principality ruler plot violence against me, and then experienced that warfare directly after. By my sharing these experiences, you hear from a witness to the actual process behind, that can confirm to you the evil behind these things are real, so in your own experiences you can have a better understanding and know the right way to deal with it, even if you never end up having your spiritual senses open.

You can take my experiences as confirmation of the warfare you may be dealing with in your own life to know these things are still going on, and in fact raging even more than when they were happening to the apostles. Back then Satan was out hindering them left and right so that sometimes they couldn't even get to where they were planning.

> Wherefore we would have come unto you, even I Paul, once and again; but Satan hindered us.
> —*1 Thessalonians 2:18, KJV*

What happened to them is real, and it still is happening now to Christians trying to do work for the Lord in any measure.

As the Scripture relates in Ephesians 6:12, we fight against the rulers and cosmic powers of darkness in the heavenly realms. While the King James states these rulers and authorities as rulers of the darkness of this world, against spiritual wickedness in high places, the Greek uses the words as shown κοσμοκράτορας τοῦ σκότους which is 'cosmic powers of the darkness' and these five, πνευματικὰ πονηρίας ἐν τοῖς ἐπουρανίοις which is 'spiritual [forces] in the heavenly realm'.

So the forces of evil that wage war against us, the rulers and the authorities of these dark forces, are not in hell as some may think, and not constrained to the earth, although Satan is the prince of the world (John 12:31), but they are out in the cosmos, and in the heavenly realms, where they will be until the Lord Jesus casts them to the Lake of Fire.

Thus, from this vantage point they wage war against us. This is where they reside until it is their time of torment. Plus, besides roving the earth to and fro for whom to destroy, Satan still goes before God to accuse us night and day (Revelation 12:10) just as he accused Job's forthrightness before God with the scheme to prove Job just as bad as any other godless man.

> Now there was a day when the sons of God came to present themselves before the LORD, and Satan came also among them. And the LORD said unto Satan, "Whence comest thou?" Then Satan answered the LORD, and said, "From going to and fro in the earth, and from walking up and down in it." And the LORD said unto

Satan, "Hast thou considered my servant Job, that there is none like him in the earth, a perfect and an upright man, one that feareth God, and escheweth evil?" Then Satan answered the LORD, and said, "Doth Job fear God for nought? Hast not thou made an hedge about him, and about his house, and about all that he hath on every side? Thou hast blessed the work of his hands, and his substance is increased in the land. But put forth thine hand now, and touch all that he hath, and he will curse thee to thy face." And the LORD said unto Satan, "Behold, all that he hath is in thy power; only upon himself put not forth thine hand." So Satan went forth from the presence of the LORD.
—*Job 1:6-12, KJV*

As Job 1 shows, the powers of darkness have access to certain information about all of us, as you can see Satan made a knowledgeable reply concerning Job, knowing his circumstances, knowing what God was doing with him, and making his assessment to God that way, from what he obviously had the ability to know about Job when God asked him if he had considered his servant Job as far as what he thought about him, which seems to be inferring what Satan thought about his righteousness.

While this kind of information may not be known to all of the demonic forces, and may be limited to the rulers and authorities in the cosmos and heavenly realms, which would explain why a demon general had to come and point out details about me which had him totally ballistic, things I didn't even know concerning my part in, and give the orders to lesser demons whom obviously this was all news to them, showing they, at least this group, did not have such information access, but had to be instructed by a higher power who did.

So in addition to pointing me out to that demon hit team, prior to that, processes were evidently put in place, perhaps by the same general or others like him, so that different problems would come together for me on that day with the plan to cause multiple overwhelming problems at the same time in order to destroy my ability to keep working on whatever was setting off that demon general's panic button to the degree I heard.

On The Dark Side's Hit List

By the end of the day, I had been slammed with several crushing troubles, some made to take me down physically and others trying to break my spirit.

The first one that slammed me was one meant to drain me physically and make me suffer mentally and emotionally as well. It involved one of my 3 dachshunds, who let out a terrible cry of pain on the way out with all the dogs for their first morning time to relieve themselves, really like screaming which led me to see he had a case of painful boils within his forepaws, in the recesses of his pads.

As Scriptures show the enemy is ruthless having no issues tormenting children by the examples of children in the New Testament under demon affliction whose parents sought to get deliverance for them, and so putting my dog through weeks of painful suffering bothers these dark powers not a bit.

That was the start of his screaming for the next 3 months each time he would rise to his feet. His cries were so bad that the other dogs stopped moving, immobilized by his cries in a kind of shock about what was going on with him.

Having no money, all I could figure was to wash his paws with antibacterial soap, and put gentian violet antiseptic on the boils as you see in this picture, and soak his paws with Epson salts, a very difficult thing to do twice a day when you are ill and the dog is heavier than you can handle, and that dog is in pain where it cries in advance of anticipating anyone coming near its infected wounds. **Enemy blow number 1.**

After the first session I lost all my energy, and could not get out of bed, not knowing then I was also officially hypothyroid despite years of meds, and felt as if I was going to perish lying there.

It was not a normal fatigue; it was abnormal one that made me feel like I was dying and I was not able to move from the exhaustion. It had an abnormal feel to it that I knew something was wrong, the kind of knocked down fatigue one gets with a tremendous case of the flu. I normally have pains and aches and tiredness from another condition for which I get disability, but this one was not my 'regular' weakness but one of the likes I had not felt since I had been diagnosed with hypothyroid in early 2000.

I was to find out 3 days later from a blood test it was because I was hypothyroid just at the level I had when I had been diagnosed

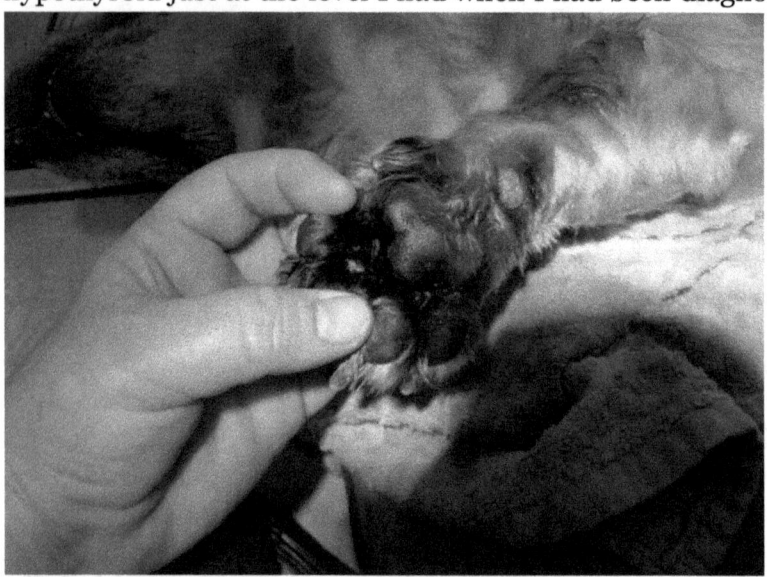

over a decade ago, even though I had been taking my medicine. It turned out to be a quality-control issue with the medication, Levoxyl, one that ended up with it being recalled because it was subpotent as listed on the fda.gov site.

I didn't know that then, only that I was downed with a kind of fatigue I had only experienced before I was diagnosed and getting treatments. Though I later filed my incident with FDA and the drug company, denials were still coming from them until an official recall was posted in their safety recalls enforcement reports a couple of months later, seemingly after they received enough complaints. **Enemy blow number 2.**

As I just lay in utter crushing exhaustion in my late husband's empty bed, downed by the work of trying to doctor my dog's paws, I had no energy, and could find no way to praise the Lord, which is a prime weapon against such enemy attacks. All I could do was feebly lift up my problem to the Lord, and feebly state I was

Chapter 10: Be Afraid, Be Very Afraid

pounding on Heaven's gate for help because if something was not done I was down and could do nothing else. I knew if I did not get help that I might not survive getting through the day.

It seemed as if the enemy would get the upper hand, and succeed in taking me down through physically binding me with more work than I could handle, using things around me to stop me from writing.

It was not easy, it did seem as if I was done for, but if this was what God wanted, then fine, and I asked God aloud if this was what he really wanted. I heard nothing back, and felt nothing.

When I could get up and get to the mail outside, I found a letter from a service I was using of which I paid monthly, which they had worded in a way that it read like a demand for the entire coming year all right then or lose the service, over $2000, even though my renewal date was 6 weeks away and I was to pay on installments. And it was Saturday, so there would be no calling up the office to try to straighten this out. **Enemy blow number 3.**

Then that same day when I checked the status of my late husband's nursing home negligence case docket online, I found that the day before one of the defendants filed a move for sanctions against me, which is a countersuit.

Finding that motion for sanctions was like one of the robbers part of the gang who killed your family member getting off because of a missed deadline, then turning around and suing you. **Enemy blow number 4.**

The defendant was taking advantage of failure of my first attorney on the case to include certain defendants within the time allowed to file.

Since there had been fraud in my husband's medical records, not dissimilar to the records fraud that months later would put the CEO of the nursing home in prison for 25 years, it clouded who were the guilty, which led the 1st attorney to withdraw, leaving me for sometime as pro se until I had proved by experts the liability of the facility to get the interest of new legal representation.

And so because of that missed deadline, the judge had ruled my new lawyers could not include this other defendant; not because the defendant had proved innocent, but because of my 1st attorney's failure to serve that defendant in the filing timeline.

That then got the defendant dismissed. So it seemed the defendant's attorney then sought to get paid by sanctions. Just an FYI that my attorneys did fight against that, and the defendant did withdraw from pursuing that, but it still led me to have to suffer the grief of the fight for the next couple of months.

In addition, I was to learn then also when browsing online that the Independent Foreclosure Review I have been counting on justice & direly needed money to have a chance to not end up in the streets, announced a few weeks before their previous payment plan has been scrapped & the banks allowed to decide who was harmed & how much to pay.

The news I read stated a new 'generic' payment plan was going to replace it, which would include adding in millions others to the plan to divvy up the same money meant to go to those whom had requested a review as myself.

Those reviews which could have resulted in fair help against the wrongful foreclosures, to which in hope I had sent them over 100 pages of documents showing the wrong in progress to me by the bank which had foreclosed on me while I was in a forbearance payment suspension through their hardship program due to my husband's death, were not going to get done, but just a general handout now given to all. **Enemy blow number 5.**

I had direly needed justice to get out of this deadly fix the bank had cornered me in: willful destruction of my credit with a foreclosure that never should have taken place, which ignored the forbearance hardship program rules, and not even the proper 30 days notice, and in addition they had just given the court a fake note with fake signatures of myself and my late husband as proof of standing.

You would think that was cut and dry justice, but due to the corruption which can be attributed to the last days mentality and hardness of heart where lawlessness increases and the love of many grow cold, the wheels of justice are proving to mostly turn in favor of the banks, with such 'evidence' overlooked, and such wrongs with zero weight.

Unless you can pay handsomely for legal recourse and pay to reinstate a loan, for the impoverished as myself, such wrongs are never reversed to force the bank to go back to the forbearance, force them to remove their wrongful willful damage of the borrower's credit, and move forward as they should. For me that has meant the inability to get any kind of housing whatsoever in my budget through a conventional loan which would have allowed me to recover from the loss of my husband.

Anyone who has gone through a foreclosure today knows you are blacklisted by that on your credit and unable to purchase any home, and often not even rent any place, and if so at much higher unaffordable rates like a bad-credit penalty.

This leaves only shelters to go to, which from all the people being displaced from their homes, are often filled up and have a backlog of homeless people on their waiting list, as in my area. And if you have pets like I do, you are really up that creek with no paddle. Thus to see all my effort had been in vain and would now result in an unjust pitiful payment that would be no help at all to overcome the harm, was one more blow.

I can certainly say the timing of my eyes falling on that information that very afternoon was demonic. As I don't read any newspaper, and I don't listen to any radio, and I do not watch any form of television, this was the first time I had come across this info. Sometimes headlines pop up into my email inbox sidebar featuring such news, and I believe this is how it caught my eyes.

To add to all of that, my printer that very day suddenly began printing with a terrible streaking problem to the point it was almost impossible to read any of the pages on my draft of this manual as I worked, a combo of streaks and faded print, even though there was plenty of toner.

Nothing I would do would solve the problem: I knew why it was happening, that the enemy was sabotaging my printer. I also was too broke to take the steps to 'fix' it, which involved putting in a new toner cartridge. **Enemy blow number 6.**

As if that were not enough, my tractor lawn mower, which I relied on to mow my lawn, not having the money since my husband passed to pay for anyone to mow my lawn, which let me mow my lawn by just sitting, turning the key and driving at slow speed the times I had the least aches and pains, I learned that day after checking how my efforts to trickle charge the battery was doing, that without a doubt the battery was dead. The dead battery was made even more than a disaster as it had already been over 7 weeks since I had mowed my lawn which in South Florida needs mowing year round, though lesser in winter.

It is not like I had just started to try to trickle charge it, it is that I had been trickle charging the battery for 3 weeks, but instead of charging, it had been failing to hold any charge, just going down in the readings. That afternoon I could see it was just not going to come back to life, even though I did try adding all the tricks suggested online to a declining battery, including Epson salts same bag as I was using on my dog's paws.

To get an equal brand battery as the one which came with the mower that had lasted me over 3 years, the cost was prohibitive, almost $100.

What was worse was it had been over seven weeks like I said since I last mowed, a South Florida lawn and it was more than overdue. To find this out at a time when I was truly sick physically was not good as I had no money to hire anyone to mow it even one-time. And I certainly didn't have the energy to use a weed whacker to tame the lawn.

What even multiplied the problem was the fiasco of a shredded hurricane tarp dangling over the front of my roof for the last few months because my insurance company denied repairing the roof damage from Storm Isaac that had loosen many shingles and had my roof leaking in several places so it rains inside the same time it rains outside.

Overgrown grass and that shredded tarp were just beacons for a city inspector to cite. So here was insurmountable **enemy blow number 7.**

I knew in order to not be crushed, to withstand these enemy blows, it was imperative I praise the Lord, because praise is a potent weapon against the enemy.

> I will call upon the LORD, who is worthy to be praised: so shall I be saved from mine enemies.
> —*Psalm 18:3, KJV*

I knew if I didn't praise I could be done in for as these were just too many things across all kinds of levels. It wasn't that these problems would disappear, as I still had to bear the burden of them, it was that it would drive the enemy away, and then I could pick up the pieces as I could without further evil assaulting me in my spirit, in my fortitude to stand, in my respite to get rest.

But if you have had the flu, you know you are so sick you can hardly speak, much less praise from the weakness, and that is what it feels like for me to be full blown-out hypothyroid, a malaise just like a bad flu that has you near death.

Because this was warfare, soon as I got enough energy, which was when I was in the kitchen, as sickness or not my pets needed water and food, here is what I did. I began to sing Amazing Grace. I could almost sense demons watching as if, "No, she really isn't going to praise with all we have hit, is she......????"

Praise is the key secret weapon to tumbling down enemy strongholds, shattering demonic oppression. When you praise God, you move God to flow His blessing to you.

> And when they began to sing and to praise, the LORD set ambushments against the children of Ammon, Moab, and mount Seir, which were come against Judah; and they were smitten.
> —*2 Chronicles 20:22, KJV*

The enemy camp knows this and tries to make situations in your life so you can't praise, so you are so overcome the last thing natural to come out of your mouth is praise. But that is the absolute worse thing you could do then is not praise. It's as essential as getting a newborn to take in its first breath; if it were stopped from that breath, it would not get life and perish, so for that baby not to breathe is the worse move, a fatal wrong.

Praise is such a key ingredient to having God release miracles to you that to not praise is for your prayers to be stillborn that is why the enemy works so hard to keep you from releasing praise to God so your prayers to God are stillborn before out of your mouth and thoughts.

Have you ever met someone who complains their prayers are never answered?

I am sure if you examine their 'praise' life in comparison to their 'prayer' life, you would see a drastically different measurement that would show anywhere from 20 to 60 percent on the prayer gauge, to 0, empty on their praise gauge. So without those praises to bring the required living ingredient to give successful birth to their prayers, those prayers they said, would show a total lack of praise.

My mother and my aunt marvel how I receive so many miracles, that my prayers are answered so often miraculously. Here is the revealing truth: I am no different than anybody else as far as having more merit, as far as more deserving, or more liked by God. As the Scripture says, God is no respecter of person (Romans 2:11).

Why then are my prayers so abundantly answered compared to my mother's or my aunt's to the point they find these occurrences very unusual?

If a praise mechanic were to come in from the military vehicle department in heaven and examine my praise fuel gauge in comparison to my relatives, he would lickety-split make his expert analysis: my gauge is sufficiently high to give proper life to my prayers.

Coming from the Catholic faith, praise is not something that is a part of everyday life for my mother. I can't even recollect my mother praising God once in a normal day routine, only after the fact in rare instances to some close call. Her prayer gauge is super low, in comparison to mine.

Now whether by design by God or not, before I learned the working principles behind successful prayers, by nature thanks spilt out of me normally from since I was a child. It has stayed with me through my life. Because of this Scripture, however, I have to believe it was by design of God so that in spite of myself, I would come to lift praise that would loosen help from God to me.

> From the lips of children and infants you have ordained praise because of your enemies, to silence the foe and the avenger.
> —Psalm 8:2, NIV

It is like I would have to slap my hand over my mouth to keep from saying thanks.

For example, whenever an employee at any fast-food drive-through gives me my drink and my food, thanks automatically comes out of my mouth, to the point I have had people chuckle in surprise at the 'thanks' as if it is something they rarely hear or expect. The thanks just come out like a force of their own, and I don't have to think about it as I genuinely feel thankful for their actions and I appreciate their service.

So by my thanks and praise 'defect' I was and have been quite ignorantly and innocently walking with my spiritual relationship with God and Jesus with my praise gauge measurably powered.

Perhaps even by God's design as I said, I may have been programmed to have praise spill out of my mouth, knowing how he works to create things for his larger goals, so that perhaps in spite of my sinner self I would give the praise due that would move him to answer my prayers, which would deliver me from a lot of troubles that could have kept me from reaching the point of my life now where I am working on this Christian material.

Thus, not because of anything noble of myself, but because God may have just instilled this in me for my better good to achieve his ultimate goal. This has led to prayers that get results since my childhood. My quirk has me thanking in advance, like in faith, and genuinely. This is the fundamental principle to praise that powers prayers.

So while my Mom's praise gauge is typical for many people, near 0, mine has been at sufficient level that unlike many of her stillborn prayers, my prayers are alive and kicking, often something fierce.

This principle is there for everyone. Everyone.

Build up your praise meter, and you, too, will have more and more of your prayers alive and kicking straight to the throne room. If your prayers have been stillborn there is a reason why as you can see from my own life example, because they lack the life of praise. Very fixable problem.

True praise is not stingy; it does not wait for God to earn it. Rather it comes out of you, thanking in advance of what you hope for from God, and in praise of God.

Praise is something you do genuinely and in advance, in faith, and not on condition of God earning your praise. Praise comes in all shapes and forms, from simple heartfelt thank-you's to God, to dedicated sessions of praise worship. The more you are in the habit of giving thanks and praise to God, the more your prayers you will see answered when you ask these things in Jesus' name.

However, in that situation I couldn't hardly sing, much less remember any lyrics, and my singing was imperfect, difficult to make myself do, morale wise, physical wise, faith wise, but I *knew* this was the way.

The more I sang the lyrics of Amazing Grace in thanks to God, the easier it got to come to a place to genuinely praise God. You see that was the key point behind my singing, so I could come to a place where praise would flow genuinely out of me. I sang two imperfectly-worded verses, but by the end I could say a genuine, Praise God, and I was genuinely grateful for His redeeming grace to me.

I can tell you that the air in the warfare surrounding me took a distinct turn at that point; the oppression in it before lifted right as I uttered that praise, and it felt distinctly lighter, and victory was on its way from that point on. I knew, I could feel that the tables were turned and I overcame the first heavy enemy skirmish, the devils defeated in that initial outright assault.

Instead of feeling defeated, I felt more determined to do the work that stirred those demonic principalities into a fearful panic, although I was still ill and had to deal with all those problems, which were taxing to overcome.

I had read previously someplace that I can't recollect now, a pastor who said he shied away from directly preaching demonic things because it would unleash terrible warfare on him and his family. I remember that as I went through this.

He said that everything in his family was hit, and I found that true, but since I do not have children, what I found is the next living things, my pets were hit, all together with problems to overwhelm me, tie me up, so all I was doing was nursing them and having no time left to work on this manuscript which was unknown to me going to evolve into what it has become.

It proved to be a benefit to me to know for certain that all that was behind it was this hit team of demons. It is not that it seemed demonic: from their visit that March 9th I actually *knew* they were demonic from the voice the Holy Spirit let me hear ordering my annihilation. Knowing this has given me the perspective to understand the deluge of problems simply demonic in nature.

It also helped me to stay motivated because I sure want to finish whatever it is that gets demons so upset. You can bet I want to live up to the trouble they are giving me. For every trouble they have given me, I look forward to the Lord sending it back to them 100fold.

Just as many people have been convinced of the reality of who Christ is just by Peter's eyewitness account of having heard the voice he understood as God on the holy mountain saying Jesus was his beloved Son in whom he was well pleased, that by hearing this supernatural voice was sufficient of the truth, so I hope you will be convinced also of the reality of the power and existence of the demonic principality, by the account I have told you I heard of a demon ruler plotting warfare against me.

> For we have not followed cunningly devised fables, when we made known unto you the power and coming of our Lord Jesus Christ, but were eyewitnesses of his majesty. For he received from God the Father honour and glory, when there came such a voice to him from the excellent glory, This is my beloved Son, in whom I am well pleased. And this voice which came from heaven we heard, when we were with him in the holy mount.
> —*2 Peter 1:16-18, KJV*

As the voice Peter heard attested to the majesty of our Lord Jesus Christ, the voice I heard attests that the schemes of the enemy to rob, kill and destroy are real.

The voice also attests of their warfare against all things leading to salvation. The voice also shows their great distress of the reality of the demonic getting known as it was known to be real in the days Jesus walked the earth. And finally, the voice I heard myself attests demons are behind problems that overwhelm, that trigger despair, that lead to destruction and bear evil timing.

You would do well to pay attention, and knowing this, deal

with such problems by overcoming them through praise and standing firm in the Word.

Now, interestingly, as I near completion of this book, it seems that it will fall exactly a year to the date when those demons came into my bedroom under the lead of a monster demon ruler come to give orders to do me in.

These ordered demon soldiers have been working to derail me since, with misery after misery. First I thought it might be this book alone as whether I liked it or not, and no matter how hard I tried to speed things up in my grueling warfare as a result of these demon antics to me, it is just all coming to be that it will be officially done a year to the date the demon general came to my room to order me destroyed, March 9th in 2013.

It is always interesting when you can see that events happening in the near future can be seen by all in the spiritual. That is why fortune tellers fed by demonic principalities can predict as they can. So apparently, before I even knew it, it was known a year before what I might finish a year later, to the day, March 9th. And that demon general definitely was an unhappy camper about whatever it was.

It may be that that is the date when I would finish it, or that somehow just this book will be a pivotal influence to another Christian as myself, or maybe even plural numbers, who in turn will do something important enough in the favor of the Kingdom of God that it has the demonic principality in a state of panic.

All I know, is from the hell these demons have put me through and continue to since that March 9th, they are still continuing in this warfare to try to take me down, derail, get me to stop somehow, with the disasters only increasing to me concerning ones of shelter and income, as it seems they are working to try to totally take me down.

So many things have happened since March 9th, 2013 to this very day, I don't have the time to pen them all. But they went along the line of this one:

At first I had thought to go it alone, as it is enough to deal with such warfare then to try to get Christians who will take it seriously and earnestly pray for you in such an ordeal. So although my church has a monthly evening when anyone can sign up for a prayer team of 2 prayer ministers per person to pray over them, I was reluctant. So I didn't seek help first.

But by the beginning of April, it seemed the Holy Spirit was urging me to do so, thus reluctantly, because I was yet very sick and still struggling to treat my dog's boils, and getting anywhere was hard, I made an appointment on April 2nd for a prayer session and was slotted for the first available night of April 26th, 8p.m..

It was hard for me to get there and I barely got there on time, and had some relief to see a handful of others waiting at the welcome desk when I came in to the entranceway. However I was soon to learn that the reason they were there is that the prayer ministers for them had not shown. In fact 10 prayer ministers had been hindered coming, and 2 of those 10 were mine.

Of course I was not surprised that the enemy would target the two ministers appointed to pray over me. However, knowing it was warfare, I straight off booked another appointment which was three weeks away.

Not to let the enemy overcome us, I suggested those of us there pray for one another, and in a group, and we did. Though all of us were in some kind of problem and need, I am sure that the Lord heard us and we were better off for those prayers than just leaving without standing in any way against the enemy. So I am not surprised again that the next time both of my prayer ministers did show up and I did get prayer concerning that issue.

Still there are demon problems that take a lot of prayer, so it was not a cure.

> And Jesus rebuked the demon, and it came out of him; and the child was cured from that very hour. Then the disciples came to Jesus privately and said, "Why could we not cast it out?" So Jesus said to them, "Because of your unbelief; ... However, this kind does not go out except by prayer and fasting."
> —*Matthew 17:18-21, NKJV*

While some interpretations omit Verse 21 altogether, the

Greek actually includes it, which is very important because if you are led to think it is only by lack of faith, but are not told the other two steps to follow, it is no wonder you will not be able to get rid of a particularly difficult demon.

So while the prayer ministers prayers I am sure afforded me aid, since I was in a situation much like Matthew 12:45 where is was not just one demon but several in this demon hit team, more than just one session of prayer that included fasting would have been needed for total deliverance.

So the trouble did continue because I was not going to stop working on these materials, like I said especially determined to do whatever it was that had them so riled. So I was sure it did not endear me to them and the warfare kept going on.

In June a city inspector knocked on my front door in order to tell me I had to remove the shredded tarp from my roof, and also

that there was an issue with all the overgrown weeds and grass.

He turned out sympathetic when I spoke to him, as I was a wreck when I answered the door, having spent the last hour on a ladder trying with a coat hanger to fish out strings of the tarp which had gotten caught into my room air conditioner just before I was set to go to bed in the early afternoon, tired already, and was

Chapter 10: Be Afraid, Be Very Afraid

sun burnt like a lobster on one half of my body and in pain from all that exhausting effort, and looking not well for certain.

I explained to him the big trouble I was in with the foreclosure and disability and due to my low income having to do all the work myself, and how the insurance company had paid for a tarp, but then had denied fixing the roof. That had left me with a tarp on the roof which slowly shredded over time that I could not take off because the installer had used rope and sandbags to fix it on the roof, tying parts to the pipes sticking out of the roof.

I asked if the city would pay for these things to be done, but he told me he would have to check, because it would put a lien on the house.

Though it seemed like a bad experience it was God-sent, because just 3 days later someone would make an anonymous report on my house to the code official, making a false story that my car had no license plate, and that my house looked like it was abandoned with no one living there, and with a tarp on too long.

It was God-sent because the inspector had just been to my house and he closed off that person's false claim. Still it was grief to know someone was acting like a pawn and making fibs about my vehicle just to draw attention of a code inspector.

Yet I did what I could to pull off the tarps hanging over the front of the house in shreds shown in this picture, which then left the roof in that area with no tarps at all, which let more rain in.

Then in July, after waiting nearly 6 years for the trial against the nursing home where my husband died, which was set for 2nd week of August 2013, to my dismay the trial was cancelled, put in limbo while waiting the outcome of the sentencing of the CEO of that facility who was separately facing sentencing for Medicare fraud come that September.

I had months before blocked off on my kitchen calendar the weeks the trial had been booked for, seeing it as a birthday present to finally see justice, so grateful it would finally see its day in court. Instead come August I was given interrogatories to fill out that took 3 weeks to do in that same time, which had come to me almost a month past their legal time to submit to the court. I wondered if the effort would be in vain if the CEO went to jail, but still had to do the work.

On September 11, 2013 I get the news that the CEO of the nursing home was whisked off to jail right from courtroom sentencing to 25 years, for that Medicare Fraud. The judge had revoked her $3 million bond, and ordered her to pay $40 million in restitution to Medicare for billing fraud.

It was this crime which led to an unexpected canceling of the long-awaited trial for my husband's case, set for the month before, August 2013. It was to lead to more painful consequences to my case against the nursing home as her incarceration led to the dissolving of the longstanding family business, meaning after all those years, and just coming to the point of justice, a justice which would have helped me to survive from the loss of my husband, fell apart on her arrest.

In that very same September and to be expected really, because the enemy didn't want me to complete these projects apparently, my computer with everything on it, my music, and all of my writings, which I really had no way to replace, got that awful blue-screen of death.

It would have been an utterly tragic loss, and the enemy would have succeeded stopping me, if I had ignored the one warning preview of that I got a few days before, on a Sunday, when for a few seconds my computer flashed that terrible blue screen, and I thought it was goners then, but thankfully I was able to recover it.

To me in hindsight, that one mini temporary death was God moving me to take action and get a hard-drive with enough space to back everything up which I had not done because I never had spare money and it meant choosing that over other necessities.

Thank God I did heed that warning flash failure, as just the very next day after I had backed everything onto the new hard-drive, my computer absolutely died, unrecoverable, nothing salvageable, almost as if an angel had kept at bay a demon power striving to do in my computer, until my data was safely moved to the new hard drive, then, boom, mission accomplished, the angel left, and the demon finished killing the computer. But I was now wiser and from then on took extra measures to do quadruple backups of my works across several thumb drives.

So, yes, the enemy took down that computer, but God had me

Chapter 10: Be Afraid, Be Very Afraid

triumph all the same, and I plugged away, now making sure to do quadruple backups like I said because power surges were now happening in unpredictable pulses, and at times, weird times, suddenly my house power would go out just before I could save what I was working on in this manuscript.

But I overcame those things by keeping my computer plugged into my still operating 5-year-old UPS battery backup, which is a miracle in itself, while I worked, and when done for the day making sure to unplug my computer from the outlet so there could be no surprise surges toasting it or viruses to find their way in while I slept.

The following month on October 8th, a party that has been trying to break into my house since after the March event, which I had suspicions was tied to the bank foreclosing on my house because each day after such attempts would appear a door hangar from the bank with a notice to call them in spite they had a Cease Desist letter from my attorney so they would only deal with him, and also having recently read a couple articles about a major

company they used to monitor houses in foreclosure accused of hiring felons to illegally break into the homes, take possessions and lock people out, had succeeded in breaking my front window with an arrow-shaped chunk of street rock asphalt shown in this photo.

I discovered this just before I was heading to bed following 24 hours of wake time as I had dealt with problem after problem that day.

So I had to force myself in pain to do whatever patchwork I could with tiles around my house to cover the broken pane, and then close the hurricane shutter over that window, which to this day stays as is, because I do not have the funds to repair it.

This same party, apparently thwarted by the closed shutters, then moved to try to force entry to my house by trying to open my front door by pulling on it hard enough that the screws in the lock face fell out.

Now mind you at the same time there were other problems going on I was having to deal with I don't even have the space or energy really to put in here. But I think from what I have here you can see it was a non-stop heavy assault coming against me, and I think you can see how they were all escalating to push me to destruction. These weren't small issues; these were big issues, one after the other.

And in the same October the insurance company gave me notice they were canceling my homeowners policy start of February 2014 because of the unrepaired roof (damage I got as I earlier wrote, from Isaac the summer before which the insurance company denied coverage to repair) at its end of life, which would fall the month I am coming close to completing this book.

Then a few days later on October 28th at 5 a.m. a great pounding came from my hallway that sounded as if someone was right in the back bedroom, making me believe for a moment the person who had been trying to break in had finally broken in through a window.

However, it turned out to be a rat which had made its way inside my roof, to the hallway closet where it was with great force trying to break its way through the closet's wooden roof. Fortunately it responded to the pounding I did with a broom on that same closet wall and left, but then I had to spend that morning sealing up all breached entries in the gutters which was how it had gotten in.

Finally, on Halloween, October 31st, a date Satan loves to give

Chapter 10: Be Afraid, Be Very Afraid

evil tricks, unexpectedly I got minimally two years early my continuing disability review (CDR), which was supposed to not come for another 2 years. So I sent it in, with the understanding from others online that the determination can come quickly or take months.

Here I am now 4 months later still hanging on whether my benefits will continue or suddenly stop without warning as others have reported can and does happen. Having no savings, this can be excessively serious 'find' in one's bank account at the start of a month.

Plus, every time it rained enough outside as I had said due to the roof damage, it rained inside feet from where I sat from leaks coming in at the nearby ceiling fan, forcing me at times to clamp a big umbrella to the table next to me in order to keep me and my computer from getting rained on as I sat working on this book. In addition, then small piles of drywood termite frass started appearing in numbers along the baseboards.

Then you have to realize that all this time I was having to deal with issues of my dogs, chronic ear infection, chronic skin infection, one dog to the point she had to wear round the clock

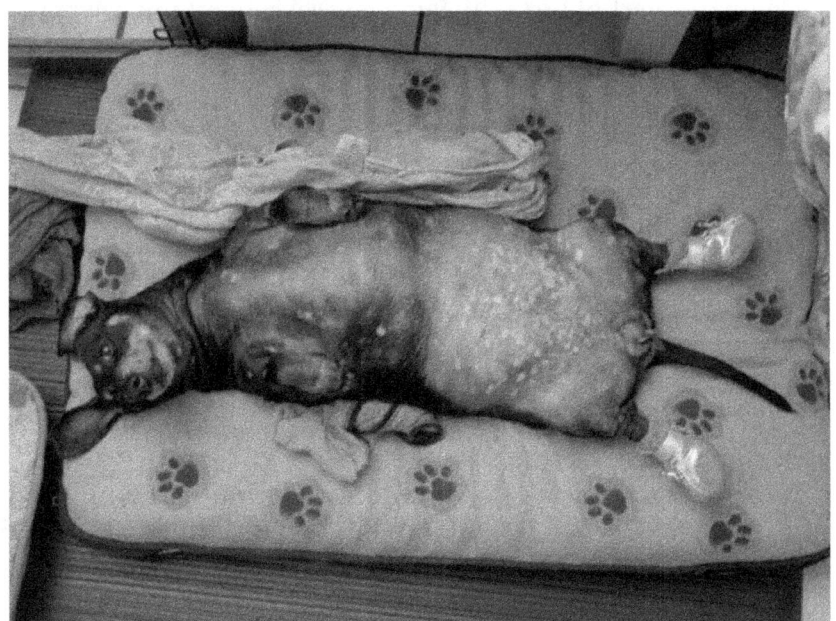

clothes and shoes, and if left unsupervised had to wear 2 of those

Elizabethan soft collars, one around her neck, one behind her forelegs, or I would find she had scratched herself as if possessed to bleeding wounds in only minutes. In this picture here she was having to lie still while the calamine lotion dried on her to help with the itches from her mystery pyoderma. This is my same dog who was in my dream with the Scholar of Seasons I wrote about in chapter 6.

I had to juggle all of these things with my normal physical limitations from my health issues and in this condition was how I was having to write, and how I had to do my album which came out the next month November, 2013.

To accomplish any of those, I had to just use whatever energy I had to work on these projects. The only way I could do that was to stay in bed until I was able to function which then had me going around the clock every week, going to bed 2 to 10 hours later each day.

But if I did not do this, in the constant barrage of problems, I would produce zero. If I had not heard those demons I might have taken it easier, but since I know they don't like something about it to a point of panic, I was going to give it my all to finish what it is.

Come the start of 2014, in January, was when I underwent my demon pawn situation with trying to get that bicycle I wrote about in chapter 9.

Same month a little later on, the party which had been trying to get into my house by force, came to a point they planned to try to really get in by shaking the door violently on January 27th Monday 2014 that would lead me to call 911.

On the Friday before that happened though, which is January 24th 2014, I had an open vision of the event, which at the time I was sitting at my computer working on that chapter, and when it had happened I had thought it was happening live, but questioned what had really happened, reality or supernatural vision because my dogs had failed to react or notice it.

In the open visions I have had, such as my encounter with God in 1972 showing me the souls of people at the world's end, there is no distinction between what the vision is showing me and my reality; what I hear and see is just like it is really happening---my only tip off it is a vision is when those around me do not see or

Chapter 10: Be Afraid, Be Very Afraid

hear it as I do, such as the case my dogs' failure to react to the door being violently shaken twelve times.

At first I thought it was really happening as I sat in view of the front door ten feet from me, watching it being shaken violently. As I said, the odd thing was my dogs lying around me had not stirred at all, and we were all right at the front door.

Because my dogs had stayed lying still as if they heard or seen nothing, and what was to come exactly three days later at the same time, I was to realize then it had been an open vision of what would happen exactly three days later to the minute, but at a very vulnerable time, when I had stepped into the shower which I believe is why God saw fit to put me on alert of this through an open vision so that I would be not slack to make sure the front door was fully locked, and also lock my bedroom door as I showered, bracing it with a bar.

It was not the first time I have had an open vision given to warn me about impending danger, as I have had several going back decades each coming at some point where my life is in danger of something that is about to happen that if I pay attention, can be averted, and because I have paid attention every time, they all have been.

On that day that I was ending my shower to retire in mid afternoon since I was exhausted, I heard a thud that sounded like someone had come into the house, slamming the door, a sound I have not heard in that way for over seven years since my late husband was alive and he might come into the house hauling groceries and just let the front door slam itself shut behind him.

Then my dogs who always lay still in their beds out in the master bedroom as I take my shower in the master bathroom, all jumped barking excitedly.

From the shower I heard the bedroom door rattle, and my dogs snorting under the door as they would if someone was on the other side, barking crazily.

Whether my dogs were rattling the bedroom door in their excitement, or someone else on the other side of it was, I could not tell. But that they were snorting as they would snort at the bottom of a door when something is right outside of it was not good.

Well you can bet I was not going to open the door. I had to call

911 as my dogs never acted like that unless someone was coming very close to the door that they could smell or hear them, which only happened at the front door of the house, and not the bedroom door as no one has ever let themselves into this house since my husband had passed away.

At the time I had made my call to 911, someone, whether the police or a neighbor, saw a black truck parked in my driveway behind my car. I didn't know that, although the 911 operator kept asking me if I was expecting any repair men or technician that day, and if I knew anyone having a black truck, which I told her no to all.

Only when I met the police outside did they tell me a black truck had been parked in my driveway just at that time.

Fortunately, it seems all the party did manage to do was shake the front door violently enough so the pounding shakes were heard in my room, but they had not been able to gain entry.

However, if I had not been on the alert from the open vision 3 days prior as I had sat writing this book, I might have not locked and tested the solidness of the front door as fully closed and locked, and they could have gained entry at a very bad time to be confronted by an intruder when I was showering.

Of course that led to my having to do all kinds of measure to further secure my door, including put up a little security camera to let the party know if they came again they would be filmed.

Then in February, my local courthouse where my foreclosure case is, started doing enforced monthly case conferences on all foreclosure cases as mine with the goal to push them through and I faced my first one on February 13th, 2014.

Early that a.m., as I tossed in bed trying to sleep, wondering if the judge would rule a default judgment as one of the legal assistants of my lawyer had said to me can sometimes happen, praying to God to help me sleep, the song I had written which I thought of as my Our Father song, titled "Lord's Prayer Indie Style," for some reason just decided to come to mind briefly when I had not thought about it for a couple of months.

True, it had been curious to me the copyright office had sent me the certificate for my album I had registered weeks after that one, yet still I had yet to receive a month later the certificate for

Chapter 10: Be Afraid, Be Very Afraid

my Our Father prayer song, now going on 3 months, but why it came to mind then I did not know as I had more pressing worries to face as in that court case meeting hours away.

When I met my lawyer at this first case management meeting I ever attended in any matter, I inquired if wouldn't the bank have to be forced to drop the foreclosure when it was shown I was under a payment suspension from forbearance.

He answered it wasn't that 'easy' that no, the bank could still end up taking my house without having to back off of the foreclosure, no matter if they had given a fake note, which they had.

On top of that, the judge had left for the day unexpectedly, forcing all afternoon conferences as mine to be rescheduled, so although we were present, we were forced to schedule to return, which the lawyer for me did, getting a date 6 weeks from then.

God Is Always Victorious

As I had driven home, relieved that no default judgment had arisen as can happen in these meetings, I drove past a church sign which read, GOD IS ALWAYS VICTORIOUS, feeling as if the Lord

was giving me that faith reminder that God wins every battle according to his will, even the ones that seem impossible, as it had seemed to me, from what the legal assistant had told me, would be the chance of my escaping a default judgment that day due to the harsh reputation the judge presiding at the time on my case was reputed to have against cases as old as mine.

It had never even occurred to me as I had tossed hours before in bed that the judge would leave the court early, and thus I had been spared of any such occurrence that day.

A few minutes later when I came to my house, and stopped my car at my curbside mailbox, and pulled out the single letter, what did I find?

The copyright certificate for my Our Father song "Lord's Prayer Indie Style," a timing that seemed to be God making his fatherly presence known to me in this time of tough battles, as a fatherly encouragement to stand in faith, he is God, including sending with a divine timing a copyright certificate with a title that would also act as an intimate uplifting message from the heavenly Father, that he is there for me, that he is aware, and that he is in control of all, and fighting the battles for me as a father does.

Yet, Satan wants to mess with all of God's plans, and unknown to me at the time, the judge canceling, then later that same day on her own reset the same conference only 2 weeks from then. So my case now had 2 conflicting mandatory conferences to go to.

If you don't go, you get a default against your case, where your house is set for auction. In my health, just on this trip to what ended up a cancelled meeting, I was drained making the drive each way, and strained financially to meet the costly court parking.

To add to the grief, the plaintiff bank set a motion for default claiming a failure to file the defenses due on my case by the ordered deadline of Feb 14th.

I had every reason to throw in the towel no matter where I was at the point of finishing this book, and put me and my survival over whatever deadline God may have.

Yet I was determined to not only finish this book by March 9th, but then to promptly begin work on another book similar to this one having other supernatural experiences of mine which further validate we are in a supernatural war between dark and light which is heating up to Armageddon with the aim to do whatever I can do as led by the Holy Spirit in order to empower you to get your house in order.

As I neared to finishing this book, the problems had gotten so bad that every day I was living in a crisis of some form or another, new ones hitting me day after day in the last two weeks before March 9th which apparently I could now see as I neared the date, had been the future date the demonic had foreseen this book would be completed.

Sleep was a challenge as I would find myself overheating as I tried to sleep from the heaping problems threatening me, leaving me in worse exhaustion than normal for me. Though I tried to sleep, my body overheated from all the problems, perhaps all the super stress taxing my immune system triggering night sweats, which can be a symptom from the IgM MGUS I have.

When I called my lawyer's office and asked about the upcoming default motion hearing, I was told by someone in the firm that they supposedly spoke with the plaintiff concerning that motion, and it was called off. But because it involves a legal proceeding you usually want to see that kind of cancellation in writing, and not believe a spoken word alone.

Thus, without such written proof of cancellation, and none visible in my case's docket, it left me forced to still go myself to the courthouse on that motion date which was Feb 27, 2014, because the status of a case management meeting for which the plaintiff may append a separate motion to the same time, was not visible online through the judge's docket.

At the time this was happening to me, I could only find this scheduling simply posted on an old-fashion typed list outside the courtroom walls on the day scheduled, and because the judge gets hundreds of emails a day, and did not want phone calls, one could only find out by making a trip to the courthouse to be sure.

And if what the party at the firm told me ended up not so, even though they had checked with the judge's office, for certain a default judgment would be made against my case, and because no defense is present, the shortest vacate time given to leave my house, of 20 days. So no matter what state of health I was on that day, Feb 27th, I had to make the 20 mile drive each way and find out.

In the interim, I directed every bit of strength I had no matter how I felt to keep moving this book forward as you can see, often having to write with double knee, back, shoulder and ankle support bands to circumvent or hold back spasms and pains that would cripple me otherwise, devices that sometimes gave me pains themselves to wear, or risk the devils would win, and that could mean people needing to hear this message never hearing it.

On the day of the motion, I struggled to make the drive, so tired I had to pray a few times to the Lord to keep my eyes alert. It seemed I would get early, but just 1 block before the turn into the parking lot for the courthouse, I found myself sandwiched in traffic before the raised bridge on that street parallel to the courthouse I did not know had a drawbridge, not familiar with that area of the city.

From the strength it took for me to hold the car brake, I felt my body growing weak as you would if you were standing on one leg for a very long train to pass after a sleepless night.

Another prayer to God to sustain me and I was able to get to the courtroom just on the minute, blessed to find a handicap parking space not far to drive my mobility scooter from which kept me from having to spend my last $10 bill for parking, which now left me with the possibility I could afford a burger meal on the long drive back, a nice blessing from the Lord.

There I discovered not to my surprise that my supposed 'cancelled' default hearing, was very on and my case #72 to be heard, making me wonder if I could last waiting for 71 cases to be heard before mine was reached.

Just at that moment, my attorney rounded the corner from the crowded courtroom, his eyes meeting mine, a God-send with all the people there, the small courtroom crowded to overflowing with people in suits as this was a 'cattle call' type of situation where almost 100 cases were heard, with 5 minutes assigned to each one.

I learned from my attorney that the plaintiff attorneys were trying to pull a super fast one, by moving for a default against my deceased husband for not filing Answers required by the court, when a death certificate was posted on my husband in the case nearly 4 years ago, July 2010, and all those years since the start of

Chapter 10: Be Afraid, Be Very Afraid

the case they were supposed to have either dropped him or appoint a court representative on his estate's behalf but never had.

Look at this: if I had not had a lawyer with me who was sharp to pick that up, dumb me might have thought it was a motion including everyone and tried to argue that my lawyer had given the papers on time and had been trying to fight against the default itself, when it was a moot point which never should have come before the judge.

This is how the banks often win, through some clever presentation that has no legal grounds.

Praise God, my lawyer jumped all over it with the plaintiff attorney, and that ended it just outside in the hallway of the courtroom, until the next case management meeting in 1 month.

Still, as you can see, even though an educated lawyer could overturn it, it still required both I and my lawyer to show up, my lawyer to be there over 2 hours, yet a second time in one month, and spend some head-scratching time over it before, and the law firm's staff to work to get it cancelled with the other side and judge, time which was moot because tenaciously it still stayed on the docket, info which could not be verified online, but required coming in person.

As I said, the only thing that matters is what is showing on the judge's docket outside the courtroom; since it was very much there, and no one showing for the defense because 'reliable' sources said it was cancelled, would have had no impact to reverse the default judgment which would have followed.

With that demonically-plotted disaster averted, I was able to more enjoy a much-needed Whopper meal, although normally it left me full, but from not having eaten well the last few days from all the high stress, it almost felt like I had just had a light snack.

The battle I went through over this default judgment is the exact battle that is happening concerning your soul. You are being fed falsehood after falsehood, lie after lie what is really going on and what is scheduled to happen to you.

Because just as you saw how till the very day, coming close to the very hour I was being given the wrong information by trusted sources, you need to take care of yourself as if the threat of getting cast to hell is true and take care of yourself same way I did, which is going to every step to make sure the threat is not real, no matter what all the people in your circles may be telling you otherwise.

It is not so much that those who gave me the false info were evil themselves, but that they were relying on sources they felt that were trusted who were giving them false information, and this can be the case with the pastor, priest or evangelist you trust in.

This is the battle surrounding the fate of your own soul, and as you can see how, as in my own situation, it requires you to stick to what you know to be true concerning what can happen, which is the Bible truth about such matters.

You need to think for yourself as I had to think for myself, and take care of yourself as I had to take care of myself to be protected from destruction.

You need to act as I had to act; you have to hold on to what you know to be true as revealed by the Bible, and keep to that information as all that matters. You need to simply get prepared to expect all that Jesus said about hell, about those who will not enter heaven, is what is scheduled to happen.

You have to close your ears to those countering that and telling you it is not so, that you do not have to take it seriously and not to worry about it, even treating you like you are hyper reacting and a thousand percent wrong.

What if I had listened to them? I would have been the only one to lose out, and it would have been utterly devastating.

It is the same situation for you here on the demon doctrines endangering the salvation of millions today and what you must do to avoid that threat, which is to ignore all the voices of the false teachers and just keep your eyes on the full truth of the Bible on what it takes to get to heaven, never wavering, no matter what mouth is speaking to you otherwise.

Seize that truth like a pit bull, just like I did, and don't relent of that grip until you have overcome, and have that crown of life on your head. If it means never turning on the television to a certain channel, then do it. If it means never stepping into a certain church again, then do it.

As far as the enemy hits coming at me since March 9th, the timing of those escalating threatening problems was so vicious, it had raised the level of hardship to work on the book to such

Chapter 10: Be Afraid, Be Very Afraid

grueling levels, and it made it like a race against hell if I could yet get it done.

It was like running a race bearing the weight of the world on my shoulders aged with arthritis and spastic muscles. But I knew something for certain: if it was God's will, it would get done. It was going to meet that upcoming March 9th date a year to the day after that demon commander appeared, a year in advance precisely on what definitely was going to become the finish date of this book.

This book in someway by its apparent synchronistic date, looked to be the something which really freaked him out, and I am not just talking like an ex-1960s flower child. This was one freaked-out monster demon, not a happy demon camper.

"Na-na na-na na-na," I taunt that monster demon, putting my thumbs in my ears and wiggling my fingers at him, now near finished, just days away from March 9th as I type this despite all the heavy artillery he'd ordered for me to be hit with at my frontline position in this enemy assault.

I may be in the Granny Unit of the Lord of Host's Army and

held together by an ADER weightlifting belt, two FUTURO™ abdomen supports, a Briggs Medical Posture Corrector, an AIRCAST™ knee band on each knee, and two ACE™ ankle wraps per ankle, but I'm not giving up, God willing, and God sure seemed to be.

The irony of it is these interferences from the enemy are actually leading to the finish date of the book to be on March 9th, as I might have finished faster if I didn't have all this grief to fight against as well.

So the finishing of this book to fall on March 9th 2014, had been no plan of mine, but instead how it was turning out to be from circumstances beyond me.

It was not planned on my end, but it seemed to be orchestrated on God's end as a sort of confirmation there was a supernatural plan to it with some kind of divine purpose to those dates matching, from the appearing of the demons on the March 9th, 2013 date with full intent to derail me from something, to the completion of this book, one year to the date, March 9th, 2014, in spite of all the things going on, and big burdens too.

I would say you can interpret the purpose of these events happening on the same day exactly a year apart, as a further conviction to receive the Lord's word, to prepare your heart, to turn from wickedness that can have the Lord find you filthy and full of blame on his return, too dirty to enter heaven.

In many different ways, God is trying to get across the message to people to repent while there is yet time; and thus you can consider this just one of those ways.

This is called grace, a period where he is extending warnings, where he is sending out calls to turn from sin, showing patience and long-suffering. For it is not his choice people should perish.

In the way he is using me, he started the thread of this mercy call in 1972 when he gave me that open vision of all the people who thought they were saved, and they were not few, but enough for nations, and yet they were far from it, as their idea of what corresponded to being saved did not correspond to the state of their depraved souls.

Grieved By Various Trials Testing Faith

From the examples of all the enemy hits you have seen I have gotten since that March 9th, you can come to know that just as the Scriptures reveal, there are times each and every one of us may find God has retracted his protective hedge from us as in Job in order that we may be tested, that the genuineness of our faith is tested.

> ...you have been grieved by various trials, so that the tested genuineness of your faith—more precious than gold that perishes though it is tested by fire—may be

Chapter 10: Be Afraid, Be Very Afraid

found to result in praise and glory and honor at the revelation of Jesus Christ,

—1 Peter 1:6-7, ESV

So here it seemed without my ability to stop it, forces were moving to have me pushed out of my house, with destroyed credit that nothing could be done to reverse.

It was a demonic timing set to take place when I may receive the news from my pending continuing disability review I had not yet heard from that my disability is stopped, and without warning that the SSA often just stops the payments so a person finds they have no money as expected, which some who have reported having their benefits mistakenly terminated this way, said took them sometimes up to 5 or more months to have them reinstated, despite how simple the SSA instructions make it seem for appeals to be made and temporary benefits in the meantime be continued.

That kind of a fight can be deadly if you are ill and with no support network that you get evicted on the street.

I had a lawyer help me to get my benefits the first time, but it is rare any lawyer will help anyone doing a continuing review because they only get paid a fixed percentage from Social Security Administration's determination of monies owed to you, and the bigger the back pay due the better for the lawyer who gets a larger payment for assisting you.

But in a CDR (continuing disability review) what is owed you could be only a month or nothing, so there is no incentive for any to aid anyone through this process.

Because of the expense to fight foreclosure, I had been unable to afford the co-pay to my hematologist for over 2 years, so that lack of paper trail in medical records was no help either in to the positive resolution of my CDR, though my primary doctor had been twice yearly checking my levels, but as it is not his specialty he hadn't input into my charts all the things my hematologist had tracked.

Even though it was a health condition that is not supposed to reverse, when you have Satan's kingdom on your back, someone can get influenced to look evilly at the reduced paper trail and decide it means I have 'recovered' and stop my disability at a deadly timing.

That left me in a position to be unable to attempt to even move, because who can sign a contract anywhere, mobile home rent or anything, when it is unknown if your SSA disability benefits will just stop cold turkey in a handful of months?

I have never had an eviction on my record, but in these days, one thing that landlords want nothing of is people with evictions. So here was a potential demonic design that I was forced into a foreclosure sale at a time when my SSA disability payments could be temporarily stopped, or even permanently if I could not wage the battle on my own to get them reinstated, and that could result in my being slammed with my first eviction, at a time I did not have the health to bounce from getting cast on the street, and then be further blacklisted by not only this foreclosure on my credit, but now a demonically-timed eviction.

I'd like to add an update to the above here on 3/3/14: after finding my local SSA office told they could not submit any kind of dire need letter to expedite the review process, I was able to obtain help from my local congresswoman. I continued to persevere to other channels of help because I knew I could stand on the truth that God is always victorious, even though everything was being "no, no, no'" just like that retail chain had been telling me concerning giving me my cash back on that bicycle story I relate in chapter 9.

The congresswoman's office was able to submit my papers on my situation to the CDR reviewer who then moved to defer my disability continuing review for another two years, so that one enemy hit set to do devastation to me at the same time I may get a foreclosure eviction was overcome.

Plus, due to that, as my contract with my current lawyer ran out and he did not like the difficulties getting stacked against lawyers in my county courthouse, and would not be taking on any more people in my area, I was able to hire a new lawyer who felt I had several strong points in my case why I should not get foreclosed on---yet even some high-priced lawyers were getting shot down in my courthouse even with good defenses, so that fate for me is still open-ended, all a God's will thing, because it would be a miracle I would get a positive resolution, but I had hope where I had none the week before.

As you see it involved my not giving up, standing firm on Jesus, even though I was getting brutal enemy hits from the front line taking a toll on my body which from the stress alone was too much.

Despite those heavy enemy assaults to do me in without relent the whole year long, you can see from the existence of this book, I had not perished from them, and instead was taking every moment of spare energy I had to get this done, because if it was God's will it like I said it would get done.

So in some ways I would like you take consolation if you are undergoing such suffering yourself in your walk of faith, that others in the Christian brotherhood around the world, also are undergoing the same kind of enemy hits.

Besides the regular reasons Christians have always been targeted by the enemy, these days, as in the last days, have an even additional trouble added to them due to the times as apostle Timothy relates in 2 Timothy 3.

> But understand this, that in the last days there will come times of difficulty. For people will be lovers of self, lovers of money, proud, arrogant, abusive, disobedient to their parents, ungrateful, unholy, heartless, unappeasable, slanderous, without self-control, brutal, not loving good, treacherous, reckless, swollen with conceit, lovers of pleasure rather than lovers of God
> —*2 Timothy 3:1-4, ESV*

Although these kinds of behaviors have always led to heartaches for people, the amount of people like this will be at an all time high, and they will be found in all types of positions, so difficulties will increase all around.

For example, where you think you will be getting help from some agencies geared to provide that help, you will end up instead getting more abuse from the wickedness of the people there, easily used by the enemy as pawns due to the legal rights the enemy has over them because of sinful lifestyles they are leading.

The kinds of troubles I have been relating to you in my direct hits from the enemy are the kinds of troubles that are last day troubles. If you are aware of this, rather than letting the enemy get you to succumb and despair, instead recognize it as warfare, and stand firm, knowing these are last days troubles the Bible has declared will come at these times..

The times will not get better; they will stay difficult because people will not turn from sin, and the hard hearts will stay hard, and the wicked will stay wicked. You are to handle it by standing firm against all these troubles meant to lead you to stumble, and hold the faith Christ will restore you in every measure on the day he comes for you, and continue to fight the good fight of faith (1 Timothy 6:12).

> Be sober, be vigilant; because your adversary the devil, as a roaring lion, walketh about, seeking whom he may devour: Whom resist stedfast in the faith, knowing that the same afflictions are accomplished in your brethren that are in the world. But the God of all grace, who hath called us unto his eternal glory by Christ Jesus, after that ye have suffered a while, make you perfect, stablish, strengthen, settle you.
> —*1 Peter 5:8-10, KJV*

That troubles will abound really is on target where we are going as far as the end times. Keep the perspective you are being tested and it will help you to keep the right mindset to persevere.

So many people do not seem to be aware of what is normal for the end times, normal as far as the difficulties, as far as the falling away of many through false doctrines, and the increase of the spiritual warfare against those holding the faith.

If they did, they would not despair so deeply, nor would they view the lack of change in their circumstances as some kind of failure of God in their lives, and a reason to lose faith. But the reality is Satan is to blame.

He is waging an end-time war to find Christians to tear asunder by testing our faith with evil attacks, and prove to God our faith is false. These are events foretold in the Scriptures so you can believe it is true. While like you I wish it was not so, it is better to

Chapter 10: Be Afraid, Be Very Afraid

face the issue rather than put your head in the sand about it, so you can deal with it, get the right mindset about it and not fall a victim to the enemy.

> Do not fear any of those things which you are about to suffer. Indeed, the devil is about to throw some of you into prison, that you may be tested, and you will have tribulation ten days. Be faithful until death, and I will give you the crown of life.
> —*Revelation 2:10, NKJV*

Thus, if you find yourself in similar hardship, don't let the enemy derail you; stay focused doing the Lord's work, trust in him. Resist the devil and stand firm, and the Lord will give you the crown of life.

As saints under the leadership of the Lord of Hosts, we are empowered to stomp on all evil.

> Behold, I have given you authority to tread on serpents and scorpions, and over all the power of the enemy, and nothing shall hurt you.
> —*Luke 10:19, ESV*

Supernatural Dates

God is the author of seasons, and he has a date and time for everything. Thus, it is not surprising some approaching dates and some exact dates can be known to the enemy, some of those visible through approaching sign and others through announcement through the Lord a specific event is on the horizon, whether imminent or a further date.

My album's creation "GODacious," experienced such a supernatural date of November 5th where early in my faith my sudden song inspirations coming to me after tithing one Sunday would lead to an album, although I had not even hummed for over ten years, I had sent what I called a 'pre-testimony' letter to my pastor dated November 5th, 2012 to save this letter so it could give glory to God later on that I was believing in faith my amateur

Christian songs would be published.

I had forgotten about that letter, except the week after the album actually was released. When I went to check that letter out to give testimony to my pastor on my completed album, I was amazed that the date of the letter was a year to the date before the album's release date of November 5th, 2013.

And now this book revealed it had a supernatural date the enemy caught an eye of on God's calendar, March 9th, 2014.

That I finished on a day when there was an official change of time, Daylight Savings Time, adds more to the message of its supernatural origin. Because of the signs of the times, where many of the signs Scriptures say announce the approach of the day of the Lord we are seeing in our generation come to pass, you should not brush off the poignancy of my finishing on a day that marks an official change of time.

You should receive it as a wake-up call to herald a message of another change of time that has also arrived and is now officially in progress, and this time now is the Season of Final Grace. After the end of this time period, it will be the season of wrath, the final time.

Now is the time to receive these revelations, and hear the message to get ready, hear the message that the Dark and Light war is real, and take the messages to heart and respond by getting your house in order to be counted on the side of the forces of Light in the Last Day.

As you can see from my March 9th demon encounter, so hard the enemy tried to do me in starting their plan a year before the end date when unknown to me this book would be finished, a book I didn't know I would write as I was writing another book still in progress.

And another supernatural date, not yet come, but will, is the day of the Lord, which has an assigned date of which only the Father knows.

But from what Jesus left behind for us in the Scriptures to have the ability to spot its looming approach, the signs are growing strong that the End Times storm has taken form and is on its way to hit all of humanity.

As I wrote before, the clock of Final Grace appears to be

Chapter 10: Be Afraid, Be Very Afraid

reaching its last ticks at the approach of the day of the Lord, a supernatural date you certainly don't want to be surprised by unprepared.

Are you ready to make it to heaven?

Will the Lord find you spotless whether on your personal day of judgment or the global judgment come the day of the Lord, your soul bright and pure from your saintly deeds of righteousness?

> And to her was granted that she should be arrayed in fine linen, clean and white: for the fine linen is the righteousness of saints.
> —*Revelation 19:8, KJV*

Or will he find you like one of the multitudes of people on the earth with their souls deformed like demons from their wicked acts as I saw in my 1972 open vision?

> He that is unjust, let him be unjust still: and he which is filthy, let him be filthy still: and he that is righteous, let him be righteous still: and he that is holy, let him be holy still.
> —*Revelation 22:11, KJV*

It is time now to establish the readiness of your heart and stand firm against all the demonic schemes working hard to prevent you from reaching heaven. Listen to the call of the Lord for readiness. Believe and receive this word from the Lord.

> He who rejects Me, and does not receive My words, has that which judges him--the word that I have spoken will judge him in the last day.
> —*John 12:48, NKJV*

Please, my friend, in Christ, renounce all that is evil, and walk like Jesus, and practice righteous deeds. As in the day of the rebellion, don't harden your heart (Hebrews 3:8).

Since everything will be destroyed in this way, what kind

of people ought you to be? You ought to live holy and godly lives as you look forward to the day of God and speed its coming. That day will bring about the destruction of the heavens by fire, and the elements will melt in the heat. But in keeping with his promise we are looking forward to a new heaven and a new earth, the home of righteousness. So then, dear friends, since you are looking forward to this, make every effort to be found spotless, blameless and at peace with him.

—2 Peter 3:11-14, NIV

***

Your Free Bonus Gift

I want you to stay motivated and keep a fighting mindset against the works of the devil and so as a bonus to this book, you can get a free mp3 audio of my song War I wrote specifically as a battle rousing song against the enemy wiles to get believers' minds psyched up to stand firm and win.

This version of my song War given to you as a bonus is a professionally performed version of my song, done by Studio A--- whereas the version on my album is me singing to the best of my amateur performance with my amateur music arrangement.

You have my permission to download this to any player of yours, whether mp3 player, tablet or computer, or cell phone for your personal use.

To download your free bonus fighting song to rev you up to resist Satan's wiles so he will flee as the Scriptures promise, go to:
www.holyforce.org/borninawar/bonus/
You will be prompted to enter a username, which is 'grace' and password which is 'resistevil', all small letters, no capitals:
USERNAME: grace
PASSWORD: resistevil

War
Lyrics and music by Vivian Gendernalik

War!
We aren't going to sit back and take it anymore
War!
We're fighting in the Army of the Lord
Listen up!

This is war, oh yeah, soldier
Don't be fooled, the Devil's real
Not fighting means ignoring ancient ordeal
Between God and Satan both active in ploy
To win your soul, one to save, one destroy

War!

Free Audio Bonus

We're terminating giving the Devil a free ride
War!
We're putting daily prayer into our lives
Pay attention!

Enemy's got one prime weapon
Control your mind through deception
Trickery, outright lies, to destruction
If you've been sleeping, now is the time to wake
Refuse to take anymore Satan's bait!

War!
We're waking from the Devil's lies that say we're all right
War!
We're shaking off the lukewarm in our Christian lives
Listen troops!

Don't buy enemy dope and lose your life
There are times it's right to fight.
Know this, know this, know this
The battle has already been won
Through the sacrifice of the Divine Son

War!
We're turning from materials made to ignite sin
War!
We're donning sword of God's Word, our weapon to win

Warfare, has no neutral ground
Serve one side or the other
Stand firm, Fight
Endure, endure, endure!
Endure, endure, endure!
Endure,
Victory is assured.

© 2013 Vivian Gendernalik -- All Rights Reserved
***

Sinner's Prayer

...when the Lord Jesus is revealed from heaven with His mighty angels, in flaming fire taking vengeance on those who do not know God...
— *2 Thessalonians 1:7*

Lord Jesus, I believe you died on the cross for me, that you shed your blood to pay for my sins. I believe you are the Messiah, the only Son of God.

Jesus, I confess my sins, and I repent of them today and ask you take every one, the ones I know about, and the ones I do not know I have in me, and ask that you wash them all from me with your blood, and purify me.

I give my life to you, to live according to your will. Help me to serve and live for you, and be a witness for you. Help me to abide in you, and be found ready when you come for me.

I thank you, Jesus, for saving me. Keep me from falling, Lord, as I know you are able to make me stand. Help me to have the personal relationship with you every believer is called to have, so I always hear your voice, and you know me to be yours.

In your holy name, Jesus, I pray.

***

AUTHOR CONTACT INFORMATION

Vivian Gendernalik
8345 NW 66 ST, Box #8434
MIAMI, FL 33166
Website: www.VivianGendernalik.com

SEED THIS BOOK TO ANOTHER SOUL
Don't let the conviction in this book stop with you! Get more copies & seed to others, while there is still time to be found a faithful servant going about your Master's work.

His lord said to him, 'Well done, good and faithful servant; you have been faithful over a few things, I will make you ruler over many things. Enter into the joy of your lord.'
—*Matthew 25:23 NKJV*

When you tell others about books teaching the uncompromised Word, you are partaking in the good works of the authors. If you have had no idea how you can be found a worthy servant by the Lord, by helping someone spread end-time warnings exposing the enemy works to lead people to salvation, you will share in that person's work for the truth.

We Christians, then, must help these people, so that we may share in their work for the truth.
—*3 John 1:8 GNT*

Get active and get counted as part of this work, by supporting it through getting the news out in the medium you are able to. In return every time you do, the Lord is recognizing your contribution to the furtherance of his warning message to have people saved from the devil's works of deception.

Whether you have the funds to give copies of this book to others or not, you can still participate and get the same reward for a prophet and for a righteous person, by telling others about it in some way, whether on a website such as Facebook.com, or you post a link in a blog that leads to the book, or you include in every item you send by postal mail a little note paper recommending the book and letting them know it can be found at Barnes and Noble website or Amazon, or direct them to www.holyforce.org/order to see current ways to obtain copies.

> And in the last days it shall be, God declares, that I will pour out my Spirit on all flesh, and your sons and your daughters shall prophesy, and your young men shall see visions, and your old men shall dream dreams; even on my male servants and female servants in those days I will pour out my Spirit, and they shall prophesy.
> —*Acts 2:17-18 ESV*

> The one who receives a prophet because he is a prophet will receive a prophet's reward, and the one who receives a righteous person because he is a righteous person will receive a righteous person's reward.
> —*Matthew 10:41 KJV*

Every time you do any of these things, you are taking an active part in this work and you are sharing in whatever reward the Lord has for getting the news out on this end time warning. This also includes leaving a review on amazon.com or bn.com on their sales page for the book, as every review helps to bring people to learn about the book and be moved to read it.

Handing out a Christian tract results in the same kind of sharing in the work for the truth. Just be careful that the tract you hand out is truly leading the person to salvation and not leading them to a deception where they believe they are saved but they are not from the partial truths some tracts promote.

So whether you decide to help promote this work, or decide to promote a tract teaching right standing with the Lord, take action now, while there is still time to be counted a worthy servant going about the business of your Master.

***

www.ingramcontent.com/pod-product-compliance
Lightning Source LLC
Chambersburg PA
CBHW071301110426
42743CB00042B/1127